Lecture Notes in Computer Science 4044

Commenced Publication in 1973
Founding and Former Series Editors:
Gerhard Goos, Juris Hartmanis, and Jan van Leeuwen

T0218639

Pekka Abrahamsson   Michele Marchesi
Giancarlo Succi (Eds.)

Extreme Programming and Agile Processes in Software Engineering

7th International Conference, XP 2006
Oulu, Finland, June 17-22, 2006
Proceedings

 Springer

Volume Editors

Pekka Abrahamsson
VTT Technical Research Centre of Finland
Kaitoväylä 1, 90571 Oulu, Finland
E-mail: pekka.abrahamsson@vtt.fi

Michele Marchesi
University of Cagliari
DIEE, Department of Electrical and Electronic Engineering
Piazza d'Armi, 09123 Cagliari, Italy
E-mail: michele@diee.unica.it

Giancarlo Succi
Free University of Bozen/Bolzano
Center for Applied Software Engineering
Piazza Domenicani 3, 39100 Bozen/Bolzano, Italy
E-mail: Giancarlo.Succi@unibz.it

Library of Congress Control Number: 2006926928

CR Subject Classification (1998): D.2, D.1, D.3, K.6.3, K.6, K.4.3, F.3

LNCS Sublibrary: SL 2 – Programming and Software Engineering

ISSN   0302-9743
ISBN-10   3-540-35094-2 Springer Berlin Heidelberg New York
ISBN-13   978-3-540-35094-1 Springer Berlin Heidelberg New York

Springer is a part of Springer Science+Business Media

springer.com

© Springer-Verlag Berlin Heidelberg 2006
Printed in Germany

Typesetting: Camera-ready by author, data conversion by Scientific Publishing Services, Chennai, India
Printed on acid-free paper   SPIN: 11774129   06/3142   5 4 3 2 1 0

Preface

Unbelievable, we have reached the seventh edition of the XP2k+n conference! We started at the outset of the new millennium, and we are still proving that agile processes were neither a millennium bug nor a YAF (yet another fad).

In its first editions, this conference was a get-together of a few pioneers who debated about how to make agile processes and methods accepted by the mainstream researchers and practitioners in software engineering. Now agile approach to software development has been fully accepted by the software engineering community and this event has become the major forum for understanding better the implications of agility in software development and proposing extensions to the mainstream approaches.

These two aspects were fully reflected in this year's conference. They were reflected in the keynote speeches, which covered the background work done starting as early as the early eighties by Barry Boehm, definition of the field by Kent Beck, a successful industrial application in a success story by Sean Hanly, the perspective and the future of agile methods in large corporations by Jack Järkvik, and even some insightful views from a philosopher, Pekka Himanen.

They were reflected in the technical sessions and in their papers, spanning from the definition and the consolidation of the theory (with specific attention to topics like pair programming, quality, experimental data) and reaching controversial areas, such as distributed agile development and new practices involving usability and security issues

The papers went through a rigorous reviewing process. Each paper was reviewed by at least three Program Committee members. Of 59 papers submitted, only 16 were accepted as full papers.

Panels, workshops, activities, and tutorials enriched the conference, introducing a wide variety of topics and of discussion techniques.

But the highest value of any conference, and especially of a XP2k+n conferences is in the people who attend it, this is why we think that this seventh edition of the conference was unique: because of its wide variety of ingenious, curious, dynamic, and nice participants.

We thank all who contributed to the XP 2006 event. The authors, sponsors, the chairs, the reviewers, and all the volunteers: without their help, this event would not have been possible.

April 2006

Pekka Abrahamsson
Michele Marchesi
Giancarlo Succi

Organization

 VTT Technical Research Centre of Finland

 University of Oulu

Executive and Program Committee

General Chair: Steven Fraser (QUALCOMM®, USA)
Program Chair: Pekka Abrahamsson (VTT, Finland)
Organizing Chair: Päivi Jaring, Finland
Organizing Co-chair: Kari Liukkunen, Finland
PhD Chair: Paul Gruenbacher, Austria
Panel Chair: Prof. Brian Fitzgerald, Ireland
Workshop Chair: Giancarlo Succi, Italy
Tutorial Co-chairs: Michele Marchesi, Italy
Tua Huomo, Finland
Poster Co-chairs: David Hussman, USA
Daniel Karlström, Sweden
Open-Space Chair: Charlie Poole, USA
Service Chair: Mike Hill, USA

Scientific Committee

Marco Abis, Italy
Pär Åkerfalk, Ireland
Mustafa Ally, Australia
Scott Ambler, Canada
Emily Bache, Sweden
Geoff Bache, Sweden
Ralf Back, Finland

Hubert Baumeister, Germany
Stefan Biffl, Austria
Laurent Bossavit, France
Anna Börjersson, Sweden
Ko Dooms, Netherlands
Yael Dubinsky, Israel
Tore Dybå, Norway

Jutta Eckstein, Germany
Hakan Erdogmus, Canada
John Favaro, Italy
Steve Freeman, UK
Jim Highsmith, USA
Mike Hill, USA
Mike Holcombe, UK
Helena Holmström, Ireland
David Hussman, USA
Tuomas Ihme, Finland
Ron Jeffries, USA
Nicolai Josuttis, Germany
Daniel Kallström, Sweden
Conboy Kieran, Ireland
Kai Koskimies, Finland
Tuomo Kähkönen, Finland

Martin Lippert, Germany
Markku Oivo, Finland
Frank Maurer, Canada
Grigori Melnik, Canada
Rick Mugridge, New Zealand
Paul Grünbacher, Austria
Barbara Russo, Italy
Outi Salo, Finland
Pinna Sandro, Italy
Helen Sharp, UK
Alberto Sillitti, Italy
Christoph Steindl, Austria
Ciancarlo Succi, Italy
Don Wells, USA
Laurie Williams, USA

Sponsors (as of April 13, 2006)

Platinium level (Main sponsor)

   Exoftware™
(http://www.exoftware.com/)

Gold level

Silver level

Partners: F-Secure Oyj, Elbit ltd.

Table of Contents

Foundation and Rationale for Agile Methods

Effects of Pair Programming

Quality in Agile Software Development

Issues in Large Scale Agile Development

New Practices for Agile Software Development

Experience Papers

Posters and Demonstrations

Panels

A Distributed Cognition Account of Mature XP Teams

Helen Sharp and Hugh Robinson

Centre for Research in Computing
The Open University
Walton Hall
Milton Keynes MK7 6AA UK
{h.m.robinson, h.c.sharp}@open.ac.uk

Abstract. Distributed cognition is a framework for analysing collaborative work. It focuses on interactions between people, between people and their environment and between people and artefacts that are created and manipulated in the course of doing work, and it emphasises information flow and information transformation. Analyses conducted using the distributed cognition framework highlight breakdowns and potential problem areas in the collaborative work being studied; distributed cognition has been used to study a wide variety of collaborative work situations. XP teams are highly collaborative, relying heavily on interactions between team members and their environment. In this paper we present accounts of four mature XP teams based on the distributed cognition framework.

1 Introduction

Distributed cognition is an approach for conceptualising human work activities that considers the people, their environment and the artefacts that are created and manipulated as one large cognitive system. The approach originated with Ed Hutchins' work on ship navigation [1] in which he explored the complex system that results in the current position and target position being identified and transformed into the required course to steer. This system involves a series of information transformations through a variety of media including the spoken word, control panel lights and dials, instruments, landmarks and so on. The approach has been used in the analysis of computer-supported co-operative work (CSCW) in order to identify the impact of new or intended technologies on collaborative work such as call centers (e.g. [2, 3]) and communities of practice (e.g. [4]), among other areas. It has also been adapted for use in HCI analyses to support the development of interactive systems (e.g. [5, 6]).

It has been argued [7] that the distributed cognition framework provides a unifying approach to studying socially complex work situations that pulls together different disciplines that have traditionally studied such phenomena, e.g. the cognitive, social and organisational sciences. The framework therefore supports analysis of a situation that takes a more holistic view of the work and its progress.

Although software engineering is recognised as a social activity by many, there have been few reported studies of software development activity using a distributed cognition approach. Flor and Hutchins' [8] study of two programmers working

P. Abrahamsson, M. Marchesi, and G. Succi (Eds.): XP 2006, LNCS 4044, pp. 1 – 10, 2006.

together during a maintenance activity is the most widely cited application of this theory to the study of software development activity. They observed and recorded two programmers working together on a maintenance task in order to characterise some of the system variables that were important for the success of the task. They did this by analysing the interactive distribution of information used in the task.

The program itself was a graphic adventure game and consisted of about 3000 lines of C code. The change to be made involved adding a 'whisper' command to the program – this command would take a string as input and send that string only to the player indicated. The programmer's interactions were recorded using videotape and all keystrokes and output at the computer terminal were logged. The analysis was performed on a written transcription of the videotape, the commands entered and the times they were entered, and interactions with documentation that were captured on the videotape. Therefore the analysis focused on the detail of the programmer's interactions, but did not consider the wider team or system context.

At the end, they had identified a set of seven properties of the cognitive system that consisted of the two programmers and their immediate environment. These properties were: reuse of system knowledge, sharing of goals and plans, efficient communication, searching through large spaces of alternatives, joint productions of ambiguous plan segments, shared memory for old plans and division of labour. Some of these properties, such as reuse of system knowledge and searching through large spaces of alternatives, have been observed before in studies of software development (e.g. [9]), and some of them have similarities to XP's practices. However Flor and Hutchins considered only one episode of collaborative programming, and they did not attempt to extend their analysis beyond this restricted view.

In this paper we broaden the scope of analysis to consider the whole XP team and its interactions over the course of a week or so rather than focus tightly on the details of one programming episode. The cognitive system under scrutiny therefore is the XP team and its environment. To do this, we discuss the results of observational studies with four mature XP teams working on different applications and in varying environments. In the next section we characterise the information flows through and around each of the four teams. Then we describe in more detail the approach to distributed cognition that we adopt in this paper. In section 4 we present distributed cognition accounts of these teams, and in section 5 we highlight breakdowns that we have observed. In the final section, we conclude that looking at teamwork through the lens of distributed cognition allows us to identify potential issues regarding information flow and transformation within and between an XP team and its environment.

2   Information Flow and Transformation Within the Four Teams

In our previous work, we have found that stories in XP are a key mechanism for capturing and propagating information throughout the XP team (e.g. [10]), and so the description of our teams and their information flows focuses on the generation and manipulation of stories. Further information about teams B, C and W can be found in [10, 11, 12, 13].

Team B produced software applications in Java to support the management of operational risk within a large bank. They were organised into two sub-teams. Stories were generated during the planning game with developers and the customers present. They were captured on index cards. The developers estimated the story cards and wrote the estimate on the cards. The cards were then dealt onto a table, sorted through and rearranged before being placed on a portable board. Throughout the iteration, the cards were treated as tokens for work to be done, and developers would take the cards off the board and use them to generate code. Continual dialogue, focused around the story card, took place between the developers and the customers in order to clarify and expand the story content.

Team C developed web-based intelligent advertisements using Java. The customer role was carried out in this team by marketing personnel who were in regular contact with the client. The marketing personnel generated the stories following discussions with the client, wrote them onto index cards, and prioritised them in the planning game. Developers wrote estimates on the cards and those for the current iteration were displayed on a common wall. At the end of an iteration a summary of the stories completed, started and abandoned during the iteration was written to a wiki site and the cards were put into storage. Cards that were obsolete or superseded were torn up and not kept.

Team S worked in a large international bank, and programmed in Java. Their project concerned the migration of database information from several smaller databases to one large database. The work to be completed was controlled by the project manager of the team, who was not himself one of the developers. The stories were developed from the overall project plan which listed the functionality to be implemented. Stories were prioritised through consultation with the business analysts and the developers. Once written on index cards, the stories were estimated and the cards displayed for all the team to see.

Team W were part of a medium-sized company producing software products in C++ to support the use of documents in multi-authored work environments. Within each iteration, the team organised itself into sub-teams oriented around the various software products or related issues. Stories were generated by the programme managers who were hybrid figures with some technical and some business expertise. They liaised with the marketing product manager on the customer side and the developers on the software side. Stories were captured and manipulated using a purpose-built software package. Developers looked at the online story and estimated the time required to complete it. Testing information was stored alongside functionality information, and the system underwent a tiered set of tests - developers were responsible for unit tests, testers (a separate element of the team) tested the stories in context, and the QA department (quality assurance) tested the whole product.

Each team was observed for about a week; our observations focused on the interactions between team members and their environment, and the data collected included contemporaneous notes, photographs and some audio recordings.

3 Analysis Approach

The initial analysis of our data followed a rigorous approach in an ethnographic tradition. This approach involves seeking counter examples to any suggested finding. For example, where we observe that developers in a team preferred to work on problems together, we also seek evidence in our data that would underpin the opposite result, i.e. examples where team members chose to tackle similar problems on their own.

A distributed cognition analysis takes the view that a cognitive system extends beyond what goes on in an individual's head and encompasses the wider interactions and information transformations that are required in order to achieve a goal. A distributed cognition analysis typically involves examining the following aspects of the cognitive system [14]:

- The distributed problem-solving that takes place;
- The role of verbal and non-verbal behaviour (what is said and what is not said, but simply implied, are equally important)
- The co-ordinating mechanisms that are used;
- The communicative pathways involved in a collaborative activity;
- How knowledge is shared and accessed

It also investigates the information flow through the cognitive system and identifies where 'breakdowns' may occur. Breakdowns are potential failures in communication or information flow that will impair the system's performance or prevent the system from achieving its goals. More formal breakdown analysis has been used to investigate collaborative software systems (e.g. [15]).

In the accounts that follow, we address each of these issues in turn, drawing on the observational data we have collected. In each case and before making an observation, we have carefully considered whether we have evidence to contradict the statement we want to make.

4 Accounts of XP Teams

Developing a software system requires access to a lot of information. Fundamentally, there is the set of requirements for the software, but in order to produce the required software, information regarding deadlines, estimates for completion, responsibilities, the status of code under development, criteria for assessing when code is complete, priorities regarding which pieces of software to work on when, technical details of a language or infrastructure, and so on. To follow the detailed information flow paths for each of these would require more space than this paper allows, and indeed our data is not detailed enough to support such an analysis. Instead, our accounts give a broader view of information flow, transformation and application. A more detailed study is left to another day.

4.1 Distributed Problem-Solving

Problem-solving was highly distributed in all of our teams, both across people and across time.

One example of this is the use of pair programming to develop code, and each of our teams saw pairing as an essential part of their normal working practice. Having said this, observed behaviour did vary. For example, Team C paired for all of their tasks with very little change from this routine, while Team S paired for the majority of tasks when there was an even number of developers available, and the smaller sub-team in Team B had an odd number of developers and hence could not work exclusively in pairs. Team W's working moved seamlessly from singletons to pairs and three-somes and occasionally into a larger group of team members. So problem-solving is usually distributed between at least two programmers, and between more than two if the situation demands it.

The distribution of problem-solving responsibility would extend to the team's customers, as needed. Each team's involvement with the customer varied, depending in part on the nature of the application and their availability. For example, Team S had very little contact with the customers of the system, but had a lot of interaction with the business analysts who knew the database structures and their uses. In this team, a discussion between a pair of developers to understand the problem was often extended to include the analysts. However analysts were not observed referring to the developers for help with solving the problems they encountered. Team W interacted mostly with the programme managers, and programme managers would frequently work with the marketing product managers.

One characteristic of problem-solving within our XP teams was that information was available from a number of sources including other members of the team, the customer, text books, intranet wikis and internet developer sites. For example, members of Team S would regularly consult a reference book, an online developer site, database documentation and the project manager in order to solve a problem.

Each person within a team was actively engaged in solving the problem as appropriate for their expertise. This manifested itself through the problem-solver actively seeking out the individual with the required expertise, but also individuals offering their help where appropriate. For example, in none of our teams did we observe a team leader nominating developers to help with an identified problem – people organised themselves to obtain and offer the appropriate advice. Where this involved one individual interrupting the work of another, both the interrupter and the interrupted respected each other's needs and worked together to find a suitable answer to the issue at hand.

This kind of distributed problem-solving, i.e. distributed across people, was observed on a daily routine basis. In addition to this, problem-solving is distributed over time. Test-first development means that the design of some code is considered before coding begins. Then, as the code evolves, we observed that issues may be raised during stand-up meetings, at iteration planning meetings and during lunch, coffee breaks and informal get-togethers. During our study of Team B, a particularly complex story exceeded its estimate and extended over more than one iteration, but the team persevered as they recognised it as a key part of the functionality.

4.2 Verbal and Non-verbal Behaviour

The character of each team we have studied is very different in terms of size, programming language, organisational setting, team composition and outlook. However each team had a keen sense of purpose and enthusiasm for their working. Team W for example appeared to work in a very solemn and serious atmosphere, while the atmosphere around Team S was much more relaxed. However all teams relied heavily on verbal communication. They were very sensitive to the need to talk with each other within the team and with customers or with others who had the right expertise. For example, when Team C faced a technical problem that they could not solve internally, they had no qualms about contacting an outside consultant for advice.

Individuals vary in how they best communicate ideas and thoughts. For example in Team S there was one individual who liked to write down notes, draw diagrams and generally doodle while exploring an issue. Any pairing session he was involved in produced and relied on a large collection of these notes and diagrams. On the other hand, another of the team members wrote only short notes on index cards, while another was not observed writing any notes at all. When these latter two team mates were pairing they did not talk very much, but often would turn to each other and appear to be seeing and manipulating an artefact in between them (which presumably represented the code, or the problem they faced). At these times, they spoke little except to make comments about the common artefact that they were both working on.

Although the purpose of pairing is to produce code, the process of pairing is fundamentally about communication – both verbal and non-verbal. We have observed elsewhere that this interaction is much like a three-way conversation [12], with developers occasionally talking directly with each other, sometimes interacting through the code and sometimes interacting directly with the code while the other developer watches. This intense three-way relationship introduces different ways of communicating; both developers typically engage in talking, typing, and gesturing - using the cursor and highlighting techniques to focus attention. In addition, the ability for pairs to overhear and be overheard appears to support the distributed nature of problem-solving where relevant expertise is offered when it is needed.

Other examples of the effect of non-verbal behaviour are the unannounced start of a stand-up meeting, and the use of a non-verbal noise to communicate information. In the former case, Team S did not often have to announce the fact that it was time for the daily stand-up meeting. When the time approached, team members would automatically congregate at the appropriate spot and the meeting would start. In Team C, a non-verbal noise was used to signify the release of tested code into the code base; in this case it was an artificial animal sound.

4.3 Co-ordinating Mechanisms

There were broadly two different types of co-ordination that we observed in our XP teams: regular and *ad hoc*. We first consider the regular mechanisms. Team C relied entirely on the manipulation and display of story cards, the planning game, and daily stand-ups for co-ordination. Team S also relied on these but in addition the project manager held the overall project plan from which story cards were generated. Team B used a similar approach to Team S. Team W did not have physical story cards, but kept their stories within the supporting software environment. This meant that the detailed manipulation of stories was not clearly visible, although they employed summary flip charts which showed which stories were being worked on and who was in which team.

All the teams were self-organising and hence there was little or no co-ordination imposed from the team's higher management. The key regular co-ordinating mechanisms were therefore the story cards, the planning game and the daily stand-ups.

Supporting this more regular co-ordination was the wide spectrum of *ad hoc* meetings, peripheral awareness, and fluid pairing situations, as we discussed above.

The stand-up meetings, for example, would be less effective if these other mechanisms were not in place.

4.4 Communicative Pathways

In general, communicative pathways in our XP teams were simple. In all cases, developers had direct and regular contact with the customer or the customer's representative, and they had clear and uncomplicated access to fellow team members and local, relevant expertise. The story was a key focus of all communicative pathways.

Within the team, communication happened through a network rather than along a single pathway. As we have discussed above, the teams all had effective ways of keeping each other informed of development issues, and the team members volunteered information when they felt it was relevant.

In Team C, if an issue arose with a customer, then the marketing person assigned to that customer would talk directly with the developer(s) working on the relevant part of the software. It was noticeable, however, that the marketing personnel would not walk straight into the developer 'pens', but would wait around outside until they were noticed by the developers (see [10] for more detail). In Team W, information regarding the wider product picture was communicated via marketing product managers or other senior staff on a regular basis, as and when there was something to report.

4.5 Knowledge Sharing and Access

Collective ownership is one of the practices that underpins XP. Hence it is no surprise that we found knowledge sharing and access to relevant expertise to be well-supported. For example, in all teams, pairs were formed explicitly on occasions to provide a balance between experience and novice status in order to expose novices to areas of the code that they did not know.

The most public evidence of knowledge sharing and access was the use of information radiators [16] to show the current status of the stories. We found these in all teams. Even in Team B where the organization rules regarding the sticking of items onto the walls prevented them from using a traditional board, they used a portable board or flipchart.

The above descriptions have painted a picture which implies that all developers are equal in terms of their capabilities and their 'specialisms'. Indeed we have not mentioned specialisms before. In Team C for example, there were eight developers, but also one graphic designer and one IT support manager. The graphic designer was not a Java programmer. She produced HTML and graphical images but in order to also gain an appreciation of the concerns of the developers, she would often pair with one of the Java programmers. In these circumstances her contribution to the development of code was minimal but the team all felt it important to share knowledge in this way. The graphic designer and IT support manager would often work together on tasks.

In other teams where 'specialists' did not pair with developers, all team members were actively involved in the daily stand-ups and other regular meetings. For example, Team W included a technical author, web developers and two testers who did not pair with developers, but they attended the meetings.

4.6 Potential Breakdowns in Information Propagation

In each team, we found evidence of breakdowns, or potential breakdowns.

Informal communication can breakdown when the parties involved don't have a common memory of the conversation and what was decided. In Team C the planning game involved estimating the cards and in order to do that it was necessary to gain a level of understanding about how to implement a solution, and that required some design. However the design used as the basis for estimating was not documented and it was not uncommon (as reported to the researcher) for a different design to be implemented and the estimate to be compromised. This illustrates the potential of collective memory to fail. This is not necessarily a problem situation provided the changed design and its rationale are communicated to others, but it is a potential breakdown.

Communication can also break down where there are 'too many' information flows. Team W did not, at the time of the study, use physical story cards, but stored information in an online internal software system. This had several advantages, including the fact that significant information could be kept alongside the main story, including acceptance tests, modifications, estimates, a history of who worked on the code, and so on. However we observed a situation where a story number was transcribed incorrectly, which led to a tester running the wrong acceptance test against a story. Due to the nature of the story and of the application it took significant time to realise that the code he had downloaded was not the code he should have been running against the given test. There are many possible ways that this could be avoided, e.g. better structuring of information online, double-checking of codes and tests, automatic linkages between code and tests, etc. However, it is interesting to note that shortly after we had completed our study in this organisation, they introduced physical story cards.

XP teams rely on self-managing and self-organising individuals who are prepared and able to take on responsibility for their work. This has significant advantages, but one consequence of this is that individuals regard their time as precious. We witnessed a situation in Team S which illustrated this. The project manager called a meeting of the developers (at the time, only four of them were in the office) in order to discuss a significant technical issue. One of the developers was unhappy as he did not understand why they were discussing this issue, nor the purpose of the meeting (i.e. what is going to be the result of this meeting). In this situation, the project manager was sharing information, but had not adequately explained the issue's significance or the meeting's purpose. Interestingly the other team members made considerable efforts to ensure that the unhappy developer was calmed.

The potential breakdown we identified in Team B revolves around the organisation's internal procedures and the team's expectation of timely feedback. Once the software had been tested internally, the software was handed over to another part of the organisation to run the acceptance tests, and this part of the organisation did not operate under XP principles. The consequence of this is that results from the acceptance tests were fed back to the developers 4 or 6 weeks after they had finished working on the software. This caused considerable consternation as the team had been working for several weeks on software that did not pass the acceptance tests.

We mentioned above the reliance of regular co-ordination mechanisms on the more *ad hoc* mechanisms. We did not see any examples of the *ad hoc* mechanisms failing, but if they did our analysis suggests that the regular co-ordination mechanisms might also suffer.

5 Discussion

One of the consequences of the XP approach to development is that much of the knowledge and expertise required to solve problems that are encountered is available quickly and easily in a form that can be immediately applied to the existing situation. For example, because one of the XP practices is collective ownership, all team members have a good understanding of the context of any problem that arises. This means that the time needed to explain the problem is minimised, and the applicability of potential solutions can be assessed rapidly. One way of expressing this is to say that the team members have sufficient common ground to be able to communicate effectively. Common ground is a key concept in co-ordination activities and without it collaborators need to express every detail explicitly [17, 18]; the discussions above indicate that XP teams need to maintain considerable common ground. There has been much debate about how to choose programmers to join an XP team. There is wide consensus that the new programmer needs to be compatible socially with the other team members, but we would also suggest that the level of common ground between the new programmer and the existing team (in terms of technical knowledge and experience, or in the specific application domain) will affect their compatibility with existing team members.

The main transformation taking place in this cognitive system is that of transforming the story into executable code. There is very little information propagation outside the story – the story remains the central focus of development from the time it is created until the code is handed over. One reason that these simple flows are sufficient for the team's needs is that the work is divided into small manageable chunks, thus restricting the amount of information needed to complete the story.

6 Conclusion

Looking at XP teams using the framework of distributed cognition shows us that XP teams use a simple flow of information that is underpinned by shared understanding of the software under development and sufficient common ground to support effective communication. To achieve their goals, XP teams tend to work in information-rich environments with easily accessible, easily applicable knowledge. Individual team members put effort into making sure the cognitive system performs as it should. The regular co-ordination mechanisms used, for example, would not be as effective if the more *ad hoc* system were to stop working. XP has a deep cultural attachment to close-knit, informal settings. In this analysis, we have indicated the benefits of this kind of setting for effective working. Potential breakdowns we have identified stem from a disturbance of the simple, coherent cognitive system we have described.

Conclusions from the work reported here fall into two areas: practical implications, and research implications. We suggest that practitioners study the potential breakdowns identified in Section 4, and consider whether any of these situations applies to their own circumstances. For researchers, we would argue that the analysis presented in this paper has shown the potential of distributed cognition to shed light on information propagation within an XP team from a novel perspective, but that this work has only just begun and there is clear scope for more, in-depth studies.

References

[1] Hutchins, E. (1995) *Cognition in the Wild*, Cambridge MA: MIT Press.
[2] Halverson, C. A., (2002) Activity theory and distributed cognition: Or what does CSCW need to DO with theories? *Computer Supported Cooperative Work*, 11:243-267.
[3] Jones, P.H. and Chisalita, C. (2005) Cognition and Collaboration – Analysing Distributed Community Practices for Design, *CHI 2005 Workshop*, April 2005, Portland, Oregon.
[4] Hoadley, C.M. and Kilner, P.G. (2005) Using Technology to Transform Communities of Practice into Knowledge-Building Communities, *SIGGROUP Bulletin*, 25, 1, 31-40.
[5] Hollan, J. Hutchins, E., Kirsch, D. (2000) Distributed Cognition: Toward a new foundation for human-computer interaction research, *ACM Transactions on Computer-Human Interaction*, 7(2), 174-196.
[6] Wright, P.C., Fields, R.E. and Harrison, M.D. (2000) Analyzing Human-Computer Interaction as Distributed Cognition: the resources model, *Human-Computer Interaction*, 15, 1-41.
[7] Rogers, Y. and Ellis, J. (1994) Distributed Cognition: an alternative framework for analyzing and explaining collaborative working, *Journal of Information Technology*, 9, 119-128.
[8] Flor, N.V. and Hutchins, E.L. (1992) Analyzing distributed cognition in software teams: a case study of team programming during perfective maintenance, *Proceedings of Empirical Studies of Programmers*, 1992
[9] Detienne, F. (2002) *Software Design - Cognitive Aspects*, Springer-Verlag, London.
[10] Sharp, H. and Robinson, H. (2004) An ethnographic study of XP practices, *Empirical Software Engineering,* **9**(4), 353-375.
[11] Robinson, H. and Sharp, H. (2004) The characteristics of XP teams, in *Proceedings of XP2004* Germany, June, pp139-147.
[12] Robinson, H. & Sharp, H. (2005) The social side of technical practices, in *Proceedings of XP2005*, LNCS 3556, 100-108.
[13] Robinson, H. and Sharp, H. (2005) Organisational culture and XP: three case studies, in *Proceedings of Agile 2005*, IEEE Computer Press pp49-58.
[14] Preece, J., Rogers, Y. and Sharp, H. (2002) *Interaction Design: beyond human computer interaction*, John Wiley & Sons, Chichester.
[15] Scrivener, S., Urquijo, S.P. and Palmen, H.K. (1993) The Use of Breakdown Analysis in synchronous CSCW system design, *Proceedings of ECSCW*, 517-534.
[16] Beck, K and Andres, (2005) *Extreme Programming Explained: Embrace Change* (2nd edition), Addison-Wesley.
[17] Clark, H. and Schaefer, E. (1998) Contributing to discourse, *Cognitive Science* 13, 259-294.
[18] Flor, N. (1998) Side-by-side collaboration: a case study, *International Journal of Human-Computer Studies*, 49, 201-222.

Foundations of Agile Decision Making from Agile Mentors and Developers

Carmen Zannier and Frank Maurer

University of Calgary, Department of Computer Science
2500 University Drive NW, Calgary, AB, CAN
{zannierc, maurer}@cpsc.ucalgary.ca
http://ebe.cpsc.ucalgary.ca/ebe

Abstract. There are few studies of how software developers make decisions in software design and none that places agile in the context of these decision making processes. In this paper, we present results of interviewing agile software developers and mentors to determine how design decision making aligns with rational decision making or naturalistic decision making. We present results of twelve case studies evaluating how agile professionals make design decisions, comparing mentor perspectives to developer perspectives. We describe our interview technique, content analysis used to analyze interview transcripts, and the interpretation of our results, to answer the question: how do agile designers make design decisions? Our results show that naturalistic decision making dominates design decision making but is supported by rational decision making.

1 Introduction

In this paper, we examine how agile software designers make software design decisions. There are three reasons to examine this topic. Firstly, little work exists concerning how decisions are made in software design [5][11], and none of this work focuses on agile methodologies, but evidence shows the ubiquity of design decisions in software development and the significant impacts of these decisions on software development [21][11][12]. As a result, there is a strong call and need to examine software design decisions [1][5][11][12][21][24]. Secondly, this topic provides insight into the important behavioral dimensions surrounding software design. Our work underscores the idea that, "the major problems of [software design] work are not so much technological as sociological in nature" [6], as well as the agile value of People and Interactions over Processes and Tools [2]. Lastly, by understanding the way that designers work and think, we can evaluate existing design processes and metrics against the way designers actually work and think, and we can motivate design processes and metrics suited to inherent work and thought processes.

Our multi-case study of twelve members of the agile community looks for consistency between agile mentors' ideas about design decisions and agile developers' practices in making design decisions. We define a design decision as the selection of an option among zero or more known and unknown options concerning the design of a

P. Abrahamsson, M. Marchesi, and G. Succi (Eds.): XP 2006, LNCS 4044, pp. 11–20, 2006.

software application [26]. We say zero or more because making no choice is still making a choice. We define an agile decision as a decision occurring in an agile environment. We define an agile *developer* as an interview subject who discussed a design decision that they championed when s/he was a member of a design team. We define an agile *mentor* as an interview subject who discussed design decisions as an abstract concept, based on the culmination of design experiences with software development teams where s/he was a coach or paid consultant. More than one design decision was discussed briefly in mentor interviews, as opposed to a detailed discussion of one design decision, in a developer interview. The abstract level at which mentors discussed design decisions allowed us to compare general understanding of agile work (e.g. agile literature and rhetoric found in the agile community) to actual practice of agile work, as reported by members of the agile community. We do not evaluate the quality of the decision.

Our empirical study provides two ground breaking results in the area of agile design decision making. Firstly, we find agile design decision making includes elements of both rational decision making (RDM) and naturalistic decision making (NDM) [14][17]. The current state of decision making literature suggests these decision making approaches are independent of each other. For example, fire-fighters use NDM [14], and operations researchers use RDM [17]. Our results show that in agile design, decisions are made using aspects of both, concurrently. This impacts the area of agile design by challenging traditional views of decisions, making agile research a forerunner in design decision making research. Our second result shows much agreement between agile developers and mentors. This impacts the area of agile design by strongly suggesting that what agile developers say they do is closely aligned with what they are seen doing. Such agreement in the agile community is a qualitative indicator of the effectiveness of agile literature and rhetoric.

Section 2 provides the background work and Section 3 describes our methodology. Section 4 describes results that emerged from our interviews. Section 5 compares quotes from agile mentors and agile developers to show similarities and differences. Section 6 discusses validity and Section 7 concludes this work.

2 Background

2.1 Decision Making

We use the concepts of rational and naturalistic decision making to provide insight on software design decision making. Rational decision making (RDM) is characterized by consequential choice of an alternative [17] and an optimal selection among alternatives. To select an optimal alternative, three features are required. First, alternatives are represented by a set of possible courses of action and potential outcomes for each action. Second, a utility function assigns a value to each possible action based on the attributes of its outcome. Third, a decision has probabilities for which outcome will occur given the selection of an alternative. Consequential choice is the analysis of alternatives and potential outcomes, typical of rational decision theory [16][17]. While consequential choice is a main factor of RDM, three other assumptions are also important. The first is the possible courses of action and the probability of specific outcomes are known. The second is a decision maker pursues optimality. The third is the large amount of time calculating alternatives is acceptable [14][19].

Naturalistic decision making (NDM) is defined by six characteristics [14]. A naturalistic decision appears in dynamic and turbulent situations. It embodies fast reactions to changes and embraces ill-defined tasks and goals. A naturalistic decision is resolved under the guidance of knowledgeable decision makers. It uses situation assessment and has a goal of satisficing design alternatives, instead of optimizing them. Situation assessment is the evaluation of a single alternative. A decision maker exercises this alternative after determining it is "good enough" [14]. Satisficing is the acceptance of a satisfactory alternative (e.g. "Good Enough Software") [14][4].

2.2 Doing Software Design

Software design is a problem structuring activity accomplished throughout the software development lifecycle [7][8][9][10]. A well-structured problem (WSP) is a problem that has criteria that reveal relationships between the characteristics of a problem domain and the characteristics of a method by which to solve the problem [22]. An ill-structured problem (ISP) is a problem that is not well structured [30].

A survey of software design studies, [1][3][5][7][8][9][10][18][21][23][24], shows that six related qualities impact software design: expertise, mental modeling, mental simulation, continual restructuring, preferred evaluation criteria and group interactions. While we do not consider this to be an exhaustive list of what impacts software design, the qualities and the studies give us some background about the way designers work. Expertise is the knowledge and experience software designers have in design [1]. Existing studies showed expertise is fundamental to design productivity [5], and that higher expertise resulted in an improved ability to create internal models and run mental simulations [1][3][23]. Mental modeling is the creation of internal or external models by a designer. A mental model is capable of supporting mental simulation [1]. Mental simulation is the "ability to imagine people and objects consciously and to transform those people and objects through several transitions, finally picturing them in a different way than at the start" [21]. Mental simulations occurred throughout the software design process at varying levels of quality dependent upon the skill of the designer and the quality of the model on which the mental simulation ran [1][5][7][8]. Continual restructuring is the process of turning an ISP to a WSP. The term "preferred evaluation criteria" refers to the minimal criteria a subject adopts to perform continual restructuring [14]. It occurred on an individual level or group level [7][24][5]. Group interactions are the dynamics of group work in software design. The terms "distributed" and "shared" cognition suggest that individual mental models coalesce via group work, resulting in a common model [7][24].

3 Methodology

We discuss our research methodology in terms of data collection and data analysis. We interviewed software designers about critical design incidents, and the decisions made concerning software design, using a critical decision method (CDM) [13]. The CDM studies "cognitive bases of judgment and decision making." [13]. The CDM contains questions regarding cues, knowledge, goals, options, experience, and time pressure surrounding a decision but the CDM is not indicative of NDM or RDM. Such indications are generated from our interpretations in Section 4. Table 1 lists the themes covered during the interview, and an example of how we asked the question. In practice the interview question was tailored to the context of the interview.

The software designers interviewed include recognized experts in successful software design, both as developers and as mentors. All of the interviewees presented in this paper were familiar with and used agile methods. In order to find new subjects to interview, we used snowball sampling "(getting new contacts from each person interviewed)" [20, p.194]. We did not restrict by age, experience, mentor versus developer roles, or by any other demographic characteristic. The comparison between 6 mentors and 6 developers emerged from a larger set of 25 interviews. Such emergence is indicative of certain formes of qualitative inquiry [20]. The interview subjects discussed varying types of software systems and we did not distinguish among the different types. The interview subjects in this paper discussed web based business applications, and/or small software systems (e.g. ~3-15 developers). Thus far we have not found any consistent differences in approaches to decision making, between web-based applications and non-web based applications.

Table 1. Design Decision Making Interview Questions

Decision
Describe how you make a design change to a system, and how you make the decision to make the change.
Cues
What do you see, hear, discuss, that suggests a change needs to occur?
Knowledge
Where do you acquire the knowledge to make the change?
Options
Discuss the extent to which you consider options in making a design change.
Experience
To what extent do specific past experiences impact your decision?
Time Pressure
How does time pressure impact decisions in design changes?
Externals
How do external goals impact decisions in design changes?

Consistent with naturalistic inquiry [14], we examined each critical design incident as an explanatory case study of the context and circumstances surrounding one or more design decisions [25]. We considered each case separately in order to allow the participant viewpoint to speak for itself. From a single case, we then made initial statements about software design decision making and then revisited the initial case and examined new cases to continuously shape the statements [25]. This pattern continued, incorporating more cases, until our theoretical propositions about design decision making were able to explain all cases [25]. This multiple-case design allows researchers to develop general knowledge about social phenomena from both the induction of data, and the deduction from theory [25].

We used content analysis [15], to identify recurring themes in the interviews to validate our theoretical propositions. Content analysis places words, phrases, sentences or paragraphs into codes which can be predefined or interactively defined [15]. Finally, for each question we used interpretations in Table 2 to decide if interview answers followed RDM or NDM.

4 Thematic Results

Using RDM and NDM to guide the generalizing of our interviewee approaches to decision making [25], we interpreted each interview question as it related to the attributes of RDM and NDM. We found differences between RDM and NDM in the *goal, method, effect of environment,* and the *nature of the knowledge* employed in the decision as shown in Table 2. In the following description of Table 2 the bold text represents data we collected during our interviews. Each of the four paragraphs contain propositions we formed, evaluated and modified as we analyzed each case.

If a decision maker's goal was to *optimize* design (rational), then **information cues** were considered to indicate *right or wrong* decisions. If the decision maker's goal was to *satisfice* design (naturalistic), then **cues** were used only to indicate *better or worse* outcomes.

If a decision maker followed *consequential choice* (rational), then s/he **discussed numerous options** surrounding the decision to make a design change. If a decision maker followed *singular evaluation* (naturalistic), then s/he **did not discuss options**.

Table 2. Foundations of Agile Decision Making

Component	1 RDM	2 NDM
Decision Goal	(1.1) *Optimizing:* Cues are right or wrong, quantifiable	(2.1) *Satisficing*: Cues are better or worse, not quantifiable.
Decision Method	(1.2) *Consequential choice*: Options are considered.	(2.2) *Singular Evaluation*: Options are not considered.
Decision Environment	(1.3) *Not concerned with computation overhead*: Time pressure is not a factor in decision making. External goals do not impact decision making. Cues are quantifiable.	(2.3) *Dynamic conditions*: External goals impact decision making. Time pressure impacts decision making. (2.4) *Real-time reactions*: Time pressure is an issue. Cues are from some trigger. (2.5) *Ill-defined tasks & goals*: Externals impact a decision. (2.6) *Situation assessment*: Cues are unquantifiable.
Decision Knowledge	(1.4) *Cognizant of all possible courses of action*: Specific experience based knowledge, explicit search of knowledge.	(2.7) *Tacit based knowledge*: Accumulation of knowledge. (2.8) *Experience-based knowledge*: Accumulation of experience.

If a decision maker was *unconcerned about time pressure* and the external environment (rational), then s/he was **unconcerned with computational overhead** and **external goals**. On the other hand, if the decision maker was *concerned about time pressure* (naturalistic), then *dynamic conditions, real-time reactions, ill-defined tasks and goals* and *situation assessment* allowed external goals to influence decision making, thus providing **little time and point** in considering detailed computations.

If the decision maker was *cognizant of all possible courses of action* (rational), then **experience, knowledge and explicit searches** were used to reach decisions. If the decision maker was *not* cognizant of all possible courses of action (naturalistic), then s/he relied on general accumulation of experience or knowledge. Given these general interpretations, more detailed results illustrate similarities and differences within and across cases.

5   Mentor and Developer Comparison

We examine each question from Table 1, across all cases, with respect to NDM or RDM and highlight similarities and differences between mentors and developers.

5.1   Cues

Every case showed that cues to design decisions were difficult to quantify, and thus needed to be qualified in some way. Feedback from people or a desire to make software code express what you want are examples of cues to a design decision. There was much agreement between the mentor perspective and the developer perspective regarding the qualitative nature of cues to a design change. For example,

Q1: "You looked at [the data model] and the picture was scrambly. It was like spaghetti code, a spaghetti data model; there were lines everywhere... And that project failed. So we worked on that project to try to do it again and it was very interesting because at the end we had something that you could look at and it was aesthetically pleasing." Mentor
Q2: "But whenever a customer comes in and says we need a new fee based on this, it's a substantial amount of work to implement if it's not something that is already supported in the old system." Developer

Given a large number of quotes such as these and our interpretations found in Table 2 (point 2.1) we conclude that cues to design decisions are more naturalistic than rational. We find consistent results between the agile mentors and agile developers.

5.2   Knowledge

The results from the knowledge question were extremely mixed. Regarding the knowledge a designer used in making a design decision, some developers reported having a general awareness of ideas, knowing only small things, or the absence of an actual search for knowledge. Given Table 2 (specifically points 2.7 and 2.8) knowledge seems to align with NDM. However, some mentors reported searching for knowledge or actively seeking it out, which aligns more with RDM (Table 2, point 1.4). There was not a clear disagreement between the mentor and developer perspective but in general the mentors spoke in a more positive fashion about actively searching out knowledge, than the developers did. For example,

Q3: "I don't think people come to a design problem and then look it up in ... [a] book. At least not when they're expected to." Mentor

Q4: "I'm appalled sometimes at how little people read, how little people go after knowledge ... in organizations." Mentor

Q5: "I'm always amazed at the teams I work with that won't read. It drives me nuts... I don't see any commonality in what people look at in books. I don't see them looking anyway – which drives me nuts! It really does." Mentor

Q6: "I never use those books. ... You talk with purists and they say ... every programmer has read 30, 50, 100 books about this and every year there's new bibles coming out...I grew up in software, I guess it comes to me naturally." Developer

Q7: "I haven't read a lot of books but there are a few that I have read ... You can read ... but until you actually put it into practice you never know, sort of wonder, if what you read is right or if you even remember it." Developer

Q8: "I went out and bought a book, the first book on XSLT that came out, a very nice book, and I just started devouring that book and started trying it out, seeing what worked. ... I bought the book to implement this design idea." Developer

We found no pattern yet as to when the pursuit of knowledge aligns more with NDM or RDM. We found no pattern among the mentors and developers, suggesting a lack of understanding of the way that agile designers learn and pursue learning.

5.3 Options

The results from the options question were mixed as well. Regarding the extent to which a software designer used consequential choice, the six mentors reported considering options as an integral step in making a design decision. Given Table 2, point 1.2, this would suggest that design decision making is rational in nature. However, the six developers reported not considering options to any large degree, choosing an option they believed would work or choosing an option based on what was the easiest at the time. Given Table 2, point 2.2 this would suggest decision making is more naturalistic in nature. For example,

Q9: "...whenever I start thinking about a problem, between the first moment the problem gets into my head and the moment my fingers hit the keyboard, I'm thinking about alternatives ...." Mentor

Q10: "[The chosen option] was pretty close to the first one that ... popped up on our radar when we started looking. [It] ended up working and it was the first one that I tried so [I] didn't really look at too many other options, no." Developer

In general we found that the larger the decision, the more the decision maker considered options. One interpretation of the mentor perspective is that mentors deal more with larger software design decisions (e.g. architecture, design patterns) than the type of decisions a developer perspective would discuss (e.g. automated refactorings), which is why we have a split between our developers and mentors in their approaches to decision making.

5.4 Experience

Similar to cues, a software designer's reliance on past experiences aligned with NDM across all cases. The case studies suggested that software designers rely on a general sense of past experiences, but also rely on assessing current situations. None of the results discussed applying specific past solutions to current design problems. There was agreement between mentor and developer perspectives. For example,

Q11: "In programming it seems to me as if everything I've ever learned is just in [my brain] ... a lot of times I know a thing but I have no idea where it came from. My brain has turned into this much of ideas that are accessible to me more or less but I don't remember the sources, I don't associate them." Mentor
Q12: "[The design decision] was generally around the problem of refactoring, so I thought our code [was] too verbose and I thought we were using the wrong solution for the problem. So yes, they were reminders of that, that's pretty generic. Where you're working in the system and you say no, we're solving this problem in the wrong way. We could solve it in a completely different way that would be much better. ... I had definitely experienced that before." Developer

From our interpretations found in Table 2 (point 2.8), we conclude that a software designer's use of past experience aligns more with NDM than with RDM. We found consistent results between agile mentors and agile developers in our study.

5.5 Time Pressure and External Goals

Time pressure did not impact decision making for the majority of the cases reporting results on time pressure and there was much agreement between the mentor and developer perspectives. Given our interpretations from Table 2 (point 1.3), we conclude that time pressure and its impact on decision making align more with RDM than with NDM. Lastly, the impact of external goals on decision making produced a 9:1:2 split NDM:RDM:N/A for the case studies, with much agreement between the mentor and developer perspectives. Given Table 2, points 2.3 and 2.5, the impact of external goals aligns more with NDM than RDM. For both time pressure and external goals we found consistent results between agile mentors and agile developers.

5.6 Design Decision

We find RDM occurring in design decision making in the form of consequential choice in large design decisions, in the absence of computational overhead involved in decision making and sometimes in the pursuit of knowledge used to make a decision. While NDM is dominant in recognizing a decision needs to be made, in the use of past experiences and in the impact of external goals, NDM is supported by RDM.

6 Validity

Given that we conducted case studies our external validity relies on generalization to theory (analytical generalization), and not statistical generalization [25]. All of our case studies align with our theory described in Section 5.6. For example, one agile developer (from Quote 8) found code "awkward" and "verbose" (qualitative cues) so he read up on XSLT as a solution to his problem (search for knowledge), "sold the idea" to business managers (external goals), and then prototyped his idea and fully implemented it once the prototype worked (singular evaluation of alternatives, satisficing). He felt little time pressure and was not reminded of specific past experiences.

7 Conclusions

We have presented results of a multi-case study with software designers concerning how they make design decisions. We conclude that NDM dominates design decision making, with support from RDM where conditions are suitable. Understanding the nature of software design decision making yields much insight into the way that people work, motivating the development of design processes and metrics tailored to our inherent approaches to decision making. For example, if a junior software designer follows a satisficing approach to his/her design decisions because s/he is under significant time pressure, and if the software engineering community cannot say that such an approach to design is right or wrong (i.e. it just _is_), then design metrics should evaluate the resulting design in light of the junior developer's knowledge/expertise/experience/etcetera and the time pressure imposed on the design decision. Comparing abstract ideas about the nature of design decisions to specific experiences in design decisions qualitatively indicates that agile rhetoric is mostly effective. As a community we lack consensual understanding of how agile designers pursue learning. This work motivates design processes and metrics that incorporate the intrinsic nature of agile software design.

Acknowledgments

We thank all of our interview participants who took time to speak with us.

References

1. Adelson B, et al. "The Role of Domain Experience in Soft. Design"; *IEEE Trans. Soft. Eng* 11 11 Nov. 1985.
2. Agile Manifesto www.agilemanifesto.org (08/17/2005)
3. Ahmed S et al. "Understanding Differences Between How Novice & Experienced Designers Approach Design Tasks"; *Res. Eng. Design* 14, 1-11 2003.
4. Bach, J. The Challenge of "Good Enough Software", *American Programmer*, Oct, 1995
5. Curtis B, et al. "A Field Study of the Soft. Des. Process for Large Systems", *Comm. ACM*, 31 11 Nov. 1988.
6. Demarco T, et al. Peopleware; 2nd Ed. Dorset House Pub. Co. NY; 1999.
7. Gasson S; "Framing Design: A Social Process View of Information System Development"; *Proc. Int. Conf. Information Systems*, Helsinki Finland, 224-236; 1998.
8. Guindon R; "Designing the Design Process" *HCI* 5, 305-344; 1990.
9. Guindon R; "Knowledge Exploited by Experts During Software Sys. Design"; *Int. J. Man-Mach. Stud.* 33, 279-304; 1990.

10. Herbsleb J, et al. "Formulation and Preliminary Test of an Empirical Theory of Coord.in Soft. Eng."; *Eur. Soft. Eng. Conf./ACM SIGSOFT Symp. Found. Soft. Eng*; 2003.
11. Highsmith J; Agile Project Management; Add-Wesley; 2004
12. Highsmith J; Agile Software Development Ecosystems; Addison-Wesley; 2003;
13. Klein G et al; "Critical Decision Method for Eliciting Knowledge" *IEEE Trans. Sys, Man and Cyber.*; 19, 3, 1989.
14. Klein G; Sources of Power, MIT Press Camb., MA; 1998
15. Krippendorff; Content Analysis; V5 Sage Pub. Lond. 1980
16. Lipshitz R; "Decision Making as Argument-Driven Action"; In: Klein et al, Decision Making in Action; NJ: Ablex Pub. Corp.; 1993.
17. Luce et al Games & Decisions John Wiley & Sons NY 1958
18. Malhotra et al "Cognitive Processes in Design" *Int. J. Man-Mach. Stud* 12 119-140 1980
19. Orasanu J et al; "The Reinvention of Decision Making"; In: Klein et al, Decision Making in Action; NJ Ablex; 1993.
20. Patton M.Q; Qualitative Research & Evaluation Methods 3rd Ed.; Sage Pub, CA; 2002.
21. Rugaber S et al. "Recognizing Design Decisions in Programs" *IEEE Software*; 1990.
22. Simon H; "The Structure of Ill Structured Problems"; *AI* V4, 181-201; 1973
23. Sonnetag S; "Expertise in Professional Soft. Design" *J. App. Psych.* 83 5 703-715 1998
24. Walz D.B, et al. "Inside a Software Design Team"; *Comm. ACM*, V.36 No.10 Oct 1993.
25. Yin, R.K; Case Study Research: Design & Methods 3rd Ed. Sage Publications, CA, 2003
26. Zannier C, et al.; "A Qualitative Empirical Evaluation of Design Decisions"; *Wkshp on Human & Social Factors of Soft. Eng.*; ACM Press: 2005

Software Development as a Collaborative Writing Project

Brian Bussell[1] and Stephen Taylor[2]

[1] Norwich Union Life, 60 Wellington Way, York YO90 1LZ
brian.bussell@norwich-union-life.co.uk
http://www.norwichunion.com
[2] British APL Association, 81 South Hill Park, London NW3 2SS
editor@vector.org.uk
http://www.vector.org.uk

Abstract. Software describes an imagined machine. To be software, the description must be executable, which means written so a computer can animate it. Non-executable descriptions (specifications, designs, &c.) are instrumental to this work; they are intermediate texts. We advance a model of software development as the collaborative writing of a series of descriptions. We propose the chief distinction of agile development to be the exclusion from this process of the human translation of intermediate texts. We distinguish supported and unsupported communication. We analyse the success of Extreme Programming in terms of avoiding unsupported communication and prioritising feedback from executable descriptions. We describe functional programming techniques to construct notations that allow programmers and users to collaborate writing executable system descriptions, collapsing distinctions between analysis, design, coding and testing. We describe a metric of code clarity, semantic density, which has been essential to the success of this work. We report the use of these techniques in the Pensions division of Britain's largest insurer, and its effect on the business.

1 Introduction

In this paper we advance a view of software development in which similarities to collaborative writing projects such as making movies or drafting legislation matter more than resemblances to civil engineering. This view is grounded in professional experience of writing software, in the mathematics of computer science, and in the philosophy of linguistics. It is contrary in general to the conventional model of software development, and in particular to what has become known as 'software engineering'.

From it we derive radical development practices and report their use at Norwich Union.

To establish common ground, we start with fundamentals.

2 Universal Turing Machines and Programs

The important characteristic of a computer is that it can be loosely thought of as a Universal Turing Machine (UTM). Without software a computer is useful only as a

P. Abrahamsson, M. Marchesi, and G. Succi (Eds.): XP 2006, LNCS 4044, pp. 21–31, 2006.

doorstop. Its real value is its ability to emulate the behaviour of other machines. The applications we run on computers are representations and emulations of the behaviour of machines.

Almost all machines emulated by computer applications are imaginary. While early word-processing applications emulated and extended the behaviour of real typewriters, modern word-processing applications now emulate machines that never have been built and never will be. Mechanical computing reached its limits with Babbage's Differential Engine; he never completed his more ambitious Analytical Engine. Our dreams exceed our abilities to press, cut and weld.

Babbage could not build his Analytical Engine with Victorian engineering and the funds he could raise; his completed machine remained a dream. But with programmable UTMs, we routinely emulate imaginary machines more complex than Babbage's.

The key is the program. A program describes the behaviour of a machine in terms that allow a UTM to animate the description. This is what programmers do – we write beforehand (*pro-gram*) executable descriptions of machine behaviour.

A UTM, like the magical character in a folk tale, grants wishes. As in the folk tales, accurately describing what you want turns out to be harder than it seems. Our dreams are light on detail and have unforeseen consequences. Software developers are the heirs of King Midas1[1].

3   Creative Writing and Translation

Here are two descriptions of a machine too complex for Babbage to have built.

```
mean=: +/ % #    NB. arithmetic mean of a list of
numbers
```

The first description (+/ % #) is executable, and written in the J programming language. The second description follows the NB. and is written in English. To a reader of both languages, the descriptions are equivalent; that is, each translates the other.

The first description can be animated with the help of a J language interpreter. A J interpreter executes C code, which becomes a new (and lengthier) description of the desired machine behaviour. A C compiler then composes an even lengthier description in a chip's instruction set. The chip is a UTM; animation can now begin.

Instructions to a chip are the final form of software. Now consider where a software development project starts; consider the following text.

---

[1] "Dionysus, who had been anxious on Silenus's account, sent to ask how Midas wished to be rewarded. He replied without hesitation: 'Pray grant that all I touch be turned into gold.' However, not only stones, flowers, and the furnishings of his house turned to gold but, when he sat down to table, so did the food he ate and the water he drank. Midas soon begged to be released from his wish, because he was fast dying of hunger and thirst; whereupon Dionysus, highly entertained, told him to visit the source of the river Pactolus, near Mount Tmolus, and there wash himself. He obeyed, and was at once freed from the golden touch, but the sands of the river Pactolus are bright with gold to this day." [1].

> Our competitors are beating us on delivery. Our process is too slow; we
> just can't get our goods out of the door fast enough. We need a new order-
> processing system.

It contains the following description of a machine: a new order-processing system. In
its likely context – a senior-management conversation – it sufficiently describes the
solution to a business problem. The description carries for that conversation the right
three facts about the solution: its behaviour will be to process orders, it will involve a
computer, and it will have to be acquired.

This description is not executable. It corresponds to many executable descriptions
– to too many. Developing the system means writing an executable description of a
machine that solves the business problem.

Note that this development process is not translation. The application code and a
new order-processing system both describe the behaviour of an imaginary machine,
but they are not translations of each other.

We propose that agile and conventional models of software development are most
clearly distinguished by the inclusion or exclusion of human translation as a project
activity.

Put another way, conventional software development projects measure their
success by whether they have accurately translated a non-executable system
description into an executable one – does the program match the specification? Agile
projects ask only – have we solved the business problem?

Of course, no one attempts to write an executable translation of a new order-
processing system. Instead, analysts meet sponsors and write specifications. Specialists read specifications and write design documents and data architectures. Analyst/
programmers write program specifications. And programmers either write program
documentation and translate it into code, or translate specifications into code and then
back into documentation. Thus the conventional model. We know that human
translation is included, because an ideal of the conventional model is to derive the
code from the program specification alone, or from the documentation alone.

4   Two Great Lies of Software Development

> *When ye sup with the Devil, use a long spoon. (Trad.)*

There are two Great Lies of software development. The first is *I can tell you what
we need*. The second is *I can tell you what it will take to build it*. Both lies contain
enough truth to nourish illusion.

A new order-processing system is the first of a series of descriptions. Each
successive description expands its predecessor. The last and longest description is
composed in a chip's instruction set; but the last several descriptions are all formal
equivalents (translations), produced without human intervention by compilers and
interpreters. Programmers make the last human contribution, by writing the first
executable description. The point to keep in mind is that from a new order-processing
system to chip instructions, is nothing but behavioural descriptions all the way
down.

The speaker of *we need a new order-processing system* will not enlarge greatly on his description. He has competent staff to do that. Describing what you want (specifying requirements) is understood to entail much discussion and analysis, balancing of priorities, and consideration of foreseeable changes in the business. But the underlying assumption is that it can be done. In most fields of activity, inability to describe what you want is a reliable indicator of incompetence.

Let us entertain the contrary, and suppose the folk wisdom is right: imagining and describing accurately a complex machine 'from thin air' is at least greatly more difficult than it appears, and perhaps too difficult for practical purposes. Here is a thought experiment.

Call the speaker of *we need a new order-processing system* the system's *sponsor*. Suppose the sponsor actually does know precisely how the system should behave. He can give consistent answers to any question on the subject; he envisages its interfaces to the user and to other systems, and understands the important implications. The sponsor is ready to write a description of the imagined machine that requires only translation into source code. Call this description the *absolute specification*.

How is he to write it? Plain English will not do; its imprecision and elegant ambiguities disqualify it for the job. Formal notations are available for different parts of the work: for example, UML for user interfaces; functional decomposition diagrams. In principle, nothing prevents the sponsor learning these notations and writing the absolute specification. But mastering them requires years of work. The sponsor will not have done this; the premise is that he is a businessman.

5   Writing Software Without Programmers

Exceptions to this are important and instructive. In the 1980s spreadsheet applications removed programmers from an entire field of software development. Using spreadsheets is not considered programming, but Taylor recalls working on an Australian government tender in the early 1990s in which the spreadsheets developed in its support exceeded in complexity most software he had previously written.

The important contribution of spreadsheets, where used, is to remove the element of human translation from software development. Microsoft has had some success in extending this with Visual Basic, making possible for users a good deal of tinkering with its products. Spreadsheet and Visual Basic users do not think of what they do as programming, nor are they encouraged to; Microsoft promotes Visual Basic as a 'productivity tool'.

We note here the bias in the usage of 'programming': what one person does for another, not what one does for oneself. A professional programmer programs machines for others to use.

Actuarial calculations provide solutions in the once stable but now fast-changing insurance business. These calculations routinely exceed the descriptive powers of spreadsheets. Actuaries have long written executable descriptions of their calculations. Bussell, an actuary, recalls writing them in APL in the 1980s. In the Pensions division he now directs, calculations are described either in APL, or by actuaries writing direct in Mathematica.

Instructive examples can also be found in the financial markets, another field in which the cost of delay has minimised or eliminated human translation in developing software. Financial traders commonly either write their own software or seat programmers in the trading room.

> When I started in this business, every trader had a Visual Basic manual on his desk; now it's more likely to be a J2EE manual. [2]

In practice, competence in the business and in writing software coincide only where the business requires mathematical skills. In consequence, highly abstract executable notations such as APL, A+, J, K, Q, R and S flourish primarily among actuaries, financial traders and statisticians.

6 Notation as a Tool of Thought

In the thought experiment above we imagined our sponsor knew exactly how the machine should behave. From this we saw the lack of a suitable notation in which to write the absolute specification as a formidable, and probably an insuperable, obstacle.

But the premise itself is untenable. It supposes the sponsor has completely imagined the desired machine, which is to say that he has an absolute specification 'in his head'.

A strong body of opinion, associated with Chomsky and Fodor [3], maintains such a mental description entails mapping to some internally coded language. Even an Andersonian realist would suppose such a description handled by the brain in the same way that language is handled. We think and speak only what can be expressed in language.

> 7. Wovon man nicht sprechen kann, darüber muß man schweigen[2].

Wittgenstein's later argument [5] against the possibility of private language further restricts the scope of thought. We know languages only by sharing them. We think only what can be expressed in languages shared with others. In studying a subject one acquires new thoughts along with the vocabulary to express them. [6]

In his later argument, Wittgenstein also came to see that the relationship between language and its referents is inexact, slippery and ambiguous; mediated by what he called our language games. We can never find in our everyday languages the precision and completeness we aspire to in mathematical notation.

> Well here again that don't apply
> But I gotta use words when I talk to you.
> …
> I gotta use words when I talk to you.
> But if you understand or if you don't
> That's nothing to me and nothing to you
> We all gotta do what we gotta do
>   *T.S. Eliot/* "Fragment of an Agon"

---

[2] 7. Whereof one cannot speak, thereof one must be silent. [4].

7   Hubris and the Children of Dædalus

> *How can I tell you what I think,*
> *till I've heard what I have to say?*
> *Anon.*

The first Great Lie of software development has two parts: *I know what I need* and *I can tell you what it is.* We have examined the difficulties of the second part while assuming the truth of the first. Now we will show what is more important: the first part is also false.

Whether writing novels, screenplays or software, we start with an incomplete vision. It is only in the process of elaboration that we understand the implications of our choices, and see, for example, that having *let everything I touch turn to gold* leads to death by starvation. Had King Midas been granted a revision of his wish, Version 2 would have included a switch to turn transmutation on or off.

Some software has to run correctly on first use – ask NASA. Such software has to be written without the benefit of feedback from use in the real world.

The legends of King Midas and Icarus [7] warn against hubris; that our dreams have unintended consequences. In pursuing our dreams, we need feedback from the world to understand their consequences. It was not the cautious craftsman Dædalus who fell to earth, but his son – carried away by his dreams.

When, sensitive to the appearance of incompetence, we subscribe to the first Great Lie and claim we know what is needed and that we can describe it, we set aside warnings from our culture's long tradition. We risk hubris rather than admit ignorance.

Even when we qualify the lie by allowing significant time to write and discuss the description, we ignore Wittgenstein's warnings about the slipperiness of language and the importance of grounding language games in reality. In thick, formal specification documents, thousands of pages of charts, tables and narratives, we detail the machines we shall conjure. So many details, so much dreaming – and no feedback.

We assert what Wittgenstein would predict: little effective communication is possible about purely imaginary machines.

8   Raiders of the Inarticulate

> *Because one has only learnt to get the better of words*
> *For the thing one no longer has to say, or the way in which*
> *One is no longer disposed to say it. And so each venture*
> *Is a new beginning, a raid on the inarticulate*
> T.S. Eliot/ *"East Coker"*

Extreme Programming (XP) shares this fear of hubris [8] and addresses it briskly. XP teams begin by building the smallest system of any possible value [9] and use that with the sponsor to conjure, explore and revise his dreams. Incremental development treats knowledge as scarce and communication as uncertain.

Communication within XP projects reflects scepticism about its value divorced from a running system. The sponsor's representative sits with the programmers at all times, to resolve immediately questions about the business values of different behaviours. These questions can always be related to the behaviour of the running system, for XP projects always have a running system. Small changes in behaviour are delivered frequently, so their consequences can be explored piecemeal. Incremental developers know that dreams turn easily into nightmares.

Everything is referred to the final human text, that is, the source code. There are no intermediate texts for humans to translate into executable notation, and against which to measure accuracy of the translation. Agile projects do not ask *did we implement the specification accurately?* but *have we solved the business problem?* Such intermediate texts as are written are destroyed after use; the running system is the starting point for any discussion of change. All changes are changes to the running system.

In similar vein, for software quality and cross-training, XP programmers collaborate upon the source code (pair programming) rather than talk or write about it.

Call communication, spoken or written, *unsupported* in the absence of its object. Talk about a system, in its absence, is unsupported. Talk about source code, in its absence, is unsupported.

Such talk is not cheap. Unsupported talk is unreliable and expensive.[3]

An engineer designing a machine minimises use of components that are unreliable or expensive. XP teams use much less communication than the conventional model. Nearly all of it is supported.

9   Shrinking the Circle

How can we use this view of software development to solve business problems faster?

The Pensions division of Norwich Union processes claims from a range of products inherited through mergers and takeovers, and supported upon a range of administrative systems. Processing the claims is relatively complex; when tackled with word-processor scripts, spreadsheets and mainframe terminal emulators, claims took about an hour to process. Clerks required six weeks training to begin handling the simpler claims of their department, and six months to be able to handle all of them. Cross-training took about three weeks, so departments were rarely able to help each other balance work loads, and backlogs were common.

Regulatory and legislative changes are now relatively frequent, as are changes to the administration of the business, and the organisation of the company. This describes an environment changing so rapidly that no conventional software development project to cut processing costs has ever been contemplated.

We have nonetheless been able to exploit insights gleaned from XP and apply them with a team initially of two programmers. The system went into production use after some months, and two years on, now processes as many pension claims as the company's core IT systems. It has halved the average processing time for claims, slashed training time to days, and eliminated backlogs. The system is now supported and developed by four programmers.

A key technique to the success of this has been programmers and users collaborating on writing the source code.

Not all of it, by any means. But key business rules, previously enshrined in user training and check lists, had appeared impractical to analyse in such an unstable environment. For example, a 5-page check list described how to determine whether a

---

[3] This is the subject of a forthcoming paper.

claim was liable to a certain penalty. An executable version of the rules was first worked out with a test battery of examples, then refactored for clarity into its present form, in which it is occasionally amended by the senior clerks and programmers together. The complete rules fit on an A4 page, and are appended.

Programmers have made this possible by constructing local, domain-specific executable notations. The vocabulary of these notations is drawn from the users' talk about the work. Our tiny team does not have an Onsite Customer; instead it works among its customers. These notations constitute the shared languages required by Wittgenstein and lauded by Whitehead.

> By relieving the brain of all unnecessary work, a good notation sets it free to concentrate on more advanced problems, and in effect increases the mental power of the race. [...] By the aid of symbolism, we can make transitions in reasoning almost mechanically, by the eye, which otherwise would call into play the higher faculties of the brain. [...] It is a profoundly erroneous truism, repeated by all copy-books and by eminent people when they are making speeches, that we should cultivate the habit of thinking of what we are doing. The precise opposite is the case. Civilisation advances by extending the number of important operations which we can perform without thinking about them. [10]

Constructing a notation is not the end of the task, but it brings the end near. Users and programmers can now converge quickly on and verify a common understanding. The notation enables them to avoid ambiguity; it is a "tool for thought" in the sense of Iverson's Turing Award lecture [11]. Because the notation is executable (and interpreted), the running system animates the described behaviour in front of them.

Taylor describes a typical scenario with an expert user, S.

> S comes and sits beside me, facing the system running in my development environment. She has not written or spoken to me about the change she contemplates. She begins by getting the system to do something she wants changed: either crashing it, or displaying or printing something other than what she wants. She can now point at the behaviour she wants changed. I use my knowledge of the source to locate the rules controlling that behaviour, and we trace execution, jointly examining how those rules are expressed and applied. We then agree an amendment, which seems to express what she intends, and resume execution. We try other examples, explore implications and revise the rules until we're satisfied the revision seems to express what S contemplated. I save the revised version where she can test and explore it further.

Working this way is insanely productive, because the system's behaviour can be revised without interrupting the conversation. If changes to the code took only an hour, the process described above would cover days. As it is, analysis, design, implementation and alpha-testing collapse into periods sometimes measured in minutes. In the last two months of 2005 the team released over 200 changes to the production system.

10 Semantic Density

Our ability to work at this speed depends on programmers and users collaborating on the source code. This in turn depends upon the value of a metric we have dubbed *semantic density*. [12]

Semantic density is the proportion of tokens in the source code that are drawn from the users' *semantic domain*; that is, the vocabulary they use to discuss the work. It ranges between 0 and 1. We are able to achieve very high values because

- functional- and array-programming techniques, and judicious use of anonymous lambdas, enable us to avoid defining terms (such as counters) outside the users' semantic domains;
- languages derived from Iverson's notation support a version of Church's lambda calculus, enabling us to define entire local vocabularies in a few lines of code;
- users ignore APL's analphabetic glyphs, which have no impact on semantic density.

11 Conclusion

A software development project imagines and describes a desired process. This is difficult work, which has become no easier since King Midas tried it. The unsupported communications and intermediate texts of software engineering do little to help this work and a great deal to prolong it. Much XP practice can be characterised as eschewing intermediate texts in favour of high-bandwidth communication between sponsor and programmer, supported by feedback from a running system. Functional programming techniques extend this by allowing sponsor and programmer to collaborate on source code, and permit radical gains in productivity. These techniques are in use in the Pensions division of Britain's largest insurer.

Acknowledgements

The authors thank Paul Berry, Chris Burke, Gitte Christensen, Romilly Cocking, Roger Hui and Charlie Skelton for comment on a draft of this paper.

References

1. Graves, R. *The Greek Myths*, London, Folio Soc., 1996, p.263
2. Mark Sykes, Director, Global Markets Finance, Deutsche Bank, London addressing Kx Systems User Meeting; see report in *Vector*, Vol.21., No.2 http://www.vector.org.uk/archive/v212/kx212.htm
3. Fodor, J., The Modularity of Mind, MIT Press, Boston, 1983
4. Wittgenstein, L., *Logische-Philosophische Abhandlung*, Cambridge, 1922
5. Wittgenstein, L. *Philosophical Investigations: German Text, with a Revised English Translation* Blackwell, Oxford, 2002
6. Taylor, S. "The Experience of Being Understood: on requirements specification as a Wittgensteinian language game" http://www.5jt.com/articles.php?article=beingunderstood
7. Graves, R. ibid., p.291
8. Beck, K. *Extreme Programming Explained: Embrace Change* Addison-Wesley, Boston, 2000, p.165
9. Beck, K. ibid. p.131&ff.
10. Whitehead, A.N. *An Introduction to Mathematics*, p59, H. Holt & Co., London, 1911 http://www.headmap.org/unlearn/alfred/1.htm
11. Iverson, K.E. "Notation as a Tool of Thought" 1979 ACM Turing Award lecture, *Communications of the ACM*, Vol.23, No. 8; see http://elliscave.com/APL_J/tool.pdf
12. Taylor, S.J. "Pair Programming With The Users", *Vector*, Vol.22, No.1 http://www.vector.org.uk/archive/v221/sjt221.htm

Appendix

A fragment of source code maintained jointly by programmers and users.

```
[0]     WillMvrApply dic
[1]
[2]     applies doesNotApply refer←1 0 ¯1                      ⍝ range of answers
[3]
[4]     ⍝ LOCAL VOCABULARY ----------------------------------------------------------
[5]     asIDN←{dft 3p#.IDNToDate ⍺ ⍺⍺ #.DateToIDN dtt ⍵}
[6]     daysAfter←+asIDN
[7]     daysBefore←-¨asIDN
[8]     oneOf←{(⊂⍺~□TC)∊⍵}
[9]
[10]    all←∧/ ⋄ not←~ ⋄ before←< ⋄ after←> ⋄ no←~∘(∨/) ⋄ and←∧ ⋄ or←∨ ⋄ any←∨/
[11]
[12]    ⍝ BUSINESS RULES START HERE -------------------------------------------------
[13]    isDeferred←OrigNRD≠Nrd
[14]    isBefore911←OrigNRD before 20040911
[15]    termOver5←OrigNRD≥5 yrsAfter StartDate
[16]    termUnder5←not termOver5
[17]    deferredBy5←Nrd≥5 yrsAfter OrigNRD
[18]    ThreePolAnniversariesBefore←StartDate∘{2 yrsBefore ⍺ ⍺⍺⍺b4 ⍵-⍴=/10000|⍺ ⍵}
[19]    oneMonthBefore←¯1∘DATE∆ADDMTHS
[20]
[21]    :If not InUWP
[22]        answer←doesNotApply
[23]    :ElseIf termUnder5 and RetirementAge≥75
[24]        answer←refer
[25]
[26]    :ElseIf RetirementAge≥75
[27]        answer←doesNotApply
[28]    :ElseIf ExitDate after oneMonthBefore 75 yrsAfter Dob
[29]        answer←doesNotApply
[30]
[31]    :ElseIf Assurer='CU'
[32]        answer←any MVRs>0
[33]
[34]    :ElseIf IsVista
[35]        answer←ExitDate before ThreePolAnniversariesBefore OrigNRD
[36]
[37]    :Else
[38]
[39]        exception←(Prepare='Quote')and(ExitDate=Nrd)and deferredBy5
[40]        exception(and)←isBefore911 or IsMvrFreePoint
[41]        :If isDeferred and not exception
[42]            answer←applies
[43]
[44]        :ElseIf (Prepare='Payment')and ExitDate before Nrd
[45]            answer←applies
[46]
[47]        :ElseIf ExitDate before 183 daysBefore OrigNRD
[48]            answer←applies
[49]        :ElseIf (Prepare='Quote')and ExitDate≠Nrd
[50]            answer←applies
[51]        :Else
[52]            useRule←deferredBy5 and(isBefore911 or(termOver5 and IsMvrFreePoint))
[53]            useRule(or)←termOver5 and not isDeferred
[54]            :If not useRule
[55]                answer←applies
[56]            :Else ⍝ SPTP rule
[57]                recentSPTP←PAYTS.EFFECTDATE after 5 yrsBefore OrigNRD
[58]
[59]                :If (all recentSPTP)and not RegPmtFlag
[60]                    answer←applies
[61]                :ElseIf no recentSPTP
[62]                    answer←doesNotApply
[63]                :Else
[64]                    answer←refer
[65]                :EndIf
[66]            :EndIf
[67]        :EndIf
[68]
[69]    :EndIf
[70]
[71]    MvrApplies←answer
```

Comparative Analysis of Job Satisfaction in Agile and Non-agile Software Development Teams

Grigori Melnik and Frank Maurer

Department of Computer Science, University of Calgary
Calgary, Alberta, Canada
{melnik, maurer}@cpsc.ucalgary.ca

Abstract. Software engineering is fundamentally driven by economics. One of the issues that software teams face is employee turnover which has a serious economic impact. The effect of job dissatisfaction on high turnover is consistently supported by evidence from multiple disciplines. The study investigates if and how job satisfaction relates to development processes that are being used and the determinants of job satisfaction across a wide range of teams, regions and employees. A moderate positive correlation between the level of experience with agile methods and the overall job satisfaction was found. The evidence suggests that there are twice as many members of agile teams who are satisfied with their jobs (vs members of non-agile teams). The ability to influence decisions that affect you, the opportunity to work on interesting projects, and the relationships with users were found to be statistically significant satisfiers.

1 Introduction

Economics is an important dimension of software engineering and it cannot be ignored. One of the issues that software teams face is voluntary turnover which has a serious economic impact. DeMarco and Lister's early work on peopleware [8] reveals a strong impact of people onto the success of software development projects. In this paper, we analyze if the development process used has an impact on job satisfaction. Concretely, we investigate agile processes and compare them to the overall industry.

Organizational psychology defines job satisfaction as a "present-oriented evaluation of the job involving a comparison of an employee's multiple values and what the employee perceives the job as providing" [12]. Even though the effect of job satisfaction on employee's performance and productivity (happy teams = productive teams) is disputed and considered by some organizational psychologists as a myth [19], [7], one particular discordant association – between job satisfaction and volunteer turnover (i.e. perceived desirability of movement) – has been consistently supported by evidence. Furthermore, job dissatisfaction is one of the most important confirmed antecedents for the high volunteer turnover [14], [17], [16]. As such it has a considerable economic effect on organizations, individuals and society[1].

---

[1] Although a positive economic effect can be achieved by the individual (i.e. increased salary), this study focuses on the societal macro aspects of the turnover, which are typically negative.

P. Abrahamsson, M. Marchesi, and G. Succi (Eds.): XP 2006, LNCS 4044, pp. 32–42, 2006.
© Springer-Verlag Berlin Heidelberg 2006

Projecting this onto the IT industry, analogous observations can be made. However comparatively less work has been done in this direction. For example, in a study of software development environments, Burk and Richardson showed that "job satisfaction relates more closely to an employee's choice to stay with the organization than does financial reward" [6]. Estimates of turnover costs in IT industry vary. For example, studies put turnover costs as much as 70-200% [10] and 150-200% of that employee's annual salary [15]. The cost of employee loss includes advertising, search fees, interview expenses (air fare, hotel etc.), manager's and team members' time spent interviewing, training and ramp up, overload on team, including overtime to get work done during selection and training of replacement; lost customers, lost contracts or business, lowered morale and productivity, sign-on bonus and other perks, moving allowance, and loss of other employees [10]. Boehm extensively discusses factors of software developers' motivation and satisfaction and their various effects in the seminal Software Engineering Economics work [4].

Agile methods – human-centric bodies of practices and guidelines for building software in unpredictable, highly-volatile environments – are gaining more popularity now. They, supposedly, increase, among other things, job satisfaction by improving communications among team members and with the customer, promoting continuous feedback, and allowing developers to make decisions that effect them.

Agilists claim that agile methods make not only the customer more satisfied but also the members of the development team. If that is the case, then the improved job satisfaction may lead to a lower turnover, which in turn results in the economic benefits discussed earlier. However, most of what we know about job satisfaction in agile software development teams is anecdotal [5]. As agile methods increase in their popularity, the benefits of higher job satisfaction mentioned have been: increased individual and team morale [11], motivation [1], performance [18], productivity [18] and retention [11], [18], [3]. With the exception of a single study by Manaro et al [13], all claims were based on anecdotes and required a leap of faith. However, if we are to really understand the impact of agile methods on employees, teams and organizations, we need to go beyond anecdote and determine employee satisfaction empirically. In the present study, we set out to investigate how employees in agile and non-agile teams perceive the quality of their work life. By restricting our attention to job satisfaction, we can sharpen the understanding of its multiple determinants and those aspects of software engineering that are most valued by the individual.

2 Research Questions, Context and Method

To structure our research, we followed the Goal/Questions/Metrics GQM) Paradigm [2]. Table 1 provides a summary of the goals, research questions and metrics. We also include our hypotheses and testing strategies. The goal of our research is to understand if and how job satisfaction relates to development processes that are being used and the determinants of job satisfaction across a wide range of teams, regions and employees based on the type of development process used. Consequently, the main research question is whether agile methods lead to higher, similar, or lower job satisfaction rates in software development teams in comparison to the IT industry in

Table 1. Research structure: Goal/Questions/Metrics with hypotheses and tests strategies

Goal	Purpose	Investigate
	Issue	the job satisfaction of individual team members related to
	Object	software development process type adopted
	Viewpoint	from the view point of agile, non-agile and general IT industry
Question	Q_1	Do members of agile software development teams experience higher, similar, or lower job satisfaction than members of non-agile teams?
Metrics	M_1	Satisfaction ratings by respondents categorized by the levels of adoption/experience with agile methods (from none to 5+ years); Spearman's measure of correspondence
Null Hypothesis	H_{01}	No relationship exists between the level of agile methods adoption and the overall job satisfaction of the individual
Test	T_1	Two-tailed Chi-square test
Question	Q_2	Are the rates of job satisfaction expressed by members of agile teams higher, similar, or lower than of IT industry in general?
Metrics	M_2	Percentage difference of satisfaction ratings; Spearman's measure of correspondence
Null Hypotheses	H'_{02}	The levels of overall job satisfaction of respondents from Agile group and General IT group are the same
	H''_{02}	The levels of overall job satisfaction of respondents from Non-agile group and General IT group are the same
Test	T_2	Two-tailed Chi-square test
Question	Q_3	Are there differences in perceptions based on the role (manager, worker, consultant)?
Metrics	M_3	Percentage differences of satisfaction ratings
Null Hypotheses	H'_{03}	Levels of satisfaction by managers and workers are the same in agile teams
	H''_{03}	Levels of satisfaction by managers and workers are the same in non-agile teams
Test	T_3	Two-tailed Chi-square test
Question	Q_4	What are the relationships between the level of experience with agile methods and individual job satisfiers (Table 2)
Metrics	M_4	Ratings for each satisfier; Spearman's measure of correspondence
Null Hypotheses $\forall s \in job\ satisfiers$	$H_{04\text{-}s}$	No relationship exists between the level of experience with agile methods and satisfiers
Test	T_4	Two-tailed Chi-square test

general. An additional objective is to discover and describe relationships between selected job satisfiers (see Table 2) and the overall job satisfaction. We distinguish job satisfiers into three groups: internal, financial and external. Financial and external satisfiers are called "factors of hygiene" [9]; for these factors "act in a manner analogous to the principles of medical hygiene". When these factors deteriorate to a level below that which the employee considers acceptable, then job dissatisfaction ensues. However, the reverse does not hold true. It is widely recognized that "when the job context can be characterized as optimal we will not get dissatisfaction, but neither will we get much in the way of positive attitudes. The factors that lead to positive job attitudes do so because they satisfy the individual's need for self-actualization at the job" [9], [4].

Additionally, we analyze satisfaction outcomes based on the employee role: *manager* (team lead, project lead, scrum master), *worker* (developer, analyst, tester, architect, user experience designer, security specialist etc.) and *consultant* (process improvement consultant, coach, facilitator) and the extent of agile process adoption (none, <6 months, 6-12 months, 1-2 years, 2-3 years, 3-4 years, 4-5 years, >5 years).

For our study, we chose quantitative survey analysis and comparative analysis as our research procedure. Two self-administered Web-based surveys were used as a research instrument. One survey – denoted as the "*main survey*" – consisted of 17 questions of both quantitative (on Likert summated scale) and qualitative (open-ended) natures. It was administered by the authors of this paper. We recognized the multidisciplinary nature of our study (among software engineering, organizational psychology, sociology, and economics) and, therefore, formulated the questions in consultation with a specialist in organizational psychology. The second survey used (henceforth referred to as *"supplementary survey"*) was a more generic IT Job Satisfaction Survey conducted by the ComputerWorld magazine (www.computerworld.com/careertopics/careers/exclusive/jobsatisfaction2003). This survey contains perceptions of a broad body of IT managers and workers (from CIO to help desk operator) employed at a wide range of industries and company sizes. The ComputerWorld questionnaire focused on job satisfaction only and was agnostic to the development process used; whereas our main survey was designed having different development processes (agile vs. non-agile) in mind. In our main survey, we included several questions that were identical (verbatim) to the questions of the supplementary survey. The objective for using these two surveys was to enable comparative analysis of the results: Agile vs General IT and Non-agile vs. General IT. Notice that both surveys were administered on the Web and during the same year.

In this paper we only discuss a subset of our findings based on the responses to questions dealing exclusively with overall job satisfaction and its determinants (satisfiers). Analysis of the data related to stress, desirability of movement, and relationship with management is left out.

Table 2. Job satisfiers

1. Opportunity for advancement
2. Ability to influence decisions that affect you
3. Ability to influence day-to-day company success
4. Opportunity to work on interesting projects
5. Salary
6. Connection between pay & performance
7. Job security
8. Workload
9. (Interpersonal) relations with IT peers
10. Relations with users (customer)

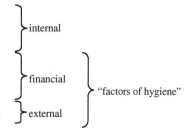

3   Data Sources

The target population for the main study is the group of software engineering professionals. The target population for the supplementary study is wider and includes IT professionals in general. Both surveys used self-selected Internet samplings.

Table 3. Suvey samples

Survey	Administered by	$N_{complete\ responses}$	$N_{partial\ responses}$	N_{total}
Main	Authors	459	286	756
Supplementary	ComputerWorld	936	-	936

Table 4. Main survey sample distribution by regions

Africa	Asia	Australia & New Zealand	Europe	Latin America & Caribbean	Middle East	North America	South America
3	35	10	135	3	2	253	18
1%	8%	2%	29%	1%	0%	55%	4%

Invitations in four languages (English, French, German, Cantonese) were posted to the most active newsgroups, mailing lists and wikis (total 51) specialized in software engineering, in general; as well as via the C2, Agile Alliance, DSDM Consortium, Canadian Agile Network. The limitations of such sampling are discussed in Section 5. Details of the sample distributions are presented in Tables 3 and 4.

4   Findings: Analysis and Discussion

4.1   Overall Satisfaction of Employees of Agile vs. Non-agile Teams

We organized our independent variable (level of experience with agile methods) in an ordered dataset as follows: 0="you don't know what agile methods are", 1="you haven't practiced agile but are interested", 2="<6 months", 3="6-12 months", 4="1-2 years", 5="2-3 years", 6="3-4 years", 7="4-5 years", 8=">5 years".

The results of the Chi-square significance test for the relationship between the level of experience with agile methods and overall job satisfaction is presented in Table 6. It reveals a statistically significant relationship at the level <.0001. Hence, hypothesis H_{01} (No relationship exists between the level of agile methods adoption and the overall job satisfaction of the individual) is rejected. In order to examine the nature of this relationship, we performed Spearman's correlation test and measured the correspondence of rank ordering. To deal with non-responses, we employed pairwise deletion. The results of Spearman's rho calculation show a moderate positive correlation between the level of experience with agile methods and the overall job satisfaction (rho_s = 0.35, 95% CI = [0.26, 0.42], 2-tailed $p<0.0001$, $N=448$). In other words, those who, reportedly, practiced agile for longer, perceived their overall job satisfaction higher. This is consistent with the claims of agilists.

4.2   Overall Satisfaction of Agile and Non-agile Teams vs. General IT Industry

The second research question we address is whether the rates of overall job satisfaction expressed by members of agile teams (group A) and non-agile teams (group B) are higher, similar, or lower than of IT professionals in general (group C). Figure 1 illustrates the perception differences about overall job satisfaction.

Comparing percentage differences between IT in general and agile teams, several important observations can be made: IT professionals in general are:

- 11 times more likely to be "very dissatisfied" compared to agile team members;
- three times more "somewhat dissatisfied";
- 50% more indifferent ("neither satisfied nor dissatisfied");
- almost twice as few "somewhat satisfied";
- almost twice as few "very satisfied".

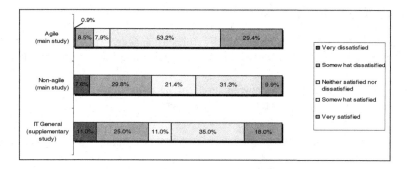

Fig. 1. Overall job satisfaction by groups: (A) members of agile teams (N=316); (B) members of non-agile teams (N=131); (C) IT professionals in general (N=936)

Comparing responses of members of agile and non-agile teams, similar trends emerge, but they are more acute:

- 8 times more very "very dissatisfied" individuals in non-agile teams;
- 3.5 times more "somewhat dissatisfied";
- almost three times more indifferent ("neither satisfied nor dissatisfied");
- almost twice as few "somewhat satisfied";
- three times as few "very satisfied".

Table 5 contains results of pair-wise chi-square tests for the set of hypotheses H_{02}. From the calculations, we reject only H'_{02}. Thus, there exists a relationship between overall job satisfaction and practice of agile methods (Agile or General IT). H''_{02} cannot be rejected, at a sufficiently small alpha level (0.05) so no strong conclusion regarding the relationship between overall job satisfaction and the group of non-agile and General IT respondents can be made.

Table 5. Chi-square test for Hypothesis H_{01} (N=448)

	Overall Satisfaction					
Level of experience with agile methods	Very dissatisfied	Somewhat dissatisfied	Neither satisfied nor dissatisfied	Somewhat satisfied	Very satisfied	Total
Don't know what agile methods are	1 (0.9)	6 (4.8)	10 (4.3)	13 (15.8)	4 (8.2)	34
Haven't practiced agile but interested	6 (2.5)	30 (13.2)	22 (12.0)	26 (43.6)	10 (22.7)	94
< 6 months	1 (1.0)	3 (5.3)	4 (4.8)	20 (17.6)	10 (9.2)	38
6 months – 1 year	1 (2.3)	9 (11.8)	5 (10.7)	47 (39.0)	22 (20.3)	84
1 – 2 years	2 (2.2)	9 (11.5)	7 (10.4)	46 (38.1)	18 (19.8)	82
2 – 3 years	0 (1.5)	5 (7.7)	7 (7.0)	27 (25.5)	16 (13.3)	55
3 – 4 years	0 (0.8)	1 (4.1)	1 (3.7)	14 (13.5)	13 (7.0)	29
4 – 5 years	1 (0.3)	0 (1.7)	0 (1.5)	3 (5.6)	8 (2.9)	12
> 5 years	0 (0.5)	0 (2.8)	1 (2.5)	12 (9.3)	7 (4.8)	20
Total	**12**	**63**	**57**	**208**	**108**	**448**
χ^2 statistic	104.67		df = 32		p	<0.0001

4.3 Overall Satisfaction by Job Roles

We examined the rates of satisfaction by roles (manager, worker and consultant) (Table 6). In addition, the main survey included a specific question that was conditionally

Table 6. Tests for relationships between levels of overall job satisfaction of employees-members of agile teams, non-agile teams and IT in general

	Non-agile	General IT
Agile	$\chi^2 = 80.96$ N=447 p<0.0001 null hypothesis rejected ✓ $rho_s = 0.39$ moderate positive association	$\chi^2 = 95.63$ N=1,252 p<0.0001 null hypothesis rejected ✓ $rho_s = 0.26$ moderate positive association
Non-agile	—	$\chi^2 = 17.15$ N=1,067 p= 0.0018 null hypothesis not rejected ✗ $rho_s = 0.05$ no association

displayed to the respondents who identified themselves as those who practiced agile at the time of taking the survey. We explicitly asked to rate individual's current experience in an agile team in comparison to the previous experiences of working in a non-agile team. The results are in Table 8. Managers of the teams who adopt agile are exceptionally positive about them (92% of "very satisfied" or "somewhat satisfied"). This is an indication that agile methods are not just a programmer-oriented movement, as some may believe. Workers (including developers and specialists) exhibit also a positive trend (80% of "very satisfied" or   "somewhat satisfied" – highlighted in green in Table 7) though there are about 12% of those who are not. Majority of them have been practicing agile for 6-12 months. Further analysis of the comments provided by these dissatisfied agile workers reveal some of the reasons for dissatisfaction. One person indicated "office politics, company movement to offshore developers, incompetent executives" as the basis for her low satisfaction ranking; while another one blamed "little real project development work" available. Several individuals indicated that they were a part of a small agile team (<10) within a larger non-agile organization and, in two cases, "management resisted agile" while the developer team "tries to sneak it in". There was one sentiment that was related to the IT crash and not agile methods per se. The person complained about working more hours leading to a lower net income – this is consistent with some of the sentiments of professional in General IT group observed in the results of the supplemental study. On the other hand, the group of workers who have not practiced agile but are interested in trying them in their organizations is largely dissatisfied with their current jobs (40%) or indifferent (27%) (highlighted in red in Table 7). Consultants, as expected, are extremely satisfied with agile methods. One data point in this category seems to be an outlier (a Telco consultant with <1 year prior experience with agile methods; who now follows a more Tayloristic process; the person provided no additional comments). Separating them from other subgroups ensures that no consultant bias is present in our analysis.

Table 7. Overall job satisfaction by job roles and levels of agile experience (N=482)

Role	Level of experience with agile	Very dis-satisfied	Somewhat dissatisfied	Overall Satisfaction Neither satisfied nor dissatisfied	Some-what satisfied	Very satisfied	Grand total
Manager	Practice agile now		2 3%	3 5%	39 60%	21 32%	65 100%
	Do not know what agile methods are	1 17%	1 17%	1 17%	3 50%		6 100%
	Haven't practiced but interested in trying	1 9%	3 27%	1 9%	4 36%	2 18%	11 100%
	Have practiced before but not now			2 33%	2 33%	2 33%	6 100%
	Have tried agile in training environment		1 25%	1 25%	1 25%	1 25%	4 100%
Worker	Practice agile now	3 1%	25 11%	19 8%	121 51%	67 29%	235 100%
	Do not know what agile methods are		5 20%	6 24%	10 40%	4 16%	25 25%
	Haven't practiced but interested in trying	5 7%	24 33%	20 27%	19 26%	5 7%	73 100%
	Have practiced before but not now	4 13%	8 27%	4 13%	13 43%	1 3%	30 100%
	Have tried agile in training environment	2 14%	3 21%	5 36%	2 14%	2 14%	14 100%
Consultant	Practice agile now			1 9%	5 45%	5 45%	11 100%
	Have practiced before but not now		1 100%				1 100%
	Have tried agile in training environment				1 100%		1 100%

Table 8. Comparative satisfaction rankings of agile vs non-agile environments by respondents who practice agile (by roles) (N=384)

Compared to your other experiences of working in a non-agile team, how would you rate your current job now?

Role	Much Better	Better	Similar	Worse	Much Worse	Grand Total
Manager	39 49%	28 35%	8 10%	4 5%		79 100%
Worker	114 39%	109 37%	47 16%	16 5%	6 2%	292 100%
Consultant	8 62%	3 23%	1 8%		1 8%	13 100%
Grand Total	161 42%	140 36%	56 15%	20 5%	7 2%	384 100%

4.4 Job satisfaction Factors

In order to answer the forth question of our study on whether there exist relationships between the level of experience with agile methods and individual job satisfiers (identified with the help of an organizational psychologist and listed in Table 2), we performed both Chi-square and Spearman's correlation tests for each of them. The results are summarized in Table 9. The relationships of the *level of agile experience* and *ability to influence decisions that affect you*, *opportunity to work on interesting projects*, and *relationships with users* were most strongly positive; while the relationships with *workload satisfaction, opportunity for advancement*, and *ability to influence day-to-day company's success* were moderately strong but, nevertheless, statistically significant at level $p<0.0001$.

Table 9. Relationships between the level of agile experience and individual job satisfiers (N=481, df=36, p<0.0001)

	Satisfiers (as per Table 2)									
	Opportunity for advancement	Ability to influence decisions that affect you	Ability to influence day-to-day company success	Opportunity to work on interesting projects	Salary	Connection between pay & performance	Job security	Workload	Relations with IT peers	Relations with users/customers
χ^2	79.92	103.24	84.05	99.18	45.28	63.96	64.34	67.42	59.43	88.82
rho_s	0.22	0.32	0.28	0.32	0.06	0.17	0.06	0.23	0.26	0.31
rel.	moderate	moderate	moderate	moderate	none	weak	very weak	moderate	weak	moderate

5   Caveats and Limitations

Among this study's main limitations is the use of self-selected sample. The way how the study was distributed (online) might have created a selection bias – an argument can be made that many developers in the industry do not check the resources were the survey invitations were sent to. The question that matters, however, is whether self-selected participants of our main survey and the supplementary ComputerWorld survey are representative of members of the target populations. We hope that it is the case: the large sizes of the samples and the breadth of the countries and organization sizes help to mitigate the risk of non-representation. All in all, we believe that our sample does not bias our significance tests substantially. Another potential caveat – ambiguity of the questions – was addressed by validating the questionnaire with two software engineers and one organizational psychologist. In addition, there is a chance of the same individual responding to both surveys. However, even if this is a case, the large size of samples compensates for this. One last caveat that we should mention is the fact that we are only looking at the start of the chain: development process $\Rightarrow$ job satisfaction $\Rightarrow$ voluntary turnover $\Rightarrow$ economic losses. We rely on interdisciplinary research to make the rest of derivations. Undoubtedly, complex relationships will emerge and those are subjects of our future studies.

6   Conclusions and Future Plans

Our research evaluated the relationship between development process and overall job satisfaction. It revealed that relationship to be statistically significant at p<0.0001 and the existence of a positive correlation between the level of experience with agile methods (from none to 5+ years) and satisfaction. Comparative analysis of the way agile teams and general IT professionals in the industry perceive their work environments revealed significantly higher rates of satisfaction by agile team members. In addition, we found not only workers but managers of agile teams are overwhelmingly satisfied with their jobs and even ten points more so. This is a clear indication that agile methods are not just a programmer-oriented movement. Lastly, it is important to recognize the complex nature of job satisfaction as no single factor usually effects satisfaction by itself. Therefore, an investigation of the relationship between the level of agile experience and individual job satisfiers was undertaken. It found the three strongest relationships were the ability to influence decisions that affect the individual, the opportunity to work on interesting projects, and the relationships with users/customers. In our future work, we'll analyze perceived desirability of movement and work stress.

Acknowledgments

Authors gratefully recognize: Dr. Theresa Kline for reviewing the original questionnaire, Dr. Harold Stolovitch and Dr. Steven Condly for discussions on the myth of "happy teams = productive teams", Dr. Hakan Erdogmus for reviewing our findings and commenting on the manuscript, and all professionals who responded to the surveys. The research is partially supported by NSERC and iCore.

References

[1] Asproni, G. "Motivation, Teamwork, and Agile Development". Agile Times, IV(1): 8–15, 2004.
[2] Basili V. "Applying the Goal/question/metric Paradigm in the Experience Factory." In Fenton et al. (Eds.) Software Quality Assurance and Measurement: A Worldwide Perspective, Ch.2, International Thomson Computer Press: 21-44, 1996.
[3] Beck, K. On Turnover in XP Teams. In Dynabok. Online: http://www.computer.org/SEweb/Dynabook/WhatIs2.htm
[4] Boehm, B. Software Engineering Economics, Prentice Hall, 1981.
[5] Boehm, B., Turner, R. Balancing Agility and Discipline: A Guide for the Perplexed. Addison-Wesley: Reading, MA, 2003.
[6] Burk, L., Richardson, J., Latin, L. "Conflict Management in Software Development Environments". Proc. PNSQC 2000 (online): 298-357, 2000.
[7] Condly, S., Melnik G. Personal correspondence. February 2005.
[8] DeMarco, T., Lister, T. Peopleware : Productive Projects and Teams, 2/e. Dorset: 1999.
[9] Herzberg, F. et al. The Motivation to Work, 2/e. Wiley: New York, NY, 1993.
[10] Kaye, B., Jordan-Evans, S. "Retention: Tag, You're It! How to Build a Retention Culture". Training & Development, April 2000: 29 –34, 2000.
[11] Larson, D. "Team Agility: Exploring Self-Organizing Software Teams". Agile Times, Vol. IV: 22–25, 2004.
[12] Locke, E. "The nature and consequences of job satisfaction." In Dunnette, M (ed.) Handbook of Industrial and Organizational Pscychology. Rand McNally: Chicago, IL, 1976.
[13] Manaro, K. et al. "Empirical Analysis on the Satisfaction of IT Employees Comparing XP Practices with Other Software Development Methodologies". Proc. XP 2004, LNCS 3092, Springer Verlag,: 166–174, 2004.

[14] March, J.G., Simon, H.A. Organizations. Wiley: New York, 1958.

[15] Meta Group. IT Labour Report. Online
      http://www.itaa.org/workforce/resources/articles.htm.

[16] Mobley, W. Employee Turnover: Causes, Consequences, and Control. Addison-Wesley:
      NY, 1982.

[17] Pettman, D. "Some factors influencing labour turnover: A review of the literature."
      Industrial Relations J., No.4: 43-61, 1973.

[18] Schiel, J. "Improving Employee Skills Through Scrum". Agile Times, Vol. VII: 37–40,
      2005.

[19] Stolovitch, H., Melnik, G. Personal correspondence. February 2005.

Investigating the Impact of Personality Types on Communication and Collaboration-Viability in Pair Programming – An Empirical Study

Panagiotis Sfetsos[1], Ioannis Stamelos[1], Lefteris Angelis[1], and Ignatios Deligiannis[2, *]

[1] Department of Informatics, Aristotle University,
54124 Thessaloniki, Greece
sfetsos@it.teithe.gr, {stamelos, lef}@csd.auth.gr
[2] Department of Information Technology, Technological Education Institute,
54101 Thessaloniki, Greece
igndel@it.teithe.gr

Abstract. This paper presents two controlled experiments (a pilot and the main one) investigating the impact of developer personalities and temperaments on communication, collaboration-pair viability and ultimately effectiveness in pair programming. The objective of the experiments was to compare pairs of mixed/ heterogeneous developer personalities and temperaments with pairs of the same personalities and temperaments, in terms of *pair effectiveness*. Pair effectiveness is expressed in terms of *pair performance*, measured by communication, velocity, productivity and customer satisfaction, and *pair collaboration-viability* measured by developers' satisfaction, knowledge acquisition and participation (collaboration satisfaction ratio, nuisance ratio, voluntary or mandatory preference, and driver or navigator preference). The results have shown that there is significant difference between the two groups, indicating better communication and collaboration-viability for the pairs with mixed personalities/temperaments.

1 Introduction

Up to now, pair programming as an intensely social and collaborative process [3], has been faced by organizations and managers as a rough technical process (not taking into consideration the human factors [16, p. 17]). But as in any software process, there exist human factors that can not be easily identified and understood well enough to be controlled, predicted, or manipulated. In pair programming although the impact of developer personalities on communication and collaboration has been recognised as the most critical success factor [3, 7, 10], it has not yet been investigated. We consider pairs as *adaptive ecosystems* (based on Cockburns' Team Ecosystems as described in [7]), in which the successful implementation of the assigned roles and tasks primary depend on developer personalities and temperaments. They are adaptive because through pair rotations, developers can create, learn and respond to change. In these adaptive ecosystems the overall development activity becomes a joint effort, a function

---

* This work is funded by the Greek Ministry of Education (25%) and European Union (75%) under the EPEAK II program "Archimedes II".

P. Abrahamsson, M. Marchesi, and G. Succi (Eds.): XP 2006, LNCS 4044, pp. 43–52, 2006.

of how paired developers communicate, interact and collaborate to produce results. However, different personalities express different natural preferences on communication, information and knowledge handling and sharing, decision making, and problem solving [7, 10]. Cockburn states that only developers with different personalities and with the same experience, if effectively combined, can minimize the communication gap [7]. This means that organizations and managers must utilize processes which first identify and understand developers' personalities and then capitalize on their potential talents and strengths, effectively combining them. Theory on pair programming does not delve in such issues. The way developers' personality and temperament types and their assigned roles, either pair[1] or functional[2], must be matched, has not been adequately investigated. Developer compatibility in pair programming is empirically investigated only in one study [11]. But, there is still no answer to the following important research question: *Do developer personalities and temperaments affect pair effectiveness and more specifically do mixed/heterogeneous developer personalities and temperaments affect pair effectiveness and especially communication, collaboration and pair viability?*

In order to answer this research question and Cockburn's claims, we conducted two experiments. In both experiments pair effectiveness is described with the same terms as the effectiveness of a team [17] (including communication and collaboration-pair viability variables). Eighty four undergraduate students from the 4th semester of the SE course participated in the experiments separated randomly into two groups of pairs according to their personality and temperament inventories. The Keirsey Temperament Sorter test [12] was used to identify and interpret students' personalities and temperaments in a separate session. Students in both experiments designed, coded and tested in Java two tasks on the well known experiment object, the Cockburn's Responsibility Driven coffee machine code [6]. The results of both experiments have shown statistically better differences for pairs with mixed/heterogeneous personalities and temperaments, i.e. they communicated better, needed less time to complete their assignments, were more effective (better grades) and produce higher quality code (better scores in acceptance tests). The results of questionnaires verified findings indicating greater member's satisfaction, knowledge acquisition and participation (collaboration-pair viability) for the pairs with mixed personalities and temperaments.

The remainder of this paper is organized as follows. Section 2 describes the identification of the students' personalities and temperaments. Section 3 describes the experiments and in section 4 we draw our conclusions and summarize our findings.

2   Identifying Personalities and Temperaments

The two widely used tools to assist in the identification of personality and temperament types are the Myers-Briggs Type Indicator (MBTI[3]) [13] and the Keirsey Temperament Sorter (KTS[4]) [12]. The MBTI, a 94-item questionnaire, is focused on four

---

[1] Roles that developers must undertake into pair, usually informally assigned (i.e. leader, mentor).

[2] Roles defined by the individual's technical skills and knowledge (i.e. tester).

[3] Myers-Briggs Type Indicator and MBTI are registered trademarks of the Myers-Briggs Type Indicator Trust.

[4] see http://keirsey.com/cgi-bin/keirsey/kcs.cgi.

areas of opposite behavior preferences, forming sixteen different personality types. It is used to identify quickly where people get their energy, how they gather information, how they make decisions, and which work style they prefer. The four pairs of preferences are: *Extroverting* (E) and *Introverting* (I), *Sensing* (S) and *iNtuiting* (N), *Thinking* (T) and *Feeling* (F), and *Judging* (J) and *Perceiving* (P). The KTS, a 70-item questionnaire, classifies the sixteen personality types into four temperament types: *Artisan* (SP), *Guardian* (SJ), *Idealist* (NF), and *Rational* (NT). We used the hardcopy of the Keirsey Temperament Sorter to identify and interpret the personality inventories of the participants. The distribution of the most numerous obtained personality types, for the students used in the experiments, is shown in Table 1. In the same table the distribution of the four temperaments in the population is also shown.

Table 1. Top four personality types and temperament types for students

Personality Type	Percent (%)	Temperament Type	Percent (%)
ESTJ	21.4	Artisan (SP)	10.0
ISTJ	20.0	Guardian (SJ)	60.0
INFJ	11.4	Rational (NT)	8.6
ESFJ	11.4	Idealist (NF)	21.4

3 The Experiments

Both experiments were conducted in controlled settings and as realistic as possible, following strict planning, operation and analysis procedures, as proposed in the literature [5, 18]. These procedures included additionally the design and preparation phase, a training session and the KTS-test session. In the design-preparation phase the used material and instrumentation, the data collection forms, the starting (kick-off) procedures and the student preparation took place. The communication transactions forms and the collaboration-pair viability questionnaires were designed as simple as possible, helping navigators to fill the forms easily (see web page: http://sweng.csd.auth.gr/wb/pages/publications/agile-methods.php). Students practiced pair programming in their laboratory assignments and were taught issues concerning communication and collaboration-pair viability during the course. The knowledge they needed to successfully participate in both experiments, was communicated to them in sufficient detail, through an informatory-training session and their access to the experiment's directory which was created in the local network, containing all the experimental material in form of text files. In this directory, all pairs had access to their own catalog in which they should save their code and the associated unit tests. The informatory-training session was executed a week before the KTS-test session. In both experiments, the students were separated into two groups of pairs (*control group*=samel personalities/temperaments, *experimental group*=mixed personalities/temperaments), according to their personality and temperament inventories (see table 2). To ensure randomness in the pair - formation and allocation process, we used a specific method which was tested in the pilot experiment.

Table 2. Control and Experimental groups of pairs for both experiments

PILOT experiment				MAIN experiment			
Control Group		*Experimental Group*		*Control Group*		*Experimental Group*	
Temperament Type	*Pairs #*	*Temperament Type*	*Pairs #*	*Temperament Type*	*Pairs #*	*Temperament Type*	*Pairs #*
NF – NF	1	NF – SJ	1	NF – NF	4	NF – SJ	6
SJ – SJ	2	NF – SP	1	SJ – SJ	13	NF – SP	1
		NT – SJ	1			NT – SJ	5
		SJ – SP	1			NT – SP	1
						SJ - SP	5
TOTAL	**3**		**4**		**17**		**18**

The pilot experiment was run with the participation of 14 students - 7 pairs (3 pairs in the control - and 4 pairs in the experimental group), a week before the main experiment. The objective of the pilot experiment was to test the experimental design, to assess the risk of failure, to discover unexpected or potential risks and gaps and test the stated hypothesis. The pilot study was successful in terms of its objective as many aspects were amended in the main experiment, according to the knowledge acquired from the pilot study. The most important amendments concerned the pair forming and pair allocation process (needed half hour to be implemented according to our method), and the acceptance tests implementation. In the main experiment, 70 students divided in 35 pairs (17 pairs in the control - and 18 pairs in the experimental group) participated. The two tasks in which students were tested were completed in two and a half hours. The data for communication transactions, velocity and collaboration-pair viability was scrutinized to check whether was correctly completed.

3.1 Definition

We used the Goal-Question-Metric (GQM) template [1, 2] to define the goals and metrics of the experiment (see Table 3). The formal definition [4] for the two experiments is the following:

Analyze:	*Developer Personalities and Temperaments and in particular how the mixed Personalities and Temperaments impact on Effectiveness and especially on Communication and Collaboration-pair Viability*
For the purpose of:	*Assessing and Improving Pair Effectiveness*
With respect to:	*Communication, Collaboration - Viability and ultimately Effectiveness*
From the point of view of:	*Researchers, Managers and Developers*
In the context of:	*Undergraduate course, fourth semester, at the Department of Informatics of the Technological Educational Institution of Thessaloniki-Greece*

Table 3. Goals, Questions and Metrics for the two experiments

Goals	Questions	Metrics
Assess the impact of developer personality and temperament types on communication.	Do developer personality and temperament types affect communication?	**(a)** # of transactions on *communication modes* including: 1. Requirements gathering trans. 2. Specification and Design changes trans. 3. Code trans. 4. Unit test trans. 5. Peer reviewing trans.
Assess the impact of developer personality and temperament types on collaboration – viability	Do developer personality and temperament types affect collaboration – pair viability?	**(b)** • Collaboration satisfaction • Knowledge acquisition • Participation (communication satisfaction ratio, nuisance ratio, and driver or navigator preference)
Ultimately: Assess the impact of developer personality and temperament types on effectiveness	Do developer personality and temperament types affect effectiveness?	• Metrics from **(a)** + **(b)** • Velocity (time to finish assignments) • Productivity (points for correct solutions) • Customer satisfaction (passed acceptance tests)

3.2 Hypothesis Formulation

Null Hypothesis: Mixed developer personalities and temperaments do not affect pair effectiveness and especially communication, collaboration-pair viability, and ultimately pair effectiveness.

Alternative Hypothesis: Mixed developer personalities and temperaments affect pair effectiveness and especially communication, collaboration-pair viability, and ultimately pair effectiveness.

3.3 Communication and Collaboration -Viability Metrics

Communication metrics are classified as process metrics, because they measure collections of software-related activities within a process [9]. These metrics have been successfully used for studying the information flow in software projects [15, 14, 8]. We used communication metrics to compute the volume of the information exchanged among developers, during a pair programming session, and to relate it to the outcome of their assignments. Two restrictions concerning communication metrics derived from the formality of the experiments. The first was that stand-up meetings were excluded and the second that only bidirectional communication could be measured. To understand the communication metrics we used, two definitions must be given:

• *Communication modes* refer to different types of information exchange that has defined objectives and scope. Communication modes are characterised as scheduled if they are planned, or as event-driven if they occur non-deterministically. We consider that most communication modes, concerning pair programming activities, are scheduled. Communication modes in our experiment are the following: requirements gathering, specification and design changes, coding, unit testing, code and design reviews. In both experiments, communication was measured by the volume of transactions in the various communication modes.

- *Communication mechanism* is a tool or procedure used to transmit and receive information and supports a communication mode. Experiment participants simply talked to each other, i.e. they used a face-to-face, synchronous communication mechanism. No other tool (e.g. collaborative CASE tool) was used.

Communication transactions were recorded in printed forms by the navigator of each pair through a log keeping process, as in the Personal Software Process (with differences in the types of the recorded data). Navigators were obligated to record the start - and finish time for each assignment and to take note in the column of the proper communication mode every time the partners were communicating. To ensure that the data collection process would be successful in both experiments, the entire process and the used forms were tested in a separate training session, before the execution of the pilot experiment. Collaboration-pair viability was measured by data gathered from a questionnaire, filled by both pair participants, after the code completion. The questionnaire contained questions concerning collaboration such as members' satisfaction, knowledge acquisition and participation (grade of communication satisfaction, grade of nuisance, voluntary or mandatory preference, and driver or navigator preference).

The classification of the *independent* and *dependent* variable was derived from the goal template. The independent variable (factor) is the same/homogeneous - or the mixed/heterogeneous personality and temperament types of the pair developers. It is of nominal type, with 2 possible values. The dependent variable is the pair effectiveness, measured by pair performance and collaboration-pair viability. Velocity is measured by the time needed for the completion of each assignment (finish time - start time). Productivity is measured by the points obtained by each pair for each assignment. The points were measured on a ratio scale, from 1 (min) to 5 (max), based on checklists to ensure objective assessment of the participants' results. Customer satisfaction was measured by the percentage of passed acceptance tests. The acceptance tests, of black-box type, were written in spreadsheets, and ran manually by the authors, after the students completed and delivered their code. A small number of representative tests were chosen to test the business value of the students' code. Data gathered by the questionnaire was measured on a ratio scale, from 1 (min) to 5 (max). Collaboration-pair viability variables were assessed both quantitatively and qualitatively. The results from the analysis of the qualitative assessment confirmed the empirical findings, but are not presented in detail due to the limited space available. Also, due to the lack of space we are not going to present the validity threats in this paper.

3.4 Data Analysis and Interpretation

For the statistical analysis of the data concerning performance variables we used a set of statistical analysis methods, namely Descriptive Statistics, Correlations between the variables, Comparisons between all variables using different Univariate statistical tests and Multivariate Stepwise Discriminant Analysis (DA), to test the discriminating power of all variables. For the statistical analysis of the data concerning collaboration-pair viability we used Descriptive Statistics and the chi-square tests.

Descriptive Statistics: The distribution (mean, median, minimum and maximum) and variance (standard deviation) of all variables separately for both tasks and groups and also for the totals of the variables, are indicating significant differences between the two groups. The box - plots and the three - dimensional scatter plot in Figure 1 confirm the significant differences between the two groups. The scatter plot shows for both tasks, in totals, the relationship between communication transactions, velocity (total time) and productivity (total points).

Correlations: The *Pearson coefficient* is significant for pairs of variables velocity (time) – productivity (points) (negative correlation, p=0.037) and communication – productivity (positive correlation, p=0.001). The non-parametric coefficients by *Kendall*

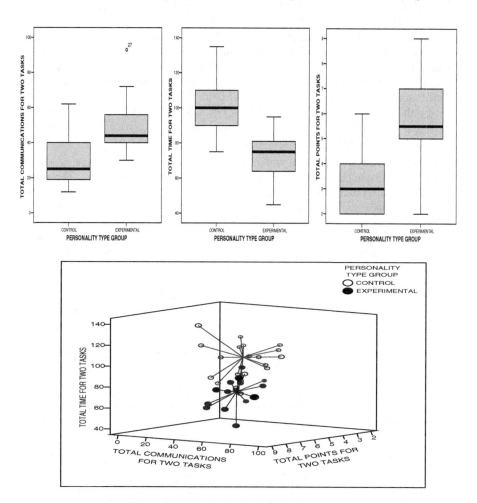

Fig. 1. Totals for both tasks and for both groups

and Spearman showed that all pairs of variables, for the first task, are significantly correlated. After calculating the same coefficients separately for each group, we found that for the control group there is some indication of negative correlation (though not significant, p=0.108) between time and productivity, while for the experimental group there is significant positive correlation (p=0.019) between communication and productivity. This shows that the experimental group performs better as the communication transactions increase, while for the control group communication seem that have no effect on the productivity. On the contrary, the increased time spent has negative results on the productivity of the control group. The same results were obtained for the second task and for the totals for both tasks. Correlation is significant between communication transactions and productivity for the experimental group. Acceptance tests are strongly correlated with the productivity. For the first task, the correlation coefficients are: *Pearson's* 0.913, *Kendall's* 0.896, *Spearman's* 0.954 (all are highly significant, p<0.0005). For the second task, the correlation coefficients are: *Pearson's* 0.948, *Kendall's* 0.907, *Spearman's* 0.955 (all are highly significant, p<0.0005).

Comparisons – Univariate statistical tests: Comparing all variables between the two groups with the *t-test* we found significant differences between the total number of communication transactions, velocity and productivity for each task and in total for both tasks. It is worth noting that only the transactions for design and code review do not differ significantly for the two groups of pairs. Exactly the same results are obtained by the non parametric *Mann-Whitney test*. The t-test for the acceptance tests showed that the differences between the means are very significant (p<0.01). The same result was obtained by the Mann-Whitney test.

Discriminant Analysis (DA): In order to test the discriminating power of all the variables together we performed the *multivariate technique Stepwise DA*. The statistics of the variables and their tests for equality of the group means have shown that the differences are significant (as in the previous tests). The stepwise DA results in a model with 4 out of 6 variables (time spent for the first task, time spent for the second task, communication trans. for the second task, points for the second task). The model based on these variables can classify correctly 97.1% of the cases in the two groups,

Table 4. Classification and cross-validation results

		Personality type group	Predicted Group Membership		Total
			Control	Experimental	
Original	Count	Control	16	1	17
		Experimental	0	18	18
	%	Control	94,1	5,9	100,0
		Experimental	,0	100,0	100,0
Cross-validated(a)	Count	Control	16	1	17
		Experimental	2	16	18
	%	Control	94,1	5,9	100,0
		Experimental	11,1	88,9	100,0

97.1% of original grouped cases correctly classified. 91.4% of cross-validated grouped cases correctly classified.

as can be seen from Table 4. The same Table contains the results of a cross-validation procedure which gives 91.4% correct classifications. Specifically, only one of the 17 control pairs is misclassified as experimental while 2 of the 18 experimental pairs are misclassified as control. Generally, the discrimination is very good and shows that the overall behavior and performance of the two groups is significantly different.

Questionnaire Results for Pair Collaboration – Viability: For the statistical analysis of the data concerned pair collaboration-viability we used Descriptive Statistics and the *chi-square tests*. The results have shown that the experimental group gives higher ratings concerning developers' satisfaction, knowledge acquisition, collaboration's satisfaction ratio and driver preference. Nuisance ratios are almost the same for both groups.

3.5 Limitations

We believe that we took care of most significant validity threats to our study during the design of the experiments and that all major risks were under control. We consider that there exist two main limitations: the short-time study on pair effectiveness (results may be different for long term collaborations or projects) and the use of students as subjects. Nevertheless, we remind the reader that, although highly desirable, such controlled experiments are difficult to conduct in an industry setting for various practical reasons.

4 Conclusions

Considering pairs as adaptive ecosystems, adopting and properly reconciling Cockburn's and Highsmith's claims, we empirically investigated how developers with different personalities and temperaments communicate and collaborate to produce results. The results from two experiments have shown better performance and collaboration-viability for pairs with mixed personalities and temperaments, leading us to the rejection of the stated null hypothesis and keeping of the alternative one. Communication variable was included in the performance variables to capture communication in real activities occurring during pair programming. The analysis of data for this variable have shown that productivity for pairs with mixed types is positively correlated with communication transactions, while the same does not hold for pairs of the same types. This important empirically supported finding by both experiments can help organizations and managers to improve pair effectiveness, by first identifying and then matching developers' personality and temperament types to their potential roles and tasks, effectively exploiting their differences in pair formations and rotations.

References

1. Basili V. and Weiss D. A Methodology for Collecting Valid Software Engineering Data. IEEE Transactions on software engineering, vol SE-10, pp. 728-738; Nov. 1984.
2. Basili V. and Rombach H. The TAME Project: Towards Improvement- Oriented Software Environments; IEEE Transactions on software engineering, 14(6): 758-773; June 1988.

3. Beck, K. Extreme Programming Explained: Embrace Change. Reading, Massachusetts: Addison-Wesley. 2000.
4. Briand, L., Differding, C., Rombach, H. Practical Guidelines For Measurement-Based Process Improvement, Software Process Improvement and Practice, 2(4), pp253-280, 1996.
5. Briand L., Arisholm S., Counsell F., Houdek F. and Thevenod-Fosse P. Empirical Studies of Object-Oriented Artifacts, Methods, and Processes: State of the Ar and Future Directions. Empirical Software Engineering, 2000.
6. Cockburn, A. The Coffee Machine Design Problem: Part 1 & 2. C/C++ User's Journal, May/June, 1998.
7. Cockburn, A. Agle Software Development. Addison-Wesley, 2002.
8. Dutoit, A. and Bruegge B. Communication Metrics for Software Development. IEEE transactions on Software Engineering, 1998.
9. Fenton, N. Software Metrics, A Rigorous Approach. Chapman & Hall, 1991.
10. Highsmith, J. Agle Software Development Ecosystems, Addison Wesley, 2002.
11. Katira, N., Williams, L., Wiebe, E., Miller, C., Balik, S., Gehringer, E. On Under-standing Compatibility of Student Pair Programmers. SIGCSE'04, 3-7, 2004.
12. Keirsey, D., and Bates, M., Please Understand Me, Del Mar, California: Prometheus Book Company, 1984.
13. Myers, Isabel, "Manual: The Myers-Briggs Type Indicator," Palo Alto, California: Consulting Psychologists Press, 1975.
14. Saeki, M. Communication, Collaboration, and Cooperation in Software Development — How Should We Support Group Work in Software Development? Proc. Asia-Pacific Software Eng. Conf. Brisbane, Australia, 1995.
15. Seaman, C., and Basili, V. "An Empirical Study of Communication in Code Inspections," Proc. 19th Int'l Conf. Software Eng., Boston, May 1997.
16. Sfetsos, P., Angelis, L., Stamelos, I. "Investigating The Extreme Programming System - An Empirical Study". Empirical Software Engineering, Vol 11, Nbr. 2, pp. 269-301, June 2006 (to appear).
17. Sundstrom, E., De Meuse, K., and Futrell, D. Work Teams, AmericanPsychologist, February, 1990, pp. 120-133.
18. Wohlin C., Runeson P., Höst M., Ohlson M., Regnell B. and Wesslén A. Experimentation in Software Engineering: An Introduction, Kluwer Academic Publishers, 2000.

The Collaborative Nature of Pair Programming

Sallyann Bryant, Pablo Romero, and Benedict du Boulay

IDEAS Laboratory, University of Sussex, Falmer, UK
s.Bryant@sussex.ac.uk, pablor@Sussex.ac.uk,
b.du-boulay@sussex.ac.uk

Abstract. This paper considers the nature of pair programming. It focuses on using pair programmers' verbalizations as an indicator of collaboration. A review of the literature considers the benefits and costs of co-operative and collaborative verbalization. We then report on a set of four one-week studies of commercial pair programmers. From recordings of their conversations we analyze which generic sub-tasks were discussed and use the contribution of new information as a means of discerning the extent to which each pair collaborated. We also consider whether a particular role is more likely to contribute to a particular sub-task. We conclude that pair programming is highly collaborative in nature, however the level of collaboration varies according to task. We also find that tasks do not seem aligned to particular roles, rather the driver tends to contribute slightly more across almost all tasks.

1 Introduction

Computer programming is known to be a complex skill that is difficult to master. Recently pair programming, formalized as one of the core practices in eXtreme Programming (XP), has been shown to assist in the production of high-quality software (e.g. [1], [2], [3]. [4], [5], [6]). Here we consider co-located pair programming, as 'two people working at one machine, with one keyboard and one mouse' [28] and use the standard terms 'driver' and 'navigator' to indicate who has control of the keyboard (the 'driver'). These existing studies indicate an improved outcome through pair programming (e.g. better quality software, faster production speed, fewer defects and greater enjoyment) and high level reports (e.g. [7]) and ethnographic studies (e.g. [8], [9]) provide useful insights into pair programming in practice. However few, if any, studies have considered in detail the process by which these improved outcomes are achieved. It has been suggested that they may be due to 'pair pressure' [7], where a programmer is more focused and thorough when being watched. Other studies have suggested pairing may be beneficial due to greater enjoyment [4], increased overhearing [8], provision of a better apprenticeship environment [29] and increased knowledge distribution. Pair programming may simply be a way of improving outcome by encouraging programmers to talk to themselves, a phenomena known in other subject areas as self-explanation (e.g. [10]). Here we consider the level of collaboration in pair programming across different types of tasks via a series of on-site studies of experience professional pair programmers 'in the wild' [11]. Via these four, one-week observational studies we

P. Abrahamsson, M. Marchesi, and G. Succi (Eds.): XP 2006, LNCS 4044, pp. 53–64, 2006.

gathered, transcribed and analyzed 36 pair programmers' conversations. Here we consider sessions where both programmers have at least six months' commercial pair programming experience, in an attempt to address the following questions:

- Do pair programmers talk to themselves while working on separate sub-tasks?
- To what extent do pair programmers actually 'collaborate' on the same task?
- Are certain types of task more collaborative than others?
- Does a particular role (driver/navigator) contribute more strongly to a particular type of task?

Section 2 provides an overview of perspectives on the effects of verbalization to oneself and others and section 3 considers how to characterize collaboration. We then go on to explain the methodology and background of our studies and in section 4 present the results of an in-depth analysis of 23 hours of pair programmers' dialogue. We conclude by considering what these results tell us about the collaborative nature of pair programming, and discussing further work which we now hope to undertake.

2 Verbalisation

Gathering and analyzing verbalizations from pair programmers seems ideal because, unlike other domains, the pair are already communicating verbally and so do not need to be asked to do so. Hopefully this minimizes the impact of the observation. Here we take verbalisation to mean any talk produced, whether directed at themselves or each other. While extra-pair communication (for example, discussion with a third party) may be an interesting area of study, it has been excluded from this analysis.

Before we can begin to address the questions we have identified, it is necessary to consider how to characterize collaboration. It has been suggested [19] that it is hard to describe the differences between explaining to oneself and explaining interactively, but that collaborative situations may be defined in terms of three factors: interactivity, asynchronicity and negotiability. Similarly it is suggested [20] that co-operative work is accomplished by the division of labour. Here, we will consider a collaborative task one to which both parties are contributing information and a co-operative task one where only one programmer contributes.

2.1 Collaboration and Verbalisation

Here we take collaboration to mean both parties contributing new information to a given task. Collaboration is widely documented as being beneficial: Suthers [17] suggests that collaboration increases learning, productivity, time focused on the task, knowledge transfer and motivation and Jeong and Chi [18] show that understanding improves after collaboration - those collaborating on a task learned more than those performing it alone. It could be suggested that collaboration decreases the probability of confirmation bias [11], where we filter information depending on what is expected and therefore are more likely to attend to items confirming our hypotheses (even if incorrect). Similarly, in pair programming literature, Williams et al. [1] suggest that collaborating lowers the likelihood of developing 'tunnel vision'.

2.2 Co-operation and Verbalisation

If pair programmers typically do not collaborate on a task, but are more likely to co-operate (that is, split the task up and work on separate subtasks) verbalisation could still affect performance. There is a body of evidence suggesting that simply talking to oneself helps improve understanding. For example, Chi et al. [10] asked a group of students to self-explain each line of a text about physics and showed that self-explanation resulted in the production of a more correct mental model and a higher gain in understanding. Ainsworth and Loizou [12] suggests that verbalization provides a form of 'computational off-load', perhaps putting part of the problem 'out in the world' rather than requiring it to be kept 'in the head'. Ericsson and Simon [13] state that verbalization provides an intermediate re-coding of information, and that in the process of this recoding, it is necessary to add further information for communication purposes which may itself prove useful. Cox [14] also shows that translation between modalities (in his work from mental to diagrammatical) improves understanding. This might all be easily extrapolated to the domain of computing and suggests that simply talking about a software development issue may assist in its understanding and ultimately its resolution. In fact there are a number of accounts of this effect including talking to a rubber duck [14] or even a poster of your favorite movie star.

Studies considering the effect of requested verbalization have also addressed this issue with somewhat different results. Such studies have questioned the use of eliciting verbal protocol (asking participants to talk to themselves as a means of gaining insight into mental processes) and considered whether talking aloud may change the manner in which a task is performed. Of particular interest, Ericsson and Polson [15] show that talking aloud has an effect no different from counting out loud while performing a task – it slows participants down but does not affect their performance.

Another group of studies of a phenomenon known as 'verbal overshadowing' suggests that verbalization may sometimes have a negative effect. Schooler et al. [16] show that verbalization may interfere with non-verbal (insight) tasks, because they rely on non-reportable mental processing. An example of these type of insight tasks are those requiring a 'eureka' moment rather than a step-by-step process of deduction.

These three schools of thought may at first seem contradictory, however if we consider task type this suggests a more complementary picture, perhaps where explaining and embellishing help in understanding non-insight problems, 'thinking aloud' has no effect, and trying to talk about an insight problem has a negative impact. This suggests that particular types of software development task may be helped or hindered by verbalization even if just talking to oneself. There may, of course, be other explanations, including the context in which the studies took place and the means by which verbalizations were elicited.

It would appear difficult to distinguish between co-operation and collaboration in pair programming sessions, however this might be achieved by considering whether the two individuals are holding a collaborative conversation or following all the rules involved in having a conversation (turn taking etc) but actually holding two separate self-conversations, or 'interleaved monologues'. The method we have used to ascertain this is to consider not only whether each party is contributing to the conversation, rather whether these contributions are 'on task'. We have particularly looked at instances of new information being added to each task in a pair programming session. This is discussed in further detail in Section 3.

3   Study Background and Methodology

In line with calls for studies of programmers working in an industrial setting [21], the analysis and results presented here are from four, one-week studies of commercial programmers working on on-going tasks in their usual environment. While a variety of levels of experience were studied (see [22] for insights about the differences in behavior between novice and more experienced pairers) this paper only considers programmers who had been commercially pair programming for a minimum of six months. The four studies were from three different industrial sectors and all the studies took place at medium to large scale companies. All of the projects encouraged or expected programmers to work in pairs whenever possible. Across the companies the pairs generally seemed empowered and were considered responsible for completing their tasks as they considered appropriate. The profiles of the session are shown in Table 1:

Table 1. Profile of the companies, projects and sessions studied

	Number of projects considered	Number of pair programming sessions considered	Agile/XP development approach?
Banking	1	3	Yes
Banking	4	12	Yes
Entertainment	2	10	Yes
Mobile communications	2	11	Yes

The methodology used followed the framework for verbal protocol analysis set down by Chi [24] in which protocols are produced, transcriptions are segmented and coded according to a coding schema, depicted in some manner and patterns are sought and interpreted. A literature review on the use of verbal protocols in software engineering is available [26], which also suggests that the analysis of verbalisation may be a useful method for use in the study of pair programmers so that 'the cognitive processes underlying productivity and quality gains can be formally mapped rather than speculated about'.

Here each one-hour recording was transcribed and segmented into utterances (an utterance typically being a sentence). A coding schema was produced by reducing the work in each of the session into a tree of numbered subtasks (e.g. see Figure 1). These subtasks were derived from the dialogue by considering what was required in order to complete the task. The derived tasks were at a level of abstraction higher (i.e. less detailed) than writing a line of code but a lower level than the overall task itself. They were typically either:

- Things which needed to be done
- Things which needed to be understood
- Things which needed to be decided
- Things which needed to be 'broadcast' (outside of the pair)

Further division into sub-sub-tasks etc. was common during the process of deriving sub-tasks.

Any utterance in which new information was added was then coded with the number of the subtask the information was contributing to, the contributor (A or B) and their role at that time (navigator or driver - note it was usual for participants to change roles several times during a session). See Table 2 for an example coding (note that line 4 is not coded as it is considered a continuance of line 2).

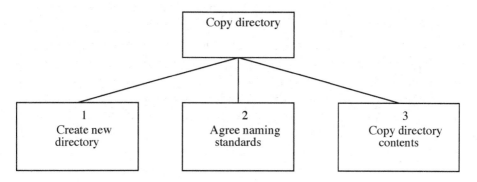

Fig. 1. Example subtask decomposition

Table 2. Example coding of dialogue

No	Participant	Role	Subtask	Generic subtask type	Utterance
1	B	Nav	1	B	So basically we can create a directory…and we can just use…
2	A	Dri	2	A	…We put the date that we are going to put the X in.
3	B	Nav	-		Right
4	A	Dri	-		So when you look at it you know that it was done on this date
5	B	Nav			Good
6	A	Dri	2	A	…Then that's a standard file
7	B	Nav	3	B	I'll just copy it all over, apart from the update.

In order to analyze the extent to which different types of subtask fostered or inhibited collaboration, the subtasks from all sessions were then used to derive a set of generic subtask types (see Table 3). The generic subtasks were then compared with those described in the literature to ensure coverage. A difference with those tasks described in [27] was the lack of a discrete 'design' category. While part of this is covered in 'agree strategy', the lack of a design category is not surprising in an XP environment, where there is no 'up-front' design task, rather design takes place as part of the coding task. The following list shows the derived generic sub-tasks used in the analysis. These cover all the tasks that were identified and therefore categories such as L (Discuss the IDE) were rarely used but are included for completeness. Instances of social chat either within or outside the pair were not considered.

Table 3. Derived generic sub-tasks

A	Agree strategy/conventions	Including approach to take, coding standards and naming conventions
B	Configure environment	Setting up paths, directories, loading software etc.
C	Test	Writing, running and assessing the success of tests
D	Comment code	Writing or modifying comments in the code
E	Correspond with 3rd party	Extra-pair communication: person to person, telephone or email
F	Build, compile, check in/out	Compiling and building on own or integration machine
G	Comprehend	Understanding the problem or existing code
H	Refactor	Re-organising the code
I	Write new code	Creating completely new code to complete the assigned task
J	Debug	Diagnosing, hypothesizing and fixing bugs
K	Find/check example	Looking at examples in books, existing code or on-line
L	Discuss the IDE	Talking about the development environment

4   Results

The pair programmers studied had all been pairing commercially for at least six months. While the introduction of pair programming was reported as having been accepted very differently (some programmers were initially very reluctant to pair, while others were keen to), all of the pairs observed behaved in a professional manner and were highly focused on the task at hand. The sessions observed showed a surprisingly high amount of verbal interaction. Pair programmers were shown to produce more than 250 verbal interactions per pair programming hour. Generally there were only very brief periods of silence. Even when a pair was awaiting a suite of tests to run, for example, they would often take the opportunity for some social chat.

The analysis performed shows that both partners contributed to more than 93% of subtasks, that is, the programming pair collaborated on 93% of the sub-tasks they performed. Similarly, when considered by role, slightly fewer, but still just more than 93% of subtasks were contributed to by the driver and by the navigator. These results suggest that pair programming sessions are highly collaborative in nature and that the programming pair really are working together on the vast majority of tasks. We will now take a closer look at the types of tasks in which more and less collaboration took place. First, in Figure 2 we consider the number of contributions made for each generic subtask type in order to ascertain which were the most common types of task for the sessions observed.

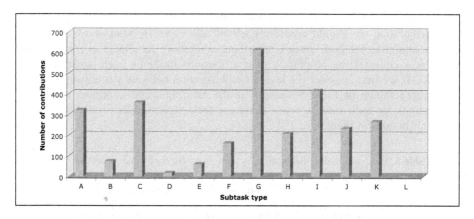

Fig. 2. Distribution of contributions amongst generic sub-tasks

It is interesting to note that the majority of contributions related to comprehension – understanding the problem or existing code. Second most common is writing new code, followed by testing (iwriting and running tests). Least common were discussing the IDE, commenting code (which is in line with the idea of self-commenting code) and corresponding outside the pair. If we normalize our data to ascertain the percentage of tasks of each type that were collaborative both across participants (i.e. both participants contributed to a task) and across role (i.e. both roles contributed) we obtain the percentages outlined in Table 4. Figures in the two columns are often, but not always the same, as a participant may contribute as both driver and navigator when roles changed mid-task.

Table 4. Percentage of tasks of each generic type that were collaborative across participants and roles

Subtask type	Percentage of tasks collaborative across participants	Percentage of tasks collaborative across roles
A - Agree strategy	91.93	91.61
B – Configure environment	81.08	81.08
C – Test	91.92	92.20
D – Comment code	83.33	83.33
E – Correspond	95	93.33
F – Build,compile,check in/out	90.68	90.68
G – Comprehension	95.11	94.94
H – Refactor	94.29	95.24
I – Write new code	94.95	94.71
J – Debug	93.56	93.56
K – Find/check example	92.48	92.48
L – Discuss the IDE	100	100

Table 4 shows that both partners contributed to almost all tasks. Only configuring the environment and commenting code had a level of collaboration below 90% and even these were over 80%, although they were rarely performed. Thus the benefits attributed to pair programming may well be due to the collaborative manner in which tasks are performed. However, in order to further understand the nature and extent of this collaboration we should consider each subtask type. In other words, since we have ascertained that both parties contribute something to almost every task, we should now consider the proportion of contributions made by each participant and each role. If we first consider the level of collaboration between participants we find the averages shown in Table 5, along with the maximum and minimum number of contributions for each subtask type. These are then expressed as percentages of the total contributions in Figure 3:

Table 5. Most and least collaboration by participant for each generic subtask type

Subtask type	Contributions by most active participant				Contributions by least active participant			
	Average	Highest	Lowest	Standard Deviation	Average	Highest	Lowest	Standard Deviation
A Agree strategy	3	13	0	2.6	1.4	8	0	1.6
B Configure environment	3	10	0	3.0	0.8	7	0	1.7
C Test	3.7	17	0	3.2	1.5	15	0	2.3
D Comment code	2.2	5	1	1.5	0.8	3	0	1.2
E Correspond	4.8	14	0	5.2	1.9	7	0	2.3
F Build, compile, check in/out	3.2	10	0	2.5	1.7	7	0	2.2
G Comprehend	5.2	32	0	5.7	2.0	12	0	2.6
H Refactor	4.1	11	1	2.6	2.2	9	0	2.4
I Write new code	3.9	14	0	3.0	1.7	8	0	1.7
J Debug	3.8	17	0	3.5	1.6	8	0	1.9
K Find/check example	4.0	19	1	3.3	1.5	10	0	2.1
L Discuss IDE	2	2	2	0	1.0	1	1	0

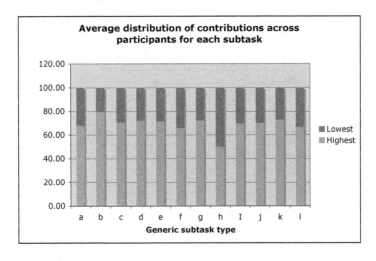

Fig. 3. Average distribution of contributions for generic subtask by participant

Interestingly, the task for which contributions are least evenly distributed (averaging nearly 80:20 between participants) is agreeing strategy. It seems that this is the task on which one person is more likely to take the lead, contrary to suggestions that pair programming lessens the chance of tunnel vision [7]. However, the activity most evenly distributed is Refactoring. This is unsurprising, given the high cognitive load associated with considering both the current and potential future organization of code. Table 6 and Figure 4 below consider the same issues according to role.

Table 6. Most and least collaboration by role for each generic subtask type

	Subtask type	Contributions by driver				Contributions by navigator			
		Average	Highest	Lowest	Standard Deviation	Average	Highest	Lowest	Standard Deviation
A	Agree strategy	2.4	13	0	2.3	2.0	13.0	0	2.3
B	Configure environment	2.6	10.0	0	3.0	1.0	8.0	0	2.0
C	Test	3.3	20.0	0	3.4	1.9	12.0	0	2.5
D	Comment code	1.8	4.0	0	1.3	1.2	4.0	0	1.5
E	Correspond	4.2	13.0	0	5.3	2.4	7.0	0	2.2
F	Build,compile, check in/out	2.8	10.0	0	2.7	2.0	7.0	0	2.2
G	Comprehend	4.8	32.0	0	5.8	2.4	12.0	0	2.9
H	Refactor	3.6	11.0	0	2.8	2.7	9.0	0	2.4
I	Write new code	3.1	10.0	0	2.5	2.5	14.0	0	2.8
J	Debug	3.1	12.0	0	3.1	2.3	13.0	0	2.6
K	Find/check example	3.2	19.0	0	3.4	2.3	10.0	0	2.4
L	Discuss IDE	1.0	1.0	1.0	0	2.0	2.0	2.0	0

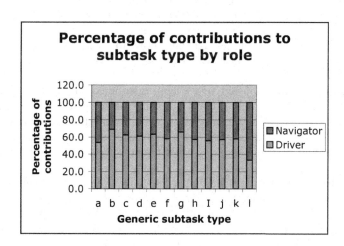

Fig. 4. Percentage each role contributed to each generic subtask type

As illustrated above, contributions were well distributed across roles with the driver contributing slightly more than the navigator across all but one subtask type,

'Discussing the IDE', which happened rarely. This suggests that the driver and navigator roles are less 'tuned to different tasks' but more a convenience in terms of who types. Considering the additional cognitive load of typing, it is surprising that drivers contributed more, however it could be that they were simply commentating on what they were doing.

The two views above (by participant and by role) indicate that the programming pair really are working together on each subtask, rather than each considering a different part of the problem and then pooling results to cover the whole task. However, when one considers more closely the level of collaboration on different types of task, it becomes clear that some lend themselves more to collaboration than others. Similarly, a particular role does not appear to dominate a particular type of task.

5 Conclusion

This report highlights pair programming as highly collaborative, with both partners contributing information to almost every sub-task, irrelevant of role. This contrasts with suggestions that the benefits of pair programming may come from encouraging verbalization, facilitating overhearing or peer pressure from being watched. The profile of the pair programming sessions showed an overall pattern with most time spent on comprehension (understanding existing code and/or the nature of the problem), followed by writing new code and then testing and least time discussing the IDE and commenting code.

While generally very high (over 80%), the level of collaboration varied according to task. Refactoring and writing new code showed the highest level of collaboration and therefore one might suggest that the challenging nature of these tasks made pairing on them most valuable. When the number of contributions per participant was considered, one person was more likely to lead on (i.e. contribute most new information to) agreeing strategy. This is a surprising and interesting phenomena that requires further investigation, as agreeing how to tackle a problem could be considered a highly complex task which one would imagine would benefit greatly from input from both parties.

The studies performed showed very evenly distributed contributions across role, with the driver contributing only slightly more than the navigator. This negates claims that the driver and navigator roles may be oriented toward different types of task, but further investigation is required if we are to fully understand whether a task benefits from the driver and navigator focusing on different aspects (e.g. working at different levels of abstraction).

It should be recognized that the companies studied were an opportunistic sample rather than chosen for being particularly representative of the pair programming community. In addition, while verbalisation occurs naturally in pair programming and the programmer is already being observed by his/her partner, one should nevertheless consider the possible effect of being observed by an experimenter. Finally, it should be noted that the coding of verbalizations as contributing to particular sub-tasks was only undertaken by one person and not blind double coded for accuracy due to resource constraints.

Although the studies report highly positively on the overall collaborative nature of pair programming, they also raise a number of further questions:

- Can software development tasks be designed to foster collaboration?
- Do the driver and navigator contribute at different levels of abstraction?
- What is the power balance in a pair – does one partner or role tend to lead decision making?
- Is collaboration the key to a 'successful' pair programming session?
- Is novice pair programming similarly collaborative in nature, and if not, can this be encouraged.

There is still much to learn about the nature of pair programming, particularly if we are to successfully foster collaborative software development in the workplace and teach it in the classroom in order to reap the many benefits it has been shown to have.

Acknowledgements

This work was undertaken as part of DPhil research funded by the EPSRC. The authors would like to thank the participating companies: BBC iDTV project, BNP Paribas, EGG and LogicaCMG.

References

1. Williams, L. et al., *Strengthening the case for pair programming*, IEEE software, 2000. 17(4): p19-25.
2. Jensen, R, *A pair programming experience*. The journal of defensive software engineering, 2003. 16(3): p.22-24.
3. Nosek, J.T, *The case for collaborative programming*. Communications of the ACM, 1998. 41(3): p.105-108.
4. Cockburn, A. and Williams, L, *The costs and benefits of pair programming*, in *Extreme Programming Examined,* G. Succi and M. Marchesi (Eds). 2001, Addison Wesley.
5. Tessem, B., *Experiences in learning XP practices: A qualitative study.* In Fourth International Conference on Extreme Programming and Agile Processes in Software Engineering, 2003.
6. Lui, K. and K. Chan. *When does a pair outperform two individuals?* In Fourth International Conference on Extreme Programming and Agile Processes in Software Engineering, 2003.
7. Williams, L. and R. Kessler, *Pair Programming Illuminated.* 2003, Boston: Addison Wesley.
8. Sharp, H. and H. Robinson. *An ethnography of XP practices.* In Fifteenth annual psychology of programming interest group workshop, 2003.
9. Bryant, S., P. Romero and B. du-Boulay, *Pair programming and the re-appropriation of individual tools for collaborative software development,* In press.
10. Chi, M., N. de Leeuw, M. Chiu and C. Lavancher, *Eliciting self-explanations improves understanding.* Cognitive Science, 1994. 18: p439-477.
11. Hutchins, E., *Cognition in the wild.* 1995, Cambridge, MA: The MIT press.

12. Ainworth, S. and A. T. Loizou, *The effects of self-explaining when learning with text or diagrams.* Cognitive Science, 2003. 27: p.669-681.

13. Ericsson, K. and H. Simon, *Verbal reports as data.* Psychological review, 1980. 87(3): p.215-251.

14. Cox, R., *Representation construction, externalized cognition and individual differences.* Learning and instruction, 1999. 9: p.343-363.

15. Ericcson, K. and P. Polson, *A cognitive analysis of exceptional memory for restaurant orders,* in The nature of Expertise, M. Chi, R. Glaser and M. Farr (eds). 1988, Lawrence Erlbaum Associates: Hillsdale, USA.

16. Schooler, J.A., S. Ohlsson and K. Brooks, *Thoughts beyond words: When language overshadows insight.* Journal of experimental psychology: General, 1993. 122(2): p166-183.

17. Suthers, D. *Towards a systematic study of representational guidance for collaborative learning discourse.* Journal of Universal Computer Science, 2001. 7(3).

18. Jeong, H. and M. Chi. *Does collaborative learning lead to the construction of common knowledge?* Twenty-second annual conference of the cognitive science society. 2000: Erlbaum, Hillsdale, USA.

19. Dillenbourg, P., *What do you mean by collaborative learning?* In Collaborative learning: Cognitive and computational approachs, D. Dillenbourg, Editor. 1999. Elsevier: London, UK. P1-9.

20. Roschelle, J. and S. D. Teasley, *The construction of shared knowledge in collaborative problem solving,* in Computer Supported Collaborative Learning, C. E. O'Malley, Editor. 1995. Springer-Verlag: Heidelberg. O, 69-97.

21. Curtis, B., *By the way, did anyone study any real programmers?* Empirical studies of programmers, E. Soloway and S. Iyengar (eds). 1986. P.256-261.

22. Bryant, S. *Double Trouble: Mixing quantitative and qualitative methods in the study of extreme programmers.* Visual languages and human centric computing. 2004. IEEE Computer Society.

23. Bryant, S., Romero, P. and du-Boulay, B, *Pair Programming and the re-appropriation of individual tools for collaborative software development* (in press).

24. Chi, M., *Quantifying qualitative analyses of verbal data: A practical guide.* The journal of the learning sciences, 1997. 6(3): p.271-315.

25. Dick, A. and B. Zarnett. *Paired programming and personality traits* in Third International Conference on Extreme Programming and Agile Processes in Software Engineering, 2002.

26. Hughes, J. and Parkes, S., *Trends in the use of verbal protocol analysis in software engineering research.* Behaviour and Information Technology, 2003, 22(2): p127-140.

27. Pennington, N., *Stimulus Structures and Mental Representations in Expert Comprehension of Computer Programs,* Cognitive Psychology, 1987, 19: p295-341.

28. Beck, K., *Extreme Programming Explained: Embrace Change,* 2000. Addison Wesley.

29. Johnston, A. and Johnson, C.S. *Extreme Programming: A more musical approach to software development.* Proceedings of the 4th International conference in XP and Agile Processes in Software Engineering, 2003. Goos, G., Hartmanis, J. and van Leeuwen, J. (eds): p325-327.

Is External Code Quality Correlated with Programming Experience or Feelgood Factor?*

Lech Madeyski

Institute of Applied Informatics, Wroclaw University of Technology,
Wyb.Wyspianskiego 27, 50370 Wroclaw, Poland
Lech.Madeyski@pwr.wroc.pl
http://madeyski.e-informatyka.pl/

Abstract. This paper is inspired by an article by Müller and Padberg who study the feelgood factor and programming experience, as candidate drivers for the pair programming performance. We not only reveal a possible threat to validity of empirical results presented by Müller and Padberg but also perform an independent research. Our objective is to provide empirical evidence whether external code quality is correlated with the feelgood factor, or with programming experience. Our empirical study is based on a controlled experiment with MSc students. It appeared that the external code quality is correlated with the feelgood factor, and programming experience, in the case of pairs using a classic (test-last) testing approach. The generalization of the results is limited due to the fact that MSc students participated in the study. The research revealed that both the feelgood factor and programming experience may be the external code quality drivers.

1 Introduction

Pair programming [1] has recently gained a lot of attention, as key software development practice of eXtreme Programming (XP) methodology [2]. The main idea of pair programming software development practice is that two programmers work together, collaborating on the same development tasks. The basic aim of pair programming, described in section 3.2, is to improve software quality.

Researchers and practitioners have reported numerous, often anecdotal and favourable studies of XP practices and methodology. Empirical studies on pair programming often concern productivity [3, 4, 5, 6, 7]. A few studies have focused on pair programming, or test-driven development, as practices to remove defects [4, 5, 8, 9], to influence the external code quality (measured by the number of functional, blackbox test cases passed) [10, 11, 12] or reliability of programs (a fraction of the number of passed tests divided by the number of all tests) [13, 14, 15] and other quality benefits [16].

In spite of a wide range of studies, there is still limited evidence concerning the role of the feelgood factor (how comfortably the developers feel in a pair

---

* This work has been financially supported by the Ministry of Education and Science as a research grant 3 T11C 061 30 (years 2006-2007).

P. Abrahamsson, M. Marchesi, and G. Succi (Eds.): XP 2006, LNCS 4044, pp. 65–74, 2006.

session [17]) and the programming experience in pair programming. The aim of this paper is to fill this gap. So far, the results obtained by Müller and Padberg [17] indicate that the pair performance is uncorrelated with the programming experience whereas the feelgood factor is a candidate driver for the performance of a pair.

The results presented by Müller and Padberg were obtained by applying a special scheme for pairing the subjects. The most skilled subject had to pair off with the lowest skilled subject, the second best skilled subject with the second lowest skilled subject, and so on. The aim was to balance the skill level across the pairs but, this special scheme for pairing the subjects might have hidden a possible correlation of pair performance with the programming experience, as the latter was averaged across pairs. In the Müller and Padberg study, the performance of a pair was measured by the implementation time [17]. In our study the implementation time is constant (eight laboratory sessions) and the dependent variable is the external code quality, measured by the number of acceptance tests passed ($NATP$), as suggested by George and Williams [10, 11] and later used by Madeyski [12]. Therefore, the research question is whether the external code quality is correlated with the pair feelgood factor, or programming experience.

2   Problem Statement

The data for this study comes from a controlled experiment performed at Wroclaw University of Technology. The purpose of the experiment was to investigate the impact of test-driven development and pair programming practices on software development products [12].

The following definition determines a foundation for our study [18]:

Object of study. The objects of study are software development products — developed code.
Purpose. The purpose is to find whether the quality of software development products is correlated with the programming experience, or the feelgood factor of pair programming.
Quality focus. The quality focus is the external code quality (measured by $NATP$).
Perspective. The perspective is from the researcher's point of view.
Context. The study is run using MSc students as subjects and the finance-accounting system as an object.

Summary: Analyse *the software development products* for the purpose of *finding correlation between quality of software development products and the feelgood factor, or programming experience* with respect to the *external code quality*, from *the researcher's* point of view, in the context of the *finance-accounting system development by MSc students*.

3   Study Description

3.1   Context Selection

The context of the experiment was the Programming in Java (PIJ) course, and hence the experiment was run off-line (not industrial software development) [18]. Java was the programming language, and Eclipse 3.0 was the Integrated Development Environment (IDE). All subjects had prior experience in at least C and C++ programming (using object-oriented approach). The PIJ course consisted of seven 90 minute lectures and fifteen laboratory 90 minute sessions. The course introduced Java programming language, using test-driven development and pair programming as key XP practices. The subjects' practical skills in programming in Java, using pair programming, and test-driven development were evaluated during the first seven laboratory sessions. The experiment took place during the last eight laboratory sessions. The problem addressed the development of the finance-accounting system. The requirements specification consisted of 27 user stories. The subjects participating in the study were mainly second and third-year (and few fourth and fifth-year) computer science MSc students. MSc programme of Wroclaw University of Technology is a 5-year programme after high school. In total, 188 students were involved in the experiment, but only 132 students were working in pairs, see table 1.

3.2   Variables and Subjects Selection

The variables considered in this study are:

- The external code quality was measured by the number of acceptance tests passed ($NATP$). This measure was proposed by George and Williams [10], [11]. The number of acceptance tests passed was collected automatically by our measurement infrastructure. In contrast to some productivity measures, e.g. Source Lines Of Code ($SLOC$) per person-month, $NATP$ takes into account functionality and quality of software development products.
- The pair feelgood factor (PFF) was measured by the mean value of the individual feelgood factors, collected by means of a post-test questionnaire. The post-test questionnaire asked how comfortable the subject felt during the pair programming session. An even number of alternatives (0–bad, 1–sufficiently, 2–good, 3–very good) was chosen, because it forces the subjects to get off the fence, and to prevent large numbers of neutral answers. The answer ranges on an ordinal scale and this metric is called the individual feelgood factor of a developer. Since our questionnaire did not ask the pairs to specify a joint feelgood factor, the mean of the individual assessments was taken as a substitute. The resulting metric is called the pair feelgood factor. This approach to calculate the pair feelgood factor was used by Müller and Padberg [15]. It may be questionable, because the individual feelgood factor is an ordinal value, but we used it for compatibility reasons.
- The mean programming experience (MPE) was measured by the mean value of the individual programming experience of each pair programmers,

collected by means of questionnaires. Not only industrial but also school (university) experience was included.

The subjects are chosen based on convenience — the subjects are students taking the PIJ course. Prior to the experiment, the students filled in a pre-test questionnaire. The aim of the questionnaire was to get a description of the students' background, see table 1. The ability to generalize from this context is further elaborated when discussing threats, see section 3.4.

In this study we analysed pairs using test-driven development practice (denoted as TP) and classic (test-last) testing approach (denoted as CP).

Table 1. The context of the study

Context factors	CP	TP
Number of MSc students:	62	70
– in the 2nd year	40	39
– in the 3rd year	18	27
– in the 4th year	3	4
– in the 5th year	1	0
– with industry experience	8	15
Median of individual feelgood factor (0–bad...3–very good)	3	3
Mean of programming experience (years)	3.61	3.86

Pair programming is a practice in which two programmers (called the driver and navigator) work together at one computer, collaborating on the same development tasks (e.g. design, test, code). The driver, is typing at the computer or writing down a design. The navigator observes the driver's work, reviews the code, proposes test cases and considers the implementations strategic implications [4, 19].

Test-driven development (TDD) is a practice based on specifying a piece of functionality, as a low level test before writing production code, on implementing the functionality, so that the test passes, and on refactoring (e.g. removing duplication) and iterating the process. The tests are run frequently while writing production code. In case of classic (test-last) development, the tests are specified after writing production code and less frequently [20].

The assignment of subjects to groups was performed first by stratifying the subjects with respect to their skill level, measured by graders, and then assigning them at random to test-driven development, or classic (test-last) testing approach teams. However, the assignment to pair programming teams took into account the people's preferences (as it seemed to be more natural and close to the real world agile software development practice). The students who did not complete the projects (did not check in the project prerequisites the final version of their program, or did not fill in questionnaires) were not included in the analysis. The outcome was an unbalanced design, with 35 pairs using TDD practice and 31 pairs using classic (test-last) testing approach.

3.3   Materials

The materials prepared for the experiment consisted of requirements specification (user stories), pre-test and post-test questionnaires, Eclipse project framework, a detailed description of software development methods, and of duties of the subjects, instructions how to use the experiment infrastructure (e.g. CVS Version Management System), and examples (e.g. sample source code of applications developed using TDD approach and JUnit tests). The number of acceptance tests passed was collected using automated infrastructure developed by e-Informatyka team members of Wroclaw University of Technology.

3.4   Validity Evaluation

The fundamental question concerning the results of each study is how valid the results are. Shadish, Cook and Campbell [21] defined four types of threats: *statistical conclusion, internal, construct* and *external validity.*

The threats to the *statistical conclusion* validity are considered to be under control. Robust statistical techniques, tools (e.g. Statistica) and large sample sizes to increase statistical power are used. The risk in the treatment implementation is that the study was spread across laboratory sessions. To avoid the risk, the access to the CVS repository was restricted to the specific laboratory sessions (access hours and IP addresses). The validity of the study is highly dependent on the reliability of the measures. The basic principle is that when you measure a phenomenon twice, the outcome should be the same. The number of acceptance tests passed is considered reliable because it can be repeated with the same outcomes.

Concerning the *internal* validity, the risk of rivalry between groups must be considered. The group using the traditional method may do their very best to show that the old method is competitive. On the other hand, the subjects receiving less desirable treatments may not perform so well as they generally do. However, the subjects were informed that the goal of the study was to measure different development methods, and not the subjects' skills. A possible diffusion or imitation of treatments were under control of the graders.

Threats to the *construct* validity are not considered very harmful. The mono-operation bias is a threat, as the study was conducted on a single software development project; however, the the project addressed a similar to real-life situation problem (the development of the finance-accounting system). Using a single type of measure would be a mono-method bias threat; however, measures used in the study were rather objective.

The largest threat to the *external* validity is that students (who had short experience in pair programming and test-driven development) were used as subjects. Kitchenham et al.[22] states that students are the next generation of

software professionals, so, they are relatively close to the population of interest. Replicated experiments by Porter and Votta [23] and Höst et al. [24] also
suggest that students may provide an adequate model of professional population.
However, it is too optimistic when we evaluate experience.

In summary, the threats are not regarded as being critical.

4   Operation

The experiment was run at Wroclaw University of Technology during eight laboratory sessions. The data was primarily collected by automated experiment
infrastructure. Additionally, the subjects filled in pre-test and post-test questionnaires, primarily to get a description of their experience and preferences.
The package for the experiment was prepared in advance and is described in
section 3.3. A few people were involved in the experiment planning, operation
and analysis.

5   Analysis

The data are analysed with scatterplot and Spearman's correlation coefficient.
Before conducting any correlational analysis, it is essential to plot a scatterplot
to look at the general trend of the data.

5.1   Discovering General Trend

A scatterplot tells us whether there seems to be a relationship between the variables, what kind of relationship it is, and whether any cases differ substantially
from the general trend of the data. We use an overlay scatterplot, as we want
to look at the role of both the pair feelgood factor and the programming experience on external code quality (but not the relationship between the pair feelgood
factor and the programming experience).

Scatterplot has been used to plot the relationship between the pair feelgood
factor and external code quality and between the programming experience and
external code quality simultaneously, see figure 1. From figure 1 it seems that
both the pair feelgood factor and programming experience are positively related
to the external code quality, at least in the case of classic (test-last) development
method used by pairs (CP). Spearman's correlations were used to follow up these
findings.

5.2   Discovering Correlations

Table 2 shows Spearman's correlations and significances for two experimental
groups (CP and TP).

In case of classic (test-last) testing approach the external code quality (measured by $NATP$) achieved by pairs is correlated with the pair feelgood factor ($p = .022$) and mean programming experience of programmers in pairs

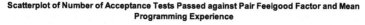

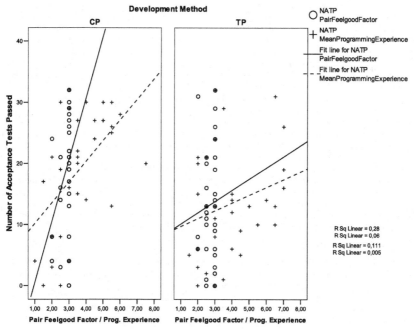

Fig. 1. Scatterplot of Number of Acceptance Tests Passed against Pair Feelgood Factor and Mean Programming Experience

Table 2. Nonparametric Correlations – Spearman's rho

		NATP$_{TP}$	NATP$_{CP}$
NATP	Correlation Coefficient	1.000	1.000
	N	35	31
Pair Feelgood Factor	Correlation Coefficient	0.121	0.364
	Sig.(1-tailed)	0.244	0.022
Mean Programming Experience [years]	Correlation Coefficient	0.222	0.512
	Sig.(1-tailed)	0.100	0.002

($p = .002$). The fact that a correlation exists is not sufficient to conclude that the feelgood factor, or programming experience, actually drivès the external code quality in case of classic testing approach e.g. it is unclear whether a pair performs well because the feelgood factor is high, or, whether the developers feel comfortable because they have the impression that the number of acceptance tests passed is high.

In the case of pairs using test-driven development practice, the effect is smaller, and the results are not statistically significant ($p > .05$). A possible explanation is that the number of acceptance tests passed is significantly affected by the software testing approach. It appeared that the number of acceptance tests passed was lower when test-driven development was used instead of the classic, test-last software development approach in case of solo programmers ($p = .028$) and pairs ($p = .013$) [12].

6   Summary and Conclusions

The previous research conducted by Müller and Padberg [17] revealed that pair performance may be uncorrelated with the programming experience, but correlated with the pair feelgood factor. A possible threat to validity of empirical results presented by Müller and Padberg is that they used a special scheme for pairing the subjects that averaged the programming experience.

The results obtained in our study suggest that both the pair feelgood factor and programming experience are correlated, in case of classic testing approach, with the number of acceptance tests passed, which is a measure of the external code quality, as suggested by George and Williams [10, 11]. Therefore, both the pair feelgood factor and programming experience may be external code quality drivers.

The existence of correlations should be considered as a basis for future research. From the correlation alone, one can not decide whether the number of acceptance tests passed is high because the pair feelgood factor or mean programming experience was high. To answer that question, further empirical studies are necessary. A further research (e.g. experiment with the pair feelgood factor in mind) is needed to establish evidence of the impact of the pair feelgood factor, and programming experience on the external code quality and to evaluate the impact of the pair feelgood factor and programming experience in other contexts (e.g. in industry).

The validity of the results must be considered within the context of the limitations discussed in the validity evaluation section.

Acknowledgments

The author expresses his gratitude to the students participating in the research, the graders and the members of the e-Informatyka team (Wojciech Gdela, Tomasz Poradowski, Jacek Owocki, Grzegorz Mąkosa, Mariusz Sadal and Michał Stochmiałek) for their help during preparations of the experiment infrastructure, and to anonymous reviewers for helpful suggestions.

References

1. Williams, L., Kessler, R.: Pair Programming Illuminated. Addison-Wesley (2002)
2. Beck, K.: Extreme Programming Explained: Embrace Change. 2nd edn. Addison-Wesley (2004)
3. Nosek, J.T.: The case for collaborative programming. Communications of the ACM **41**(3) (1998) 105–108

4. Williams, L., Kessler, R.R., Cunningham, W., Jeffries, R.: Strengthening the case for pair programming. IEEE Software **17**(4) (2000) 19–25
5. Williams, L.: The Collaborative Software Process. PhD thesis, University of Utah (2000)
6. Nawrocki, J.R., Wojciechowski, A.: Experimental evaluation of pair programming. In: ESCOM '01: European Software Control and Metrics. (2001) 269–276
7. Nawrocki, J.R., Jasiński, M., Olek, L., Lange, B.: Pair Programming vs. Side-by-Side Programming. In Richardson, I., Abrahamsson, P., Messnarz, R., eds.: EuroSPI. Volume 3792 of Lecture Notes in Computer Science., Springer (2005) 28–38
8. Williams, L., Maximilien, E.M., Vouk, M.: Test-Driven Development as a Defect-Reduction Practice. In: ISSRE '03: Proceedings of the 14th International Symposium on Software Reliability Engineering, Washington, DC, USA, IEEE Computer Society (2003) 34–48
9. Maximilien, E.M., Williams, L.A.: Assessing Test-Driven Development at IBM. In: ICSE '03: Proceedings of the 25th International Conference on Software Engineering, IEEE Computer Society (2003) 564–569
10. George, B., Williams, L.A.: An Initial Investigation of Test Driven Development in Industry. In: SAC '03: Proceedings of the 2003 ACM Symposium on Applied Computing, ACM (2003) 1135–1139
11. George, B., Williams, L.A.: A structured experiment of test-driven development. Information and Software Technology **46**(5) (2004) 337–342
12. Madeyski, L.: Preliminary Analysis of the Effects of Pair Programming and Test-Driven Development on the External Code Quality. In Zieliński, K., Szmuc, T., eds.: Software Engineering: Evolution and Emerging Technologies. Volume 130 of Frontiers in Artificial Intelligence and Applications. IOS Press (2005) 113–123
13. Müller, M.M., Hagner, O.: Experiment about test-first programming. IEE Proceedings - Software **149**(5) (2002) 131–136
14. Müller, M.M.: Are Reviews an Alternative to Pair Programming? In: EASE '03: Conference on Empirical Assessment In Software Engineering. (2003)
15. Müller, M.M.: Are Reviews an Alternative to Pair Programming? Empirical Software Engineering **9**(4) (2004) 335–351
16. Hulkko, H., Abrahamsson, P.: A Multiple Case Study on the Impact of Pair Programming on Product Quality. In: ICSE '05: Proceedings of the 27th International Conference on Software Engineering, New York, NY, USA, ACM Press (2005) 495–504
17. Müller, M.M., Padberg, F.: An empirical study about the feelgood factor in pair programming. In: METRICS '04: Proceedings of the Software Metrics, 10th International Symposium on (METRICS'04), Washington, DC, USA, IEEE Computer Society (2004) 151–158
18. Wohlin, C., Runeson, P., Höst, M., Ohlsson, M.C., Regnell, B., Wesslén, A.: Experimentation in Software Engineering: An Introduction. Kluwer Academic Publishers, Norwell, MA, USA (2000)
19. Williams, L.A., Kessler, R.R.: All I really need to know about pair programming I learned in kindergarten. Commun. ACM **43**(5) (2000) 108–114
20. Erdogmus, H., Morisio, M., Torchiano, M.: On the Effectiveness of the Test-First Approach to Programming. IEEE Transactions on Software Engineering **31**(3) (2005) 226–237
21. Shadish, W.R., Cook, T.D., Campbell, D.T.: Experimental and Quasi-Experimental Designs for Generalized Causal Inference. Houghton Mifflin (2002)

22. Kitchenham, B., Pfleeger, S.L., Pickard, L., Jones, P., Hoaglin, D.C., Emam, K.E., Rosenberg, J.: Preliminary Guidelines for Empirical Research in Software Engineering. IEEE Transactions on Software Engineering **28**(8) (2002) 721–734
23. Porter, A., Votta, L.: Comparing detection methods for software requirements inspections: A replication using professional subjects. Empirical Softw. Engg. **3**(4) (1998) 355–379
24. Höst, M., , Wohlin, C., Thelin, T.: Experimental context classification: incentives and experience of subjects. In: ICSE '05: Proceedings of the 27th International Conference on Software Engineering, New York, NY, USA, ACM Press (2005) 470–478

Leveraging Code Smell Detection
with Inter-smell Relations

Błażej Pietrzak and Bartosz Walter

Institute of Computing Science, Poznań University of Technology, Poland
{Blazej.Pietrzak, Bartosz.Walter}@cs.put.poznan.pl

Abstract. The variety of code smells deserves a numerous set of detectors capable of sensing them. There exist several sources of data that may be examined: code metrics, existence of particular elements in an abstract syntax tree, specific code behavior or subsequent changes in the code. Another factor that can be used for this purpose is the knowledge of other, already detected or rejected smells. In the paper we define and analyze different relations that exist among smells and provide tips how they could be exploited to alleviate detection of other smells.

Keywords: Refactoring, bad code smells, inter-smell relations.

1 Introduction

The quality of source code is one of the factors affecting the software maintenance cost [1]. Poor quality results both in short term in increased fault ratio and on the long run in higher expenditure on modifications and further development of the product. Code quality is then a costly, although valued attribute of software, which gives a chance for savings and profits in further software maintenance, but requires considerable initial investments.

High quality source code is particularly important in agile methodologies. eXtreme Programming (XP) [2], the most popular among them, diminishes the importance of documentation in favour to the source code readability and comprehension. Any factors that do not contribute to these values are considered potential threats and are candidates for improvement. Although there exist numerous different source code flaws that can negatively affect the software quality, XP covers all of them by a vague term of *bad code smell* [2]. Smells are defined as constructs in the code that "suggest (sometimes scream for) the possibility of refactoring" [3]. This deliberate imprecision, which puts stress on the human judgment based on experience and the sense of aesthetics, leads to significant problems with automated detection and identification of smells. It is illustrated by the diversity of over 20 bad smells identified by Fowler, which differ in importance, complexity and localization. The range of code elements affected by them spans from entire modules or class hierarchies (*Parallel Inheritance Hierarchies, Message Chain*), through single classes and objects (*Feature Envy, Divergent Change, Large Class*), then methods (*Extract Method, Long Parameter List*), ending up with individual variables, statements and expressions (*Primitive Obsession, Temporary Field*). As a result, there exists no

P. Abrahamsson, M. Marchesi, and G. Succi (Eds.): XP 2006, LNCS 4044, pp. 75–84, 2006.

general method of smell detection. Each smell describes a distinct flaw, related to either improper structure, communication between objects, low readability and other aspects. In turn, each smell is revealed with multiple symptoms of various nature and require a unique mechanism of identification.

In attempt to capture the subtle, complex nature of smells, in [4] we proposed a multi-criteria, holistic model of smell detection, which combines various sources of information. We identified six such sources considered useful for smell detection:

- Programmer's intuition and experience,
- Metrics values,
- Analysis of a source code syntax tree,
- History of changes made in code,
- Dynamic behavior of code,
- Existence of other smells.

Apart from the programmer's intuition, another four data sources are measurable or at least intuitively comprehensible. The last one is special as it reuses information about the already discovered smells, so that they can be exploited again in further examination. It comes from the observation that smells are not independent, separated phenomena and their presence or absence often carries knowledge about other smells. Therefore, it is possible to support code smells detection process with already available information about the relations existing between smells. Our initial thoughts on the smell dependencies have been presented in [11].

In this paper we continue the research and examine some relations existing among code smells, presenting how they could be exploited for more effective smell detection.

The paper is structured as follows. Section 2 describes seven identified relations among bad code smells. It also suggests how the relations could be exploited in smell detection. In section 3 we attempt to evaluate the relevance of the relations on selected classes taken from Jakarta Tomcat project [5]. The paper is concluded with a summary presented in the section 4.

2   Inter-smell Dependencies

Even a superficial analysis of Fowler's bad smells descriptions reveals that most of them are related to each other: some appear in groups, while others exclude one another. In general, the already confirmed presence or absence of a particular smell may carry information about others. It is Fowler who noticed the existence of relations and dependencies between smells: "When a class is trying to do too much, it often shows up as too many instance variables. When a class has too many instance variables, duplicated code cannot be far behind" [3].

The nature of the relations varies: some smells share a common flaw as an origin, whereas others are revealed by similar symptoms or can be eliminated with a single transformation. The kind of relationship suggests also the way it could be exploited. We focus on the relations that (1) contribute to identification of other smells and (2) their elimination.

In [11] we proposed five coarse relations that describe dependencies between smells. The extended and updated list now contains six relations:

- Plain support,
- Mutual support,
- Rejection.
- Aggregate support,
- Transitive support,
- Inclusion.

In order to measure the effectiveness of the relations we need a metric reflecting their strength. Strength of the plain support relation, which also makes a basis for the other ones, can be measured with the certainty factor [12]. Certainty factor for the relation $r(A, B)$ is interpreted as a number of objects incriminated with the smell B in the set of objects featuring the smell A. The notion of the factor is used in the remaining relations respectively.

2.1 Plain Support

Plain support relation is the simplest relation that may be identified. A smell B is supported by A if the existence of A implies with sufficiently high certainty the existence of B. B is then a companion smell of A, and the program entities (classes, methods, expressions etc.) burdened with A also suffer from B. The relation makes a basis for many other relations analyzed below.

The importance of the relation comes from observation that in A is often an easy to detect smell with few symptoms, while B is a more complex one, embracing various aspects and showing up with different symptoms. Thus, A can be utilized for diagnosing B without delving into its complex nature.

As an example, let us consider the relation between *Data Class* and *Feature Envy*. A *Data Class* is a class inappropriately used as a data container [3], which may evince through one of the following:

- Class contains public fields,
- Class improperly encapsulates a collection,
- Class is structure equivalent and features with only getting and settings methods.

We only analyze the structure equivalent violations, because the other are not related to the *Feature Envy* smell. The exemplary structure equivalent symptom, taken from Tomcat's code base (*org.apache.catalina.deploy.FilterMap* class), is provided below.

```
public class FilterMap implements Serializable {
    ...
    private String filterName = null;
    public String getFilterName() {
        return (this.filterName);
    }
    public void setFilterName(String filterName) {
        this.filterName = filterName;
    }
    private String servletName = null;
    public String getServletName() {
```

```
        return (this.servletName);
    }
    public void setServletName(String servletName) {
        this.servletName = servletName;
    }
    ...
}
```

A method that is more interested in a class other than the one it actually belongs to, is an example of a *Feature Envy* smell [3]. It indicates that the responsibility is improperly distributed among classes. *Feature Envious* methods should be moved to the class that they reference the most. The exemplary *Feature Envious* method taken from Tomcat's *org.apache.catalina.core.ApplicationFilterFactory* class is presented below.

```
public final class ApplicationFilterFactory {
    ...
    private boolean matchFiltersServlet(
        FilterMap filterMap, String servletName) {
        if (servletName == null) {
            return false;
        } else {
            if (servletName.equals(
                filterMap.getServletName())){
                return true;
            } else {
                return false;
            }
        }
    }
    ...
}
```

The *matchFilterServlet()* method checks if the actual servlet name matches the filter's servlet name. It makes no use of any of its enclosing class' fields and methods. There are two objects referenced by it: *filterMap* and *servletName*, each of them referenced twice. Since *servletName* is of a standard type *java.lang.String* and cannot be modified, then *filterMap* object is considered the possible owner of the method. Thus, the method could be moved to the *FilterMap* class, which is a *Data Class*. As a side effect, the latter smell would be removed as well.

Of course, there exist several design patterns, like *Strategy* and *Visitor* [8], which are used primarily to combat the *Divergent Change* smell [3], that violate this rule. In this article we did not take these cases under consideration.

The conclusion is that the structure equivalent version of the *Data Class* smell is closely related to the *Feature Envy* smell. If there exist a *Data Class*, there is usually also another class that uses its data. The client almost certainly contains methods that are *Feature Envy* candidates.

2.2 Mutual Support

This relation is a symmetric closure of the plain support: both related smells support each other. It is not only simply equivalent to two plain support relations, but also suggests that the related smells share common roots and originate from the same code flaw. Removing the reason may result in reduction or even removal of both smells.

Seemingly, it gives a powerful ability to attain two goals with a single action. However, among the smells identified by Fowler there are no two odors mutually supporting each other with considerable certainty. That observation is justified, as different smells, although often related to each other, describe at least slightly, yet different anomalies. Therefore, even if a smell A supports smell B, the reversed relation (if exists) is weaker. Should any such smell be defined in future, it would resemble the existing ones so much, that the gain from removing it along with others would be negligible.

Unfortunately, we cannot provide any examples of the mutual support relation.

2.3 Rejection

Rejection yields the negative information about smells presence: a smell B is rejected by a smell A, if the presence of A excludes the existence of the smell B. Knowing that, we may restrict the exploration area to remaining smells and limit the computational complexity of the detection process.

Noticeably, this relation, unlike others, is symmetric: if A rejects B, then B rejects A. Presence or confirmed absence of any of smells participating in the relation carries information about the other one.

For example, a *Lazy Class*, which has no or only limited functionality, cannot be simultaneously an over-functional *Large Class*. *Lazy Classes* are relatively easy to identify, because there exist few symptoms of low functionality. Therefore, for classes diagnosed as lazy there is no need to look for *Large Class* signs. The latter smell embraces multiple subtle symptoms, which are much harder to detect than *Lazy Class*, like multiple interfaces, multiple instances, multiple subclasses, so the knowledge of the *Lazy Class* presence allows giving up further exploration towards *Large Class*.

2.4 Aggregate Support

Aggregate support generalizes the plain support and rejection relations to a case of multiple source smells. A finite sets of detected smells A_1, A_2, ..., A_m and absent smells B_1, B_2, ..., B_m support a smell C as an aggregate, if they all support the existence of the smell C with higher certainty than any of individual smells A_i does or the smell C rejects the existence of any of smells B_j. Colloquially speaking, it is the synergy of several source smells (both present and absent) that increases the probability of existence of the target smell.

Aggregate support in several cases provides a stronger premise for many smells to exist. Source smells usually combine a broader spectrum of symptoms, which gives higher accuracy of the final result. The price for that is higher complexity of the detection process, resulting from the necessity of analyzing multiple source smells.

As an example, let us consider the following relation: if the given class is simultaneously composed of setters and getters, is not *Inappropriately Intimate*, and is the target of *Move Method* performed to remove a *Feature Envious* method, then it is a *Data Class*. The certainty factor for that relation is then higher than it would be without some of the supporting symptoms.

2.5 Transitive Support

The relation is a specific example of aggregate support with source smells depending on each other. Provided that there exist two plain support relations *p*: *A* supports *B* and *q*: *B* supports *C*, we can deduce the presence of a relation *r*: *A* supports *C*.

As an example we found the chain *Data Class* supports *Feature Envy* supports *Large Class*. *Large Classes* are classes that bear too much functionality. The over-functionality may result from improper class abstraction and combining several classes together. Other reasons include the presence of *Feature Envious* methods or *Inappropriate Intimacy* with other classes. Such a class needs to be split into smaller classes. Therefore, *Data Class* suggests the presence of the *Large Class*, because *Data Class* is related to *Feature Envy* (see 2.1) and the *Feature Envy* is related to *Large Class*.

2.6 Inclusion

Inclusion is a directed relation between smells *A* and *B*, in which *A* is a particular case of *B*. It means that every symptom revealing the smell *A* is also a sign of *B*'s presence. Therefore, by detecting the smell *A* we always find also the smell *B*.

Inclusion is slightly related to plain support, with exception that the special smell entirely fulfills symptoms specific to the general one.

Fowler's catalog contains a few examples of included smells. For instance, *Parallel Inheritance Hierarchies* is a special case of *Shotgun Surgery* smell.

2.7 Common Refactoring

The relations presented above concentrate on direct dependencies between smells. There exist other relations, which connect smells indirectly. One of binding elements is a common refactoring that once applied, affects all smells involved, either removing them or removing some and introducing the other.

For example, a *Move Method* applied to a *Lazy Class* may result in *Feature Envy* smell, because *Move Method* transfers the envious method outside, possibly reducing responsibility carried by that class.

3 Evaluation

To evaluate impact of our findings, we performed experiment on 830 classes coming from Apache Tomcat 5.5.4 [5] codebase. The project was selected for evaluation due to its high quality source code [9].

In subsequent sections we provide examples of how the information about smells could be exploited to detect other smells.

3.1 *Data Class* and *Feature Envy* **Plain Support**

In order to select *Data Class* candidates, we employed a simple getter/setter measure. We assumed that a class is a structure equivalent if the ratio of such methods is at least 80%. Other symptoms (improper encapsulation of fields and collections) were ignored. Candidates were then manually inspected to determine actual *Data Class* smell representatives. We also considered a method to be *Feature Envious* if it referenced other classes more frequently than its own class methods.

During inspection we found 26 classes, which had at least 80% of setter/getter methods, and as such were identified as *Data Classes*. Among them, 24 were referenced in *Feature Envious* methods. Therefore, it yields a high certainty factor (equal to 92%), which strongly suggests that the relation exists.

3.2 **Plain Support of** *Large Class* **for** *Feature Envy*

We analyzed the plain support relation between *Large Class* and *Feature Envy*. To measure class functionality we adopted four popular object-oriented metrics [6,7]. Their definitions and accepted thresholds taken from NASA's historical metrics database [10] are presented in Table 1.

Table 1. Metrics used for measuring functionality and their accepted thresholds (source: [6,10])

	Description	Max. accepted
NOM	Number of methods in the class	20
WMC	Sum of cyclomatic complexities of class methods	100
RFC	Number of methods + number of methods called by each of these methods (each method counted once)	100
CBO	Number of classes referencing the given class	5

We assumed that a class is considered large if at least one metric value exceeds the accepted threshold. Moreover, we also experimentally found that a *Large Class* has at least one *Feature Envious* method. Table 2 depicts the results of the evaluation. There exist 230 classes classified by common detectors as large. Out of these, 205 referenced *Feature Envious* methods. As we supposed, it turns out that most *Large Classes* have at least one *Feature Envious* method (certainty factor is equal to 89%), which helps in detecting the smell.

Table 2. Analysis of *Large Class*, *Inappropriate Intimacy* and *Feature Envy* smell relations (source: [11])

Metric	Value
Total number of analyzed classes	830
Number of classes with *Feature Envious* methods	463
Number of *Inappropriately Intimate* classes	159
Number of *Large Classes* found with common detectors	230
Number of *Large Classes* found exploiting relations between smells	501

3.3 Rejection

The rejection relation was analyzed with *Inappropriate Intimacy* and *Data Class* smells. *Inappropriately Intimate* classes "spend too much time delving in each other private parts" [3]. There are two violations covered by this smell:

- Bi-directional associations between classes, and
- Subclasses knowing more about their parents than their parents would like them to know.

Data Classes are mere data holders and thus do not have bi-directional associations with other classes. In other words, if a class is *Inappropriately Intimate*, then it cannot simultaneously be a *Data Class*.

Due to difficulties with automatic detection of the latter symptom of *Inappropriate Intimacy*, we considered only bi-directional associations between classes. Even a single association was considered to be smelly. The evaluation revealed 159 of 830 inspected classes to have such association. The number of possible checks for the *Data Class* smell was therefore reduced by 19%, because *Inappropriate Intimacy* excludes that smell.

3.4 Aggregate Support

As an example of this relation we evaluated *Data Class* structure equivalent smell [3]. A simple detector based on the setter/getter ratio found 66 candidates, out of which, after manual verification, only 26 have been found actually smelly (39% of accuracy).

We used this result to verify a hypothesis that information about support and rejection relations of other smells with *Data Class* smell may increase the accuracy of the detector, leaving the programmer with the smaller list of refactoring candidates to manual assessment. Therefore we evaluated the following aggregate relation: if a class has at least 80% of getter/setter methods, and is not *Inappropriately Intimate* smell, and is the target of *Move Method* refactoring of the *Feature Envy* method, then it is a *Data Class*.

Among 26 actual smell classes from 66 candidate classes we found 24 *Data Classes* referenced by *Feature Envy* methods and simultaneously being not *Inappropriately Intimate*. Another 12 were *Data Classes* referenced by *Inappropriately Intimate classes*. Therefore, there are only 30 classes left (out of 66) for manual inspection. The certainty factor for the analyzed aggregate support relation is then 92% (24 out of 26 candidate classes featured that smell).

3.5 Relations with a Common Refactoring

The knowledge about the relations between smells may be helpful also while removing them, i.e. at refactoring. We evaluated *Feature Envy* smell removal with *Move Method* transformation. Moved methods targeted also 21 *Data Classes* and simultaneously minimized the number of these smelly classes from 26 to 7. More details can be found in [11].

4 Conclusions

Every code smell is characterized by a different set of symptoms. To alleviate smell detection, we exploit the fact that some of them are related to others and carry information about them. The existence of already discovered smells becomes then a valuable indicator of other flaws. Whereas it infrequently plays a primary role in smell detection, it could be successfully utilized as an auxiliary source of smell-related data.

In the paper we identified six distinct inter-smell relations that appeared useful for smell detection. Another one relates smells through a common refactoring. The experiment showed that the use of the knowledge about already identified smells in Jakarta Tomcat code supports the detection process. We found examples of several smell dependencies, including simple, aggregate and transitive support and rejection relation. The certainty factor for those relations in that code suggests the existence of correlation among the dependent smells and applicability of this approach to smell detection.

Several activities benefited from the dependency analysis: in most cases it improved effectiveness and efficiency of the smell detection process; in others it suggested a single refactoring to remove several smells at once. Therefore, there are multiple applications of the inter-smell relations.

Future research plans include examination of other smells and their relations, and development of a tool for assisting a programmer in smell detection utilizing the presented approach.

Acknowledgements

The work has been supported by the Rector of Poznań University of Technology as a research grant BW/91-429.

References

1. Pearse T., Oman P.: Maintainability Measurements on Industrial Source Code Mainte-nance Activities. In: Proceedings of International Conference of Software Maintenance 1995, Opio (France), pp.295-303.
2. Beck K.: Extreme Programming Explained. Embrace Change. Addison-Wesley, 2000.
3. Fowler M.: Refactoring. Improving Design of Existing Code. Addison-Wesley, 1999.
4. Walter B., Pietrzak B.: Multi-criteria Detection of Bad Smells in the Code. In: Proceedings of 6th International Conference on Extreme Programming, 2005, Lecture Notes in Computer Science 3556, pp.154-161.
5. The Apache Jakarta Project: Tomcat 5.5.4, http://jakarta.apache.org/tomcat/index.html, January 2005.
6. Chidamber S.R., Kemerer C.F.: A Metrics Suite from Object-Oriented Design. IEEE Transactions on Software Engineering, Vol. 20, No. 6, 1994, 476-493.
7. Marinescu R., Using Object-oriented metrics for Automatic Design Flaws Detection in Large Scale Systems. ECOOP Workshop Reader 1998, Lecture Notes In Computer Science; Vol. 1543, pp.252-255.

8. Gamma E., Helm R., Johnson R., Vlissides J.: Design Patterns. Elements of Reusable Object-Oriented Software. Addison-Wesley, 1995.
9. Tomcat Defect Metric Report, http://www.reasoning.com/pdf/Tomcat_Metric_Report.pdf, visited in April 2005.
10. NASA Software Assurance Technology Center: SATC Historical Metrics Database, http://satc.gsfc.nasa.gov/metrics/codemetrics/oo/java/index.html, January 2005.
11. Pietrzak B., Walter B.: Exploring Bad Code Smells Dependencies. In: Zielinski K., Szmuc T. (eds.): Software Engineering: Evolution and Emerging Technologies. Frontiers in Artificial Intelligence and Applications, Vol. 130, pp.353-364.
12. Łukasiewicz J.: Die logischen Grundlagen der Wahrscheinilchkeitsrechnung. Kraków, 1913, in: L. Borkowski (ed.), Łukasiewicz J.: Selected Works. North Holland Publishing Company, Amsterdam, London, Polish Scientific Publishers, Warsaw, 1970.

Studying the Evolution of Quality Metrics in an Agile/Distributed Project*

Walter Ambu[2], Giulio Concas[1], Michele Marchesi[1], and Sandro Pinna[1]

[1] Dipartimento di Ingegneria Elettrica ed Elettronica, Universitá di Cagliari,
Piazza d'Armi, 09123 Cagliari, Italy
{concas, michele, pinnasandro}@diee.unica.it
http://agile.diee.unica.it
[2] AgileTec, Via G. Murat, 26
09134 Cagliari, Italy
w.ambu@agiletec.it
http://www.agiletec.it

Abstract. This paper analyzes the development of a project initiated by a co-located agile team that subsequently evolved into a distributed context. The project, named JAPS (Java Agile Portal System)[1], has been monitored on a regular basis since it started in January 2005, collecting both process and product metrics. Product metrics have been calculated by checking out the source code history from the CVS repository. By analyzing the evolution of these metrics, it has been possible to evaluate how the distribution of the team has impacted the source code quality.

1 Introduction

In recent years many projects have been developed in a distributed context using agile practices [2][3][4][5]. Obviously opportunities for a co-located team differ from those for a dispersed team. Some XP/agile practices can be adopted at the same level in both contexts, while others cannot [6][5]. Several case studies have been published reporting experiences in applying agile practices in distributed projects, but as far as we are aware nothing has been published to date concerning the analysis of the evolution of source code quality metrics in this kind of project.

1.1 CK Metrics

The quality of a project is usually measured in terms of lack of defects or maintainability. It has been found that these quality attributes are correlated with specific metrics. For Object Oriented systems the Chidamber and Kemerer metrics suite [7] [8], usually known as the CK suite, is the most validated. The CK suite is composed of six metrics:

---

* This work was supported by MAPS (Agile Methodologies for Software Production) research project, contract/grant sponsor: FIRB research fund of MIUR, contract/grant number: RBNE01JRK8.

P. Abrahamsson, M. Marchesi, and G. Succi (Eds.): XP 2006, LNCS 4044, pp. 85–93, 2006.

- **Weighted Methods per Class (WMC):** a weighted sum of all the methods defined in a class. Chidamber and Kemerer suggest assigning weights to the methods based on the degree of difficulty involved in implementing them [7]. Since the choice of weighting factor can significantly influence the metric value, this is a matter of continuing debate among researchers. Some researchers resort to cyclomatic complexity of methods while others use a weighting factor of unity for validation of OO Metrics. In this paper we also use a weighting factor of unity, thus WMC is calculated as the total number of methods defined in a class.
- **Coupling Between Object Classes (CBO):** a count of the number of other classes with which a given class is coupled, hence it denotes the dependency of one class on other classes in the system. To be more precise, class A is coupled with class B when at least one method of A invokes a method of B or accesses a field (instance or class variable) of B.
- **Depth of Inheritance Tree (DIT):** the length of the longest path from a given class to the root class in the inheritance hierarchy.
- **Number of Children (NOC):** a count of the number of immediate child classes inherited by a given class.
- **Response for a Class (RFC):** a count of the methods that are potentially invoked in response to a message received by an object of a particular class. It is computed as the sum of the number of methods of a class and the number of external methods called by them.
- **Lack of Cohesion of Methods (LCOM):** a count of the number of method-pairs with zero similarity minus the count of method pairs with non-zero similarity. Two methods are similar if they use at least one shared field (for example they use the same instance variable).

1.2   Literature on CK Metrics

CK metrics have been widely validated in the literature. In a study of two commercial systems, Li and Henry [9] explored the link between CK metrics and the maintenance effort. Similarly, based on an investigation of several coupling measures (including CBO) and the NOC metric of the CK suite in two university software applications, Binkley and Schach [10] found that the coupling measure was associated with maintenance changes made in classes. Studying eight medium-sized systems Basili et al. [11] observed that several of the CK metrics were associated with class fault proneness. In a commercial setting, Chidamber et al. [12] noticed that higher values of the coupling and cohesion metrics in the CK suite were associated with reduced productivity and increased rework/design effort. Cartwright and Shepperd [13] studied a medium-sized telecommunications system and found that the inheritance measures of the CK suite (DIT, NOC) were associated with class defect density.

2   JAPS Process Evolution

JAPS is an open source j2EE solution for building web portals, integrating services and handling contents through a content management system (CMS). The project was started in January 2005 by the agile team of AgileTec [14], an IT company based in Italy. JAPS was conceived as a result of some team members' experience in developing web portals and CMS with open source and legacy software. The goal was to create an adaptive, non predictive system that was simple, flexible and easily adaptable to customer needs.

The JAPS kernel was first built by a co-located team of two experienced software engineers applying agile practices. These practices include pair programming, testing, refactoring, planning game, short iterations [15][16]. After two months the team released a prototype of the system.

Subsequently, a partnership agreement was drawn up with an IT company and a commitment made to build two portals. As a result the number of team members was increased from two to seven. As the new members came from different IT companies, it was decided to adopt an open source-like development model. In particular the team applied dispersed agile development [4] where developers were physically alone most of the time and connected through communication channels. Thus, in this phase the team started working in a distributed context. In defining an agile methodology for this context and integrating agile practices with open source principles [17], they allowed for the fact that all team members lived in the same city. For instance, in order to share knowledge and experience, it was decided to meet once or twice a week. Being located in the same city also made it possible to schedule pair programming sessions as needed. The lack of face to face communication in the distribution, made it necessary to define effective communication strategies. Voip systems, e-mail and mobile phones allowed the team to communicate [18] effectively during development sessions even if this involved several iterations.

Frequent releases with working functionalities allowed continuous customer feedback. Requirements were gathered by using a prioritized backlog list shared among team members [19]. After a first tuning phase, requirement management using the backlog list became effective.

The other agile practices had to be adapted to the new distributed context. This required several iterations before the team developed maturity in adopting agile distributed practices.

The distributed phase initiated with an already defined test infrastructure. This included testing frameworks for web-applications, xml and mock objects. Several iterations were needed for the new team members to effectively implement the testing practices in a JAPS context. Once the team had become more comfortable with test harnesses, refactoring practices were applied more effectively.

The JAPS development process is thus characterized by two distinct phases. In the first phase, the team experimented and optimized some key agile practices in a distributed context. In the second phase, the team developed maturity in implementing these practices. The main phases of the evolution of the JAPS process are summed up below:

- phase 0 (January 2005-February 2005). The kernel was built by a co-located team of two experienced programmers using agile practices.

- phase 1 (March 2005-July 2005). The 7-strong team, (2 kernel developers + 5 new members), experimented key agile practices in a distributed context.
- phase 2 (August 2005- January 2006): the team developed maturity in the application of key practices.

In the next section, we will analyze how the source code quality metrics evolved during phases 1 and 2.

3   JAPS Metrics Evolution

In this section we analyze the evolution of source code metrics at regular two-week intervals. Each source code snapshot has been checked out from the CVS repository and analyzed by a parser that creates an xml file containing the information needed for calculating the metrics. This xml file is parsed by an analyzer that calculates all the metrics. Both the parser and the analyzer have been developed by our research group as a plug-in for the Eclipse IDE. The analyzed metrics are: Number of Classes, Class Size, Number of Test Cases, Number of Assertions, WMC, RFC, LCOM, CBO, DIT, NOC.

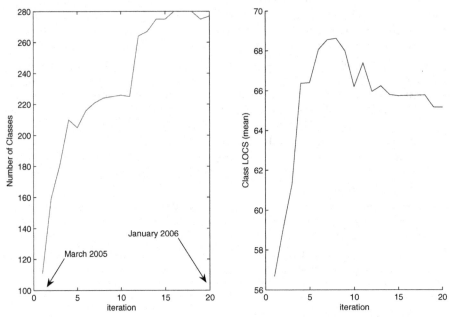

Fig. 1. Total number of classes and lines of code per class evolution (1 iteration = 2 weeks)

Number of Classes. This metric measures the total number of classes (abstract classes and interfaces are included) and is a good indicator of system size. When the distributed phase started, the system comprised 111 classes, then evolved

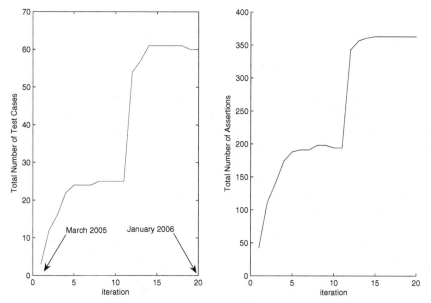

Fig. 2. Number of test cases and number of assertions for each iteration (1 iteration = 2 weeks)

rapidly as shown in fig. 1. The last CVS snapshot consists of 277 classes, indicating that the system doubled in size during the distributed phases (phases 1 and 2).

Class size. The size of a class has been measured by counting the lines of code (LOC), excluding blanks and comment lines. The mean value of class LOC has been plotted in Fig 1 for each iteration. It is known that a "fat" class is more difficult to read than an agile one. High values of this metric indicate a bad code smell that should be corrected using refactoring technics. Fig 1 shows a first phase in which the metric grows rapidly followed by a second phase in which it decreases.

Number of test cases. The number of test cases may be considered as an indicator of testing activity. As shown in fig. 2, the metric increases more rapidly in the second phase than in the first one. This might be explained by the faster growth of the total number of classes in the second phase but examination of the plot in fig 1 shows that this hypothesis can be reasonably ruled out. The main reason is certainly the maturity developed by the team in the second phase, that enabled them to write more tests during development.

Number of Assertions. Simply using the number of test cases, however, could be considered a poor indicator of testing activity. In fact, new test methods could be added to existing test cases without increasing their total number. The number of test methods might be a better indicator of testing activity than the simple test case count. On the other hand, a test method may have

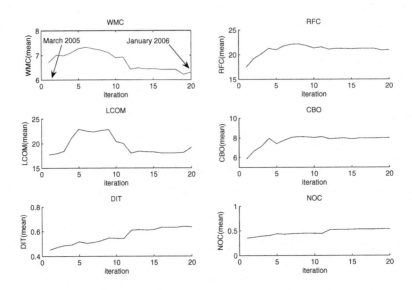

Fig. 3. CK Metrics Evolution (1 iteration = 2 weeks)

one or more assertions that compare expected and actual values. An assertion is a call to those methods of TestCase that have a name beginning with the string "assert"(assertEquals, assertSame, assertNotNull.....). The total number of assertions may be regarded as a more comprehensive indicator of testing activity. This metric, reported in fig. 2 shows the same trend observed for the number of test cases.

LCOM and WMC. The evolution of LCOM reported in fig. 3 shows a first phase where classes are characterized by low cohesion and a second phase where this metric has been progressively improved through refactoring. The same considerations discussed above also apply to WMC: a first phase characterized by a growing number of methods per class and a second phase where fat classes were split into cohesive classes with a small number of methods.

CBO. The evolution of this metric reported in fig. 3 shows a first phase where class complexity increases followed by a second phase where this metric remains approximately constant. The mean value increases from 6 to 8 during phase 1 and stabilizes at 8 during phase 2.

RFC. As previously mentioned, the response for a class is calculated by summing the number of methods and the number of calls to external methods. The RFC evolution (fig. 3) shows an initial increasing phase followed by a second phase in which the metric decreases slightly. This decrease could be explained by the strong reduction of WMC and an approximately constant trend of coupling between objects.

DIT and NOC. These metrics, that measure class inheritance characteristics, exhibit an increasing trend during the distributed phase.

4   Discussion

In this section we attempt to match the observed metrics evolution with the development process phases. To do this we can group metrics exhibiting similar behavior.

LCOM, WMC. The initial increasing phase can be explained by the lack of rigorous application of certain key practices like testing and refactoring. In the second phase, the team was able to reduce these metrics by applying simple refactoring practices. The bad smell was due essentially to the large number of methods and their low cohesion. These smells were eliminated by splitting the fat classes into classes with a small number of more cohesive methods, and by eliminating duplicated code. This also resulted in a reduction in the number of lines of code, as shown in fig. 1.

CBO, RFC. The interesting consideration that emerged from observation of these metrics lies in the second part of the plots. In fact, the effective adoption of key practices by the distributed team did not lead to the expected reduction in coupling and response for a class. This might be explained by the very nature of these metrics, that measure class interrelationship. To reduce this metric it is necessary to modify not only the single class but also the complex relationships with other system classes. Distribution of the team resulted in the programmer developing specialized knowledge on specific modules. Each time a programmer performed refactoring he did so on components of his competence. Programmers were apprehensive about changing something they knew little about. Their uneasiness grew as system complexity increased. It should also be noted that the kernel was built by two senior programmers and several meetings were planned at the beginning of the distributed phase to disseminate knowledge to new team members. Weekly meetings and a number of pair programming sessions did not enable effective knowledge sharing across team members in the distributed environment. This specialization resulted in the impossibility of reducing those metrics that depend on class interrelationships.

DIT and NOC. The same considerations made above hold here too. In fact, refactoring a class hierarchy requires a broad vision of the system and this is exactly what the distributed team did not have.

5   Conclusions

In this paper we have analyzed a project initiated by a co-located team and subsequently developed in a distributed manner. We have also presented the strategies employed by the team to effectively implement agile practices in the distributed context. The project has been divided into three main phases:

- phase 0: A co-located team developed the kernel.
- phase 1: The team experimented and optimized agile practices in a distributed environment.

– phase 2: The team applied agile practices effectively despite not being co-located.

The project was monitored by calculating product metrics during its development. These metrics include the CK suite of quality metrics. Analyzing the evolution of these metrics we found that in phase 1 the team increased system complexity. In phase 2 we observed that the effective implementation of agile practices resulted in system simplification. However, we also observed that the team was unable to improve all metrics to the same extent. In particular it proved impossible to reduce the value of those metrics that measure class inter-relationships (CBO, DIT, NOC). This is likely due to the specialization of team members in specific components of the system. Therefore, in our experience, the adoption of agile practices in a distributed context may be effective only in reducing a subset of complexity metrics. Moreover, in the initial experimental phase of agile distributed practices system complexity was found to increase significantly. This study has given the team an opportunity to reflect on how to improve knowledge dissemination in a dispersed development environment. The JAPS project has now been released as open source [1] and we will continue monitoring both the process and metrics evolution in this new "phase 3".

References

1. JAPS: Java agile portal system. Url: http://www.japsportal.org (2005)
2. Poole, C.J.: Distributed product development using extreme programming. In Eckstein, J., Baumeister, H., eds.: Extreme Programming and Agile Processes in Software Engineering. (2004) 60–67
3. Fowler, M.: Using an agile software process with offshore development. http://www.martinfowler.com/articles/agileOffshore.html (2004)
4. Braithwaite, K., Joyce, T.: Xp expanded: Distributed extreme programming. In Baumeister, H., Marchesi, M., Holcombe, M., eds.: Extreme Programming and Agile Processes in Software Engineering. (2005) 180–188
5. Baheti P., Williams L., G.E., D., S.: Exploring pair programming in distributed object-oriented team projects. In: OOPSLA Educator's Symposium. (2002)
6. Maurer, F.: Supporting distributed extreme programming. In: Proceedings of the XP/Agile Universe 2002: Second XP Universe and First Agile Universe Conference. (2002)
7. Chidamber, S., Kemerer, C.: Towards a metrics suite for object oriented design. Proc. Conf. Object Oriented Programming Systems, Languages, and Applications (OOPSLA'91) **26**(11) (1991) 197–211
8. Chidamber, S., Kemerer, C.: A metrics suite for object-oriented design. IEEE Trans. Software Eng. **20** (1994) 476–493
9. Li, W., Henry, S.: Object oriented metrics that predict maintainability. J. Systems and Software **23** (1993) 111–122
10. Binkley, A., Schach, S.: Validation of the coupling dependency metric as a predictor of run-time failures and maintenance measures. Proc. 20th Int'l Conf. Software Eng. (1998) 452–455
11. V. Basili, L.B., Melo, W.: A validation of object oriented design metrics as quality indicators. IEEE Trans. Software Eng. **22** (1996) 751–761

12. S.R. Chidamber, D.D., Kemerer, C.: Managerial use of metrics for object oriented software: An exploratory analysis. IEEE Trans. Software Eng. **24** (1998) 629–639
13. Cartwright, M., Shepperd, M.: An empirical investigation of an object-oriented software system. IEEE Trans. Software Eng. **26**(7) (2000) 786–796
14. AgileTec: Agiletec it company. Url: http://www.agiletec.it (2005)
15. Beck, K.: Extreme Programming Explained: Embrace Change. Addison-Wesley (1999)
16. Beck, K., Andres, C.: Extreme Programming Explained: Embrace Change- Second Edition. Addison-Wesley (2004)
17. Koch, S.: Agile principles and open source software development: A theoretical and empirical discussion. In Eckstein, J., Baumeister, H., eds.: Extreme Programming and Agile Processes in Software Engineering. (2004) 85–93
18. Steven Fraser, Angela Martin, M.A.C.C.D.H.M.P.M.S.: Off-shore agile software development. In H. Baumeister, M. Marchesi, M.H., ed.: Extreme Programming and Agile Processes in Software Engineering. (2005) 267–272
19. Bent Jensen, A.Z.: Cross continent development using scrum and xp. In Marchesi, M., Succi, G., eds.: Extreme Programming and Agile Processes in Software Engineering. (2003) 146–153

The Effect of Test-Driven Development on Program Code

Matthias M. Müller

Fakultät für Informatik, Universität Karlsruhe,
Am Fasanengarten 5, 76 131 Karlsruhe, Germany
muellerm@ipd.uka.de

Abstract. Usage of test-driven development (TDD) is said to lead to
better testable programs. However, no study answers either the question
how this better testability can be measured nor whether the feature
of better testability exists. To answer both questions we present the
concept of the controllability of assignments. We studied this metric on
various TDD and conventional projects. Assignment controllability seems
to support the rules of thumb for testable code, e.g. small classes with
low coupling are better testable than large classes with high coupling.
And as opposed to the Chidamber and Kemerer metric suite for object-
oriented design, controllability of assignments seems to be an indicator
whether a project was developed with TDD or not.

1 Introduction

Test-driven development (TDD) is besides pair programming one of the main
programming techniques in extreme programming. However, test-driven development has not been studied as thoroughly as pair programming. Studies dealing
with test-driven development have focused on the development cost or the quality
of the written tests [1, 2, 3, 4, 5]. Nobody investigated the structure of programs
developed with test-driven development although it is claimed that "Test-first
code tends to be more cohesive and less coupled than code in which testing isn't
part of the intimate coding cycle" [6, p. 88].

This paper uses the concept of controllability [7] to investigate the effect of
test-driven development on program code. Controllability means that the program can be put in every legal state by only altering the inputs. This concept is
applied to assignments. Controllability of an assignment means that the operands
on the right hand side are input parameters of a method or these operands can
be calculated from these parameters. We present a new metric called *assignment
controllability* (AC) which quantifies this property for methods and classes. The
assignment controllability is compared to the Chidamber and Kemerer metric
suite for object-oriented design [8] using a set of TDD and open-source projects
As a result, assignment controllability seems to support the rules of thumb of
testable code, i.e. fewer number of methods and low coupling, and assignment
controllability seems to be an indicator whether a project was developed using TDD or not. Throughout the paper we refer to projects which have been
developed with test-driven development as TDD-projects.

P. Abrahamsson, M. Marchesi, and G. Succi (Eds.): XP 2006, LNCS 4044, pp. 94–103, 2006.

2   The Metric

2.1   Controllability

Controllability is a concept from the design of digital circuits. For example Abramovici et al. [9] define controllability as 'the ability to establish a specific signal value at each node in a circuit by setting values on the circuit's inputs.' The transformation of controllability to an object oriented program means that all input parameters are known and that these parameters provide enough information to describe the state and the behaviour of the program. In this paper, we concentrate on assignments as they provide the only means to change the state of objects which represent the state of a program. Invocations of methods which do not return any value are ignored by our analysis, so far.

2.2   Controllability of Assignments

The calculation of controllability is a data-flow problem. First of all, all parameters of a method as well as private or public instance or class variables are controllable. These elements form the basic blocks for the calculation. Table 1 shows the rules for the remaining parts of an assignment. The result of an assignment,

Table 1. Controllability of Operations

Operation	Controllability of the result
$lhs := rhs$	The left hand side of an assignment is controllable if the right hand side is controllable.
$exp_1 \oplus exp_2$	The result of an arbitrary binary operation $\oplus$ is controllable, if both operands exp_1 and exp_2 are controllable.
$\oplus\ exp_1$	The result of an arbitrary unary operation $\oplus$ is controllable, if the operand exp_1 controllable.
$obj.foo\,(\,a,\,b\,)$	The result of a function call controllable, if obj and parameters a and b are controllable.

i. e. the left hand side, is controllable if its right hand side is controllable. An expression is controllable if all its identifiers are controllable. The conditional assignment is a special case, see Figure 1. The object a in line 6 is controllable only if either *both* expressions exp_1 and exp_2 in the lines 2 and 4 are controllable, or, the condition in line 1 and *one* of the expressions exp_1 or exp_2 is controllable. All constants and all messages send to `this` are not controllable.

2.3   Calculation

The controllability of a method m is the ratio of controllable assignments to all assignments in m. We call this metric *Assignment Controllability AC*:

$$AC(m) = \frac{\text{number of controllable assignments in method } m}{\text{number of all assignments in method } m}$$

```
1    if ( cond ) {
2        a = exp1;
3    } else {
4        a = exp2;
5    }
6    b = ... a ...
```

Fig. 1. Conditional Assignment

Its range varies between 0 and 1. The controllability of a class c is the average controllability of its methods. For a class c having n methods m_i $(i = 1 \ldots n)$ the assignment controllability is

$$AC(c) = \frac{1}{n} \sum_{i=1}^{i=n} AC(m_i) \tag{1}$$

Methods without any assignments are ignored in the calculation.

A program to calculate the assignment controllability metric was implemented using the *Byte Code Engineering Library* (BCEL) [10] of the Jakarta Apache Project.

3   Data Set

Table 2 lists the projects used for this analysis. The type of project is given in

Table 2. Overview of Projects

| | | Number of | |
Name	TDD	Classes	Packages
Webtest	yes	149	21
XPChess1	yes	63	8
XPChess2	yes	48	8
XPChess3	yes	68	8
Yaps	yes	100	16
Sum		428	61
Ant	no	372	22
JUnit	no	75	7
Log4j	no	228	19
Sum		675	48

the second column. The columns 3 and 4 present the number of classes and the number of packages for each project. Webtest [11] is a testing tool for web applications. The projects XPChess1, XPChess2, and XPChess3 are student projects from the extreme programming lab course held in the summer term 2005 at the

Universität Karlsruhe. These programs are chess engines with command line interface. Yaps is a portal framework of a medium-sized company. Ant [12] is the Apache platform independent implementation of make. JUnit is the Java testing framework of the xUnit family. Log4j [13] is the Java implementation of the protocol framework from the Apache project. The number of classes and packages refer to the size of the application. The test classes were omitted because the test classes were not part of this study.

4   Results

4.1   Metrics Used in This Study

The assignment controllability metric is compared to the following eight metrics. The first six metrics are known as the Chidamber and Kemerer metric suite for object oriented design [8]. The suite contains the weighted sum of methods of a class (WMC). As the weights of the sum are set to one, the weighted method per class metric simply presents the number of methods of a class. The depth of a class in the inheritance tree (DIT) is the next metric. The third metric is the number of children of a class (NOC). For the number of children only the direct subclasses are count. The coupling of a class c (CBO) is the number of classes from which c uses methods or variables. The response set of a class c (RFC) is the number of all methods which are called directly from c. The lack of cohesion of methods (LCOM) of a class c is the difference between the number of method pairs of c that do not share an instance variable of c and the method pairs of c that do share an instance variable of c. The difference is cut off at zero to prevent negative values. The last two metrics do not belong to the Chidamber and Kemerer metric suite. They are the number of assignments (Assign) and the number of byte code statements (Size) of a class.

4.2   The Projects from the Metrics' Point of View

Table 3 presents the metric values for the TDD-projects and the conventional projects. The table lists the minium, the median (med), the maximum, and the mean ($\overline{x}$). We used the two-sided Wilcoxon test [14, pp. 106] to look for differences in the data samples. The last column of Table 3 shows the p-values. Values smaller than the 5 percent significant threshold are marked. The Wilcoxon test shows a difference for all but two metrics: the depth in the inheritance tree (DIT) and the weighted method per class.

4.3   Assignment Controllability on Method Level

Here, we focus on the values of the assignment controllability on method level. Figure 2 which is located at the end of the paper shows for each project the distribution of the assignment controllability. Two characteristics can be seen. First, most methods have a value for the assignment controllability of 0 or 1. This means that each project has a large number of methods most of which

Table 3. Metric values for the projects

| Metric | conventional | | | | TDD | | | | Wilcoxon |
	min	med	max	$\overline{x}$	min	med	max	$\overline{x}$	p-Value
AC	0	0.42	1	0.45	0	0.51	1	0.54	<0.01
LCOM	0	0	741	3.37	0	1	325	7.28	<0.01
RFC	1	10	197	14.35	1	8	91	11.26	<0.01
CBO	2	8	165	10.81	2	6	60	8.5	<0.01
DIT	1	2	11	2.15	1	1.5	10	2.16	0.32
NOC	0	0	52	0.35	0	0	31	0.48	<0.01
WMC	1	5	133	8.29	1	4	59	6.95	0.6
Assign	0	5	273	14.11	0	3	239	6.95	<0.01
Size	2	67	2178	140.18	3	57	1762	90.65	<0.01

either do not contain any controllable assignment (AC=0, left most bar in each histogram) or in which all assignments are controllable (AC=1, right most bar). A second characteristic is the height of the two bars. Each conventional project has more methods without any controllable assignment than methods in which all assignments can be controlled. This observation holds for Webtest as well, but not for the other TDD-projects. To investigate this topic further, we look at the figures presented in Table 4. It lists for each project the number of methods with at least one non-controllable assignments (AC<1) and the number the methods in which all assignments are controllable (AC=1). We look at the

Table 4. Percentages of controllable methods per project and project group

| | Methods with | | | | |
| | AC < 1 | | AC = 1 | | |
Project	number	%	number	%	sum
Webtest	353	58.3	253	41.7	606
XPChess1	46	53.5	40	46.5	86
XPChess2	39	50.6	38	49.4	77
XPChess3	52	47.7	57	52.3	109
Yaps	138	59.0	96	41.0	234
TDD	628	56.5	484	43.5	1112
Ant	1144	63.1	669	36.9	1813
JUnit	146	68.9	66	31.1	212
Log4j	619	73.0	229	27.0	848
conv	1909	66.4	964	33.6	2873
all	2537	63.7	1448	36.3	3985

TDD-projects. Here, 43.5 percent of all methods have assignments which are completely controllable. See the fourth value in the row labelled TDD. The conventional projects achieve a value of 33.6 percent. The fraction of methods

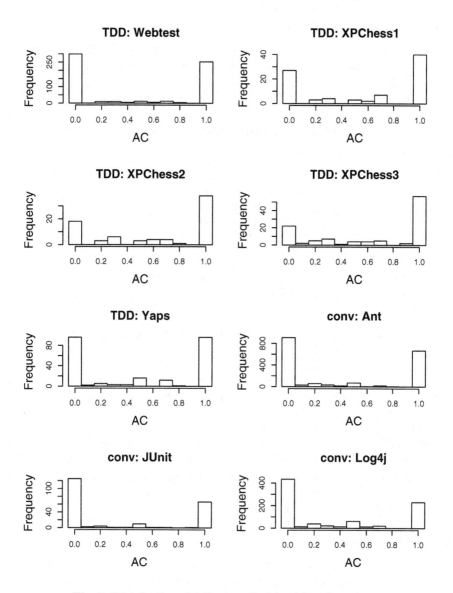

Fig. 2. Distribution of AC on method level for all projects

where all assignments are controllable to methods where at least one assignment is not controllable is $484/628 = 0.771$ for the TDD-projects. The fraction for the conventional projects is $964/1909 = 0.505$. The fraction for the conventional projects is smaller than for the TDD-projects. The fraction for the whole data set is $1448/2537 = 0.571$. Finally, the fraction for the TDD-projects is $0.771/0.505 = 1.526$ times larger than for the conventional projects.

4.4   Correlation Analysis on Class Level

This section analyses the correlation of the assignment controllability to the other metrics used in this study. Correlation analysis was performed using Spearman's method. Table 5 shows the correlation coefficients for the corresponding data sets. The column labelled *all* shows the results for the pooled data set. The

Table 5. Correlation analysis on class level

	AC		
	all	TDD	conv.
Assign	-0.30	-0.19	-0.32
Size	-0.34	-0.32	-0.35
WMC	-0.20	-0.19	-0.26
DIT	-0.22	-0.26	-0.20
NOC	-0.07	-0.22	0.02
CBO	-0.27	-0.20	-0.30
RFC	-0.32	-0.31	-0.32
LCOM	-0.23	-0.21	-0.29

following columns list the results for the TDD-projects and the conventional projects, respectively. Two effects can be seen. First, all absolute values are smaller or equal 0.35. These small values indicate a low correlation and it seems as if assignment controllability covers a property which is not covered by the other metrics analysed in this paper. And second, there is a negative correlation of the assignment controllability to all other metrics for the *all* and the *TDD* data sets. The negative correlation of the size metric means for example, that small classes tend to have more controllable assignments in their methods than large classes. A similar statement holds for classes with a small number of assignments (Assign), for classes with a small depth of inheritance (DIT), and for classes with low coupling (CBO). It seems as if the assignment controllability metric supports the rules of thumb for testable code.

4.5   Logistic Regression

The applicability of the assignment controllability as indicator for the usage of test-driven development is analysed. Logistic regression is used for this analysis [15]. Logistic regression is an extension of linear regression to values on a nominal scale. The type of the project is coded by a binary variable. All classes from projects developed with test-driven development are coded with TDD=1. The remaining classes are coded with TDD=0. The logistic model is as follows:

$$P(TDD = 1 | X_1, \ldots, X_9) = \frac{1}{1 + e^{-f(X_1, \ldots, X_9)}}$$

$$f(X_1, \ldots, X_9) = \alpha + \sum_{i=1}^{9} \beta_i X_i$$

The enhance readability, the variables X_i $(i = 1, \ldots, 9)$ represent the metrics used in this study. We are looking for parameter values with whom we can estimate the probability whether a project was developed with test-driven development or not. We are not interested in the actual values of α and the β_i. We would rather like to know which metric plays a role in the model and how large its impact on this model is. We estimate the parameters (β_i and α) for two data sets. The data set D_{All} contains all classes while the data set $D_{Assign>0}$ contains only those classes containing at least one assignment.

Table 6 lists for each data set the estimated parameter values and the corresponding standard error. The p-values in the last column refer to the hypothesis test that the parameter has no impact on the model. These p-values are interesting for this analysis. Only α and the assignment controllability have an

Table 6. Logistic model parameter estimates

Parameter	D_{All}			$D_{Assign>0}$		
	Estimated	Std. Err.	p-Value	Estimated	Std. Err.	p-Value
α	-1.1955	0.2042	<**0.001**	-0.7337	0.2129	<**0.001**
AC	0.7171	0.2136	<**0.001**	0.8884	0.2306	<**0.001**
Assign	-0.0393	0.0123	**0.001**	1.9888	62.9964	0.974
Size	0.0013	0.0013	0.312	-1.9909	62.9964	0.974
WMC	0.0134	0.0160	0.402	0.0159	0.0161	0.324
DIT	0.0609	0.0503	0.225	-0.0034	0.0533	0.949
NOC	0.0245	0.0294	0.404	0.0246	0.0308	0.424
CBO	-0.0006	0.0209	0.975	0.0163	0.0226	0.468
RFC	0.0082	0.0201	0.683	-0.0058	0.0203	0.773
LCOM	0.0070	0.0051	0.169	0.0069	0.0051	0.180

impact on the model for both data sets (p<0.001). The number of assignments is significant for the D_{All} data set as well. All other p-values are larger than 10 percent. Looking at the classes with at least one assignment our data set suggests that the assignment controllability metric is a better indicator for the usage of test-driven development than all the other metrics used in this paper.

4.6 Validity

There are two major threats concerning the validity of the results. First, the data set of the TDD-projects is smaller than the data set of the conventional projects. The main reason for this difference was the absence of industrial TDD-projects. To overcome this shortcoming, we added the three student projects to our analysis. Adding the student projects to the analysis increases the data set. But now, we have three projects from the same problem domain. However, the three projects have been developed by different student groups.

The next problem originates from the usage of student projects. It is unclear how projects developed by developers experienced in test-driven development differ from projects which have been developed by developers new to test-driven development. Students have problems getting accustomed to the test-driven development process [16, 17]. But whether their program code differs from that written by professional developers is not known so far. Thus, the shown differences might not only be caused by the usage of test-driven development but also by the differences caused by the usage of projects developed by students.

5   Conclusions

This paper investigated the assignment controllability of methods. We compared projects which have been developed using test-driven development to conventional projects. Our data set supports the following results:

- The number of methods where all assignments are completely controllable is higher for projects developed with test-driven development than for conventional projects.
- The metric assignment controllability is negatively correlated to all other metrics studied in this paper. The negative correlation supports the rule of thumb of testable programs.
- Assignment controllability is the only parameter that has a significant impact on the predictability whether a project was developed with test-driven development or not.

This study is a first step towards an understanding of the effects of test-driven development on the program code. Further studies should repeat this analysis with a larger data set to increase the validity of the results. Other metrics should be incorporated into the analysis as well, such as complexity metrics or coverage measures of existing tests.

Acknowledgement

I would like to thank Guido Malpohl for proof reading a previous version of this paper and Christian Frommeyer for implementing the assignment controllability calculator.

References

1. Müller, M., Hagner, O.: Experiment about test-first programming. IEE Proceedings Software **149**(5) (2002) 131–136
2. Pancur, M., Ciglaric, M., Trampus, M., Vidmar, T.: Towards empirical evaluation of test-driven development in a university environment. In: EUROCON 2003. Computer as a Tool. The IEEE Region 8. Volume 2. (2003) 83–86
3. George, B., Williams, L.: An initial investigation of test driven development in industry. In: ACM symposium on Applied computing, Melbourne, Florida, USA (2003) 1135–1139

4. Geras, A., Smith, M., Miller, J.: A prototype empirical evaluation of test driven development. In: International Symposium on Software Metrics (Metrics), Chicago, Illinois, USA (2004) 405–416
5. Erdogmus, H., Morisio, M., Torchiano, M.: On the effectiveness of the test-first approach to programming. IEEE Transactions on Software Engineering **31**(3) (2005) 226–237
6. Beck, K.: Aim, fire. IEEE Software **18**(5) (2001) 87–89
7. Binder, R.: Design for testability in object-oriented systems. Communications of the ACM **37**(9) (1994) 87–101
8. Chidamber, S., Kemerer, C.: A metrics suite for object oriented design. IEEE Transactions on Software Engineering **20**(6) (1994) 476–493
9. Abramovici, M., Breuer, M., Friedman, A.: Digital Systems Testing and Testable Design. Computer Science Press (1990)
10. Apache: Byte code engineering library (BCEL). (http://jakarta.apache.org /bcel/index.html)
11. Canoo: Webtest. (http://webtest.canoo.com)
12. Apache: Ant. (http://ant.apache.org/)
13. Apache: Log4j. (http://logging.apache.org/)
14. Hollander, M., Wolfe, D.: Noparametric Statistical Methods. 2nd edn. John Wiley & Sons (1999)
15. Kleinbaum, D.: Logistic regression: a self-learning text. Springer (94)
16. Wilson, D.: Teaching xp: A case study. In: XP Universe, Raleigh, NC, USA (2001)
17. Müller, M., Link, J., Sand, R., Malpohl, G.: Extreme programming in curriculum: Experiences from academia and industry. In: Conference on Extreme Programming and Agile Processes in Software Engineering (XP2004), Garmisch-Partenkirchen, Germany (2004) 294–302

Configuring Hybrid Agile-Traditional Software Processes

Adam Geras[1], Michael Smith[2], and James Miller[3]

[1] Ideaca Knowledge Services, Calgary, Alberta, Canada
adam.geras@ideaca.com
[2] Department of Electrical and Computer Engineering, University of Calgary, Calgary, Alberta, Canada
smithmr@ucalgary.ca
[3] Department of Electrical and Computer Engineering, University of Alberta, Edmonton, Alberta, Canada
jm@ece.ualberta.ca

Abstract. The traditional versus agile project debate is most often represented in terms of polar positions of the life cycle – the process is either traditional or agile, waterfall or highly iterative. This may be effective in intellectual discussions, but it is highly unlikely to be useful to practitioners, especially those practitioners that are facing traditional project pressures and trying to find the "home ground" for their situation that will increase the likelihood that they will succeed. In this paper, we discuss extensions to Boehm and Turner's five dimensions for determining a project's "home ground" – that is, the process configuration that might best fit the situation at hand. We have added dimensions to the basic framework provided by Boehm and Turner and have considered the process configuration question as a process itself and increased its scope to include both management and engineering key practice areas.

1 Introduction

As agile processes enter the mainstream, it is becoming increasingly clear that many organizations will attempt at least some, if not all, agile practices, especially given the increasing pressure on software development organizations to be adaptable [1]. Boehm and Turner specify the dimensions of method selection as "criticality, size, personnel, dynamism and culture" [2]. In this paper, we first evaluate, by drawing upon both personal expertise and knowledge provided by a number of project managers, the re-categorization of software process determinants into two broad categories: customer/ developer concerns, and product/environment concerns. Then we will describe a process for configuring hybrid agile-traditional software that uses those determinants. By characterizing the customer/developer and the product/ environment, we are enabling a software process that is discovered and applied based on its context – a context-driven software process.

2 Software Process Determinants

In this section, we will describe the software process determinants used and the categories into which these are placed, as sh own in the Kiviat charts for the customer/ developer profile (Fig. 1) and the product/environment profile (Fig. 2).

P. Abrahamsson, M. Marchesi, and G. Succi (Eds.): XP 2006, LNCS 4044, pp. 104 – 113, 2006.

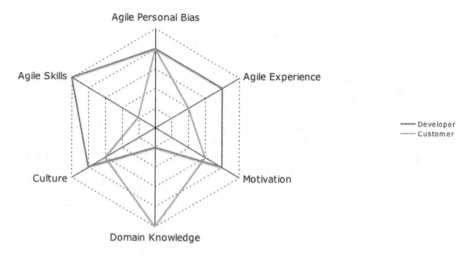

Fig. 1. The Customer / Developer Profile - The intent is to create one profile for each of the customer and developer, so that any highlighted distinctions can be addressed as risks and deviations from the ideal agile or ideal traditional home grounds can be assessed

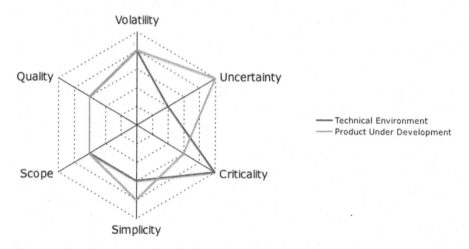

Fig. 2. The Product / Environment Profile - The intent is to create one profile for each of the product and the technical environment it will ultimately operate in, so that again any highlighted distinctions can be addressed as risks

2.1 The Customer/Developer Profile

The process determinants in the customer/developer profile describe the customer and developer in terms of their culture and values, skill, and history. Illustrative of the importance of the customer, most adaptive processes rely on user involvement as a key principle. Dynamic Systems Delivery Method (DSDM) uses "Ambassador User" and "Advisor User" roles as the archetype of all customers on the project [3] to again signify that user involvement is a key to the success of the project. Similarly, Highsmith states that agility involves much more than reducing documentation or being lean - it's also about working collaboratively [4]. Cockburn incorporates the customer profile as part of the "personal anchors" in [5].

Boehm similarly includes the customer profile as part of the "culture" dimension in [2]. Both Boehm and Cockburn cite the culture of the customer organization as possibly distinct from the culture of the supplier organization; reinforcing the point that identifying and characterizing the culture of the customer is just as important as understanding the culture of the supplier. Boehm acknowledges that the customer representative becomes the primary stress point for agile methods [2], a point that highlights the relevance of the customer's *domain knowledge* as a process determinant. He further characterizes the importance of the customer relationship but unfortunately, his argument inappropriately boils down to talk of contracts and customer relationships that are characterized by formal agreements. The "human" side of the customer relationship should also be considered significant! The people fulfilling the customer/end-user role may not be in their comfort zone when working on the project, and preparing for their potential reactions to unforeseen events may prove fruitful in maintaining progress. They are, after all, domain experts and not necessarily software project experts. Hence, our primary customer profile process determinants, differ from Boehm and Turner, and are illustrated in Fig. 1.

The customer's *agile personal bias* indicates their particular experiences in previous software projects. If the projects were successful, then there may be a personal or even collective bias towards project styles and techniques that were successful. Even without this history, the customer's *agile project experience* level will also partly drive the determination of the optimal project style. For example, given a customer that has successfully accepted software in the past, the team may approach them to be more highly involved in decision-making. A customer that has less experience and tends to 'panic' at the slightest sign of trouble may be treated differently. On one project we witnessed the team instituting an additional testing level to shield the customer from the daily builds to counter the customer's panic that ensued from finding cosmetic errors.

Some projects also reported that customer availability is a limiting factor on their ability to use agile processes. Getting timely feedback is critical on the project, but sometimes it just isn't logistically or politically possible to have the customer/end users available as full-time members of the team. In many organizations, for example, the customer still has their regular, full-time job, alongside participating as the key user representative on the project. Both agile and non-agile processes would benefit from a high level of user involvement so a low ranking on this dimension should be treated as a risk on the project and an appropriate response designed-into the process. Availability is considered part of the '*motivation*' axis on the chart in Fig. 1.

A customer's personal style also plays an important part in determining an optimal software process. We have called this '*culture*' on the chart. People and organizations that struggling with accommodating or embracing change will find working with an agile method difficult. Similarly, if they have trouble with ambiguity then a development style that involves discovery (iterative and evolutionary) again might not work for them. This interpretation of 'culture' is identical to [2] except we apply it to the individuals and the organization separately. We have placed significance on the separation of these two criteria based on experience with agile teams within non-agile organizations. In observing the behavior of the agile team and its customer within the non-agile environment, we concluded that the individuals on the team drove much of the agility despite the non-agile surroundings. We found agile projects thriving within non-agile organizations, and therefore concluded that making generalizations about a given organization does not serve software process configuration well.

The corporate and IT culture of the organization will also play a part in setting the software process. In many organizations, the funding for projects is based on a satisfactory (and approved) business case. This funding model is a precursor to a fixed-price, fixed-scope contract, even if the developer organization is an internal one. This type of contract makes agile development difficult (not impossible, but difficult) since the primary lever of control – variable scope – is less available. Similarly, IT culture may end as constraints on the project processes. Agile projects rely on multiple releases to achieve shorter time-to-benefits periods and to give the development team early feedback. If there is a rigorous environment change control process that any changes to production have to go through, then there may be some tension between the project and the organizations that enforce the change mechanism. The interactions between the project team and other IT organizations have to be considered in the configuration of the process. If not, the likelihood of creating an adequate development process decreases.

Finally, we have included a dimension on *agile skills*. In our experience, the agile project places significant technical demands on the people fulfilling the customer role. This is particularly notable in the areas of requirements management, change management, and testing. All modern software processes require user involvement, but some of the agile methods – extreme programming in particular – makes them part of the team with specific responsibilities for prioritizing user stories (requirements) and for developing and running customer tests. This dimension is not so much an assessment of the customer's ability to use computers, as much as it is an assessment of their skills in the agile practices that they must use to drive the project. If the customer were more familiar with and skilled in agile project practices, then they would receive a ranking on the periphery of the dimension. As with the customer agile skill assessment, the developer's agile skills are again not assessed from good to bad, but instead ranked based on their experience with an agile toolset and techniques (xUnit, FIT, refactoring, pair-programming, etc.). The ranking should reflect the developer's comfort with the agile practices and associated tools. If a team is not familiar with refactoring and test-driven development, then asking them to use these techniques to design and deliver a mission-critical system will not be optimal!

2.2 The Product/Environment Profile

The product profile is illustrated in Fig. 2 and shows a number of dimensions that are identical to what Boehm and Turner used in [2], specifically dynamism (relabeled as *volatility* in our figure), *scope*, and *criticality*. We have re-labeled the rating scales for complexity as '*simplicity*' to reflect the agile axiom for "keeping things as simple as possible" [6]. From the product perspective, the simplicity rating should reflect the amount of simplicity that the team can get away with and still deliver an adequate solution. The environment perspective, on the other hand, should reflect the simplicity of the technical environment that the product will have to operate in. For example, certain systems may have low computational complexity but be required to inter-operate with several existing systems, making it's architecture more complex.

In relating Boehm's "dynamism" dimension to project managers, they often break it down further into two concerns –volatility and uncertainty. Volatility represents an assessment of the extent of changes that may appear over the course of the project. Uncertainty is related to other changes, such as architectural uncertainty, manpower issues or changes in the business climate.

In summary, we have found it beneficial to characterize the customer, the developers, the product and the technical environment by creating two profiles and then suggesting use of the resulting chart shapes to devise an appropriate starting software process for projects. The determinants presented here are examples of what could be done in any given setting – the actual choice of dimensions would be left to the person or organization performing the process configuration. With the profiles prepared, the process configuration can occur as part of a workshop at the beginning of the project. A proposed process for completing the configuration is presented in the next section.

3   Proposed Configuration Process

A person or team that has above-average communication and analysis skills is needed to complete the process configuration. Much of the information to be collected in order to construct the profiles is not readily available – it will take a number of interviews and a healthy dose of interviewing skill to be able to accurately assess many of the dimensions. In particular, the profile dimensions related to project histories and experience level. Few people want to talk about previous projects that have gone badly, even in project retrospectives. To obtain this information early in a new project may therefore require advanced communication skills.

In this section, we will discuss when a software process should be configured and the following steps in detail: *profiling* the project context, *aligning* the key practice areas with the profiles, *preparing* the team for the project, *running* the project, and then *checking* the configuration at regular points throughout the project. Configuring a process to suit a project is one of the highlights of Cockburn's work in [7]. Essentially what the process 'configurator' is seeking is a set of levers that can be adjusted, ultimately creating an initial process that the team can use as a starting point. The inputs to setting the 'levers' are the profiles discussed above.

3.1   Step 1 – Profiling

This step consists of conducting the necessary interviews, workshops, meetings, so that the customer, developer, and product profiles can be built. This may be difficult for a number of reasons. First, the customer may not be readily available for profiling. In competitive bidding, for example, the suppliers have to somehow envision the customer and product profiles based on the information they are given in the Request for Proposal (RFP).

In other situations, the profiling step can easily be incorporated into the existing scoping and requirements identification steps. Workshops set up to craft the first-stage business models and any other information-gathering sessions that are conducted can include considerations for gathering the profile information. Another guideline is that anything that would be useful for estimating is also useful for process configuration – especially in terms of risk. In this paper, we've avoided mentioning risk since its role in process configuration is well described in [2]. The intent there is that any dimension is a risk if it gets assessed as outside of the "home ground" that is ultimately chosen for the project.

3.2 Step 2 – Aligning

Aligning the process to the profile has been simplified in [2], making it sound like a simple binary decision between plan-driven and agile, and that anything in between can be handled as a risk. This warrants further discussion, and to handle that discussion in meaningful pieces, we have to break the project activities down further. The goal is to define a set of 'levers' that can be adjusted to define a process that will deliver a desirable product, and there are many aspects of that ecosystem that can be tailored and adapted. It's not an "all or nothing" decision. There is even a strong argument for suggesting that much of the future enterprise development will be done using hybrid agile and plan-driven methods [7].

We propose using some of the Capability Maturity Model (CMM[sm]) Key Practice Areas (KPA) as the basis for identifying project activities that can act as the 'levers' for configuring the software process. The CMM KPA's that are organizationally-focused (technology change management, process change management, organization process focus, organization process definition, and training program) are excluded given that we're configuring a process for a project, not an organization. Similarly, defect prevention and software quality management are excluded on the basis that they don't have agile and plan-driven extremes, unlike other engineering-related KPA (product engineering and peer reviews). We have also added iteration duration to the list given that we have witnessed organizations use it as a benchmark of agility for their active projects. The set of activities that we have used is listed in Table 1.

Table 1. Project activities based on the CMM Key Practice Areas (KPA) can be used as 'levers' that the team or 'process configurator' can adjust to match the project context

Project Activity	More Agile	Less Agile
Iteration Duration	2 weeks or less	8 weeks or longer
Requirements Management	User stories on cards	Use case descriptions
Software Project Planning	Entire team involved	PM/Tech Lead involved
Software Project Tracking	Burn-down charts, tests	Earned Value
Software Quality Assurance	Entire team involved	Separate team
Software Configuration Mgmt	Continuous integration	Periodic integration
Peer Reviews	Pair Programming	Formal Inspection
Product Engineering	Test-driven	Test-last

Iteration duration was added to the list because of its impact on the overall approach taken to the project. Shorter iterations imply a more advanced level of agility. Not all agile teams are able to sustain short-duration iterations such as 1 week. For most teams, even 4-week iteration durations are challenging at first, until the team gains some practice and establishes an increasing number of lean techniques.

Change management and release management were mentioned as primary concerns for many project teams. In terms of the KPA, change management fits mostly in *Requirements Management* and release management fits mostly in *Software Configuration Management*. There are significant differences between "low ceremony" and "high ceremony" change/release management. The high influencers for change/ release management are going to be the cultural dimensions and the developer technical skills. A low-ceremony change management approach would use more face-to-face conversations to describe changes and a prioritized feature list to maintain the order of new and changed features as compared to the existing backlog. A high-ceremony change management approach would involve completing a change request form and basically instantiating a workflow to qualify, approve, schedule, and assign the change. There may even be monetary compensation involved for making approved changes in a high-ceremony change management approach. Developer skills are a high-influencer because of the extent that agile teams automate the build process – some teams implement the agile practice of "continuous integration" using solutions such as Cruise Control that creates a new build and runs associated tests on every source code check-in event. However, these approaches have a steep learning curve.

The first activity to be aligned to the profiles is iteration duration. This assumes that at least some form of iteration is going to be used, a relatively safe assumption. Few organizations are willing to plan for a completely non-iterative project. Instead, the question has really turned into a debate over the length of the iteration more than a decision to develop iteratively or otherwise. To align the iteration duration with the profiles, the first step is to look at the 'high influencers' – that is, the profile dimensions that influence the iteration duration the most.

The high-influencers for iteration duration are probably customer bias, customer motivation, culture, customer agile skills, developer bias, developer agile skills, volatility, uncertainty, and criticality. You can use either another Kiviat Diagram or a weighted ranking to determine the final outcome. As Boehm suggests, if any of these dimensions fall outside the stated decision, then they can be handled as risks [2]. Once the high-influencers are identified and ranked, then the optimal iteration length can be derived from the rankings. The underlying assumption here is that you decrease the length of the iterations if you can, to a minimum of 1-2 weeks.

Once iteration duration is configured then the other KPA can be configured using similar steps. The Change and Release Management KPA are closely related to iteration duration, so it might be appropriate to configure them next, but at the end of this step, all of the KPA should be addressed holistically to ensure that the proposed configuration of each one of them is appropriate – again bringing up connotations of Highsmith's ecosystem [9,10].

The ecosystem approach to the practices within a team is particularly acute in considering the Product Engineering KPA. In this area, requirements analysis, design, construction and testing are all considered as related activities. Taken together, the activities could implement a test-driven development, or a highly iterative test-last method. To establish a thriving ecosystem, the configuration of the product engineering practices then has to be integrated with the other KPA, in particular the Quality

Assurance, Software Configuration Management, and Project Planning and Tracking/ Oversight KPA. The high influencers on the Product Engineering KPA are the developer technical skills, the developer experience level, the developer's domain knowledge, and the volatility and uncertainty associated with the product.

In conclusion of the Aligning step, the team should have a shared vision of the development workflow. It might even make sense to informally model this workflow and display it publicly so that the team has an easily accessible depiction of the workflow to discuss. The underlying sensibility of the workflow is "practice makes perfect" – so that once development begins, the team can start practicing the intended workflow and over time – get better and better at it, fine-tuning it as the project proceeds.

3.3 Step 3 – Preparing

Even if the team actively participated in the process configuration profiling and aligning steps, they may still need to be prepared in order to make the envisioned process a reality. The best way to complete this preparation is by running Iteration 0 – an iteration that delivers nothing of value to the customer but allows the team some practice time. This is especially critical if all the members of the team are not familiar with all the underlying tools. The length of Iteration 0 does not have to conform to the same length as the rest of the development iterations - if it extends beyond two weeks, there is probably something else going on other than preparation.

3.4 Step 4 – Running

Once prepared, the development iterations can be launched, and the team can start performing the activities that comprise the envisioned workflow. As the team completes the workflow, their progress should be measured in an unobtrusive manner in order to feed the next phase, checking.

3.5 Step 5 – Checking

Checking is confirming that the current process and development workflow is optimal. This should be done periodically, probably at a greater frequency than iteration cycles (especially, if the iteration length is longer than 4 weeks). Checking enables the entire team to assess the earlier rankings and to fine-tune the development workflow and project technical processes as required.

3.6 Challenges

Configuring the process in this manner is difficult for a number of reasons, but the greatest danger comes from not knowing the individuals that will comprise the team at configuration time. Many software development organizations don't make explicit resource plans until after the project is confirmed. In competitive bidding situations, for example, the project configuration is done and offered to the customer as part of the bid process. Placing personnel on the team then has to be done with the promised software process in mind. In addition, the development team may not meet the individuals that will ultimately fulfill the customer role on the project until the project is launched. This will make tailoring the process for their personal bias impossible.

Other challenges to this process are on the relative uncertainty over the influence of certain dimensions. Take the 'Motivation' dimension of the developer profile as an example – there are sure to be differing opinions on how to deal with this. Some will say that an agile approach is better for dealing with this since then the effects of the low motivation (poor productivity) would be noticeable sooner. Others will say that the 'empowered teams' of agile is less likely to be effective when the team members have little motivation. This is just an example – the point is that the influencing dimensions and their effects are probably not universally applicable.

4   Future Work

The proposed configuration process is being used in an industrial setting in two ways – to configure projects as outlined here, and to help existing teams create a test strategy that matches the existing project context. A qualitative analysis of these projects will follow pending ethics and the participating companies' approvals.

5   Summary

Boehm and Turner specified five dimensions – size criticality, dynamism, personnel, and culture as the keys to finding a project's "home ground" [2]. This home ground represents the optimal balance between agile and plan-driven processes, with the exceptions being managed as risks. This approach is an exceptional contribution to the notion of tailoring the software process to match the project context. In this paper, we have extended the tailoring process in two ways – by first articulating dimensions of more resolution and second by proposing a process for conducting the configuration that considers the additional dimensions and the key practice areas that they might influence.

The underlying assumption is that hybrid projects are most likely to be the primary means that large organizations will be using to deliver working software to their users for the foreseeable future. Purely plan-driven processes are increasingly rare. Even if they are advertised, they are less likely to be followed to the letter. Even traditionally non-agile companies are starting to try out some aspect of agile software development. Based on this increasing need, a strong understanding of the relationship between the configuration criteria (dimensions) and the key practice areas is required. If we have this understanding, then we have a better grip on what sort of process might be optimal for any given customer/developer and product/environment combination.

References

[1] Correia, J. Recommendation for the Software Industry During Hard Times. Gartner Data-quest Report, June 6, 2002.
[2] Boehm, B. and R. Turner (2004). Balancing Agility and Discipline: A Guide for the Perplexed. Toronto, Addison-Wesley.
[3] DSDM Consortium. (2005). DSDM Lifecycle. DSDM Consortium. http://www.dsdm.org/tour/process.asp. Accessed 2005.

[4] Highsmith, J. (2005). AgileVsSelfAdapting. Alistair Cockburn.http://alistair.cockburn.us/crystal/wiki/AgileVsSelfAdapting. Accessed 2005.

[5] Cockburn, A. (2000). Just-In-Time Methodology Construction. Alistair Cockburn. http://alistair.cockburn.us/crystal/articles/jmc/justintimemethodologyconstruction.html. Accessed 2005.

[6] Beck, K. (1999). Extreme Programming Explained. Don Mills, Addison-Wesley Publishing Co.

[7] Cockburn, A. (1999). A Methodology Per Project. Alistair Cockburn. http://alistair.cockburn.us/crystal/articles/mpp/methodologyperproject.html. Accessed 2005.

[8] Barnett, L. and U. Narsu (2003). Planning Assumption: Best Practices for Agile Development. Cambridge, Mass., Forrester Research, Inc.

[9] Highsmith, J. (2004). Agile Project Management. Toronto, Addison-Wesley.

[10] Highsmith, J. A. (2000). Adaptive Software Development. New York, Dorset House Publishing Co., Inc.

Rolling the DICE® for Agile Software Projects

Bartłomiej Ziółkowski[1] and Geoffrey Drake[2]

[1] Nokia Networks
Düsseldorf, Germany
bartlomiej.ziolkowski@nokia.com
[2] Managed Design
UK
geoffd@mandes.com

Abstract. The DICE[1] framework provides means for predicting the outcome of change management initiatives. The four factors: duration, integrity, commitment, and effort are evaluated and a score is calculated. The DICE® score is used to classify projects into win, worry, or woe zones. In this paper, we apply the DICE® framework to predict the outcome of a software project that is migrating from waterfall to agile practices. We propose fine-tuning of the four factors to improve the score and show how to use DICE® for communication with the stakeholders. Finally, we make a claim that evaluation against the DICE® framework confirms that agile projects have a higher chance of success than traditional waterfall projects.

1 Introduction

Despite the success of the software projects following the iterative & incremental development processes [1], most of the big companies still use pure waterfall methodologies or at least the ones that give a feeling of command-and-control. We recently carried out research on the software job market. This showed that among the biggest and most successful software development companies only one was actively looking for project managers that are familiar with IID practices. Developers have it a bit better as there are many openings for people familiar with, for example, eXtreme Programming [2]. That opens a question of how agile programmers are managed.

Currently, we are involved in a change initiative at one of the top telecommunication companies where the goal is to use agile software development practices to create a new product. Previously, the company followed a strict waterfall process that led to long delays. Moreover, the developers were not familiar with agile practices and did not regularly present the results of their work to the stakeholders. The change was driven by middle management and upper management agreed to try out strict time boxing and IID methodology to increase the rate of software delivery.

Whilst the change came from the software group, we searched for a general change management evaluation technique. Change is not simply a software problem and we needed to convince business people that agile methodology would introduce higher

---

[1] DICE is a registered trademark of The Boston Consulting Group, Inc.

P. Abrahamsson, M. Marchesi, and G. Succi (Eds.): XP 2006, LNCS 4044, pp. 114–122, 2006.
© Springer-Verlag Berlin Heidelberg 2006

level of success. This also would help us to prove that agile is not just hype but has sound business roots for its success. During this search, we came across DICE® from The Boston Consulting Group [4].

2   The DICE® Framework

Every change initiative is a painful process for an organization. Despite the common understanding of the need for constant change in every aspect of human life, the changes in organizations are usually not welcome. Most of the time people in affected organizations believe that a little tweaking here and there would solve the biggest problems whereas the change initiators (i.e., the management) strive to change everything. Sometimes it is the opposite, people expect an organizational shake-up and the management proposes just touching the surface.

In order to address people's issues, there should be enough focus on the soft aspects of change management like culture, leadership, and motivation [5]. As much as those elements are important, focusing on them does not guarantee the success of the initiative. Moreover, the soft aspects are hard to qualify and measure.

The hard factors of change management like time, resources, and business goal are easier to measure and organizations are more often able to influence them quickly. The research shows [3] that companies not paying enough attention to the hard issues are bound to fail even if the soft factors are handled properly.

The DICE® framework [3], created by The Boston Consulting Group, provides a means for predicting the outcomes of change initiatives and is based on evaluation of the hard issues, namely:

- The *duration* (D) – either the time needed to complete the change initiative, or the time between reviews or milestones.
- The *integrity* (I) – the project team's ability to complete the initiative on time.
- The *commitment* of the management team (C_1) and the commitment of the people affected by the change (C_2).
- The additional *effort* (E) that employees must make to cope with the change.

In order to calculate the DICE® score, the following equation is used:

$$\text{DICE}^® \text{ Score} = D + (2 * I) + (2 * C_1) + C_2 + E \qquad (1)$$

For every factor the score from 1 to 4 is used, where 1 is the best and 4 is the worst score. The resulting DICE® score is in the range from 7 to 28.

In the Figure 1, the DICE® scores and the actual outcome of 225 change initiatives are plotted [3]. The highly successful projects had the DICE® score between 7 and 14 and are in the Win zone. The projects with scores between 14 and 17 were more unpredictable and are in the Worry zone. The projects in the Woe zone had the DICE® scores above 17 and were more consistently unsuccessful.

Since the completion of the initial study, the BCG has used the DICE® factors to predict the outcomes and support the execution of more than 1,000 change management initiatives all around the world and in a broad range of industries. So far, no other hard factors have been found that predict outcomes nearly as good at the four DICE® factors.

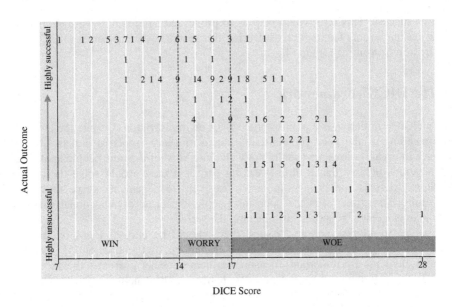

Fig. 1. DICE® scores of 225 change initiatives [3]

3 Applying DICE® to Agile

Any change brings about conflict and turmoil as people try to reconcile new ways of working and integrate the new techniques into their current skill set. In addition, these techniques are rarely introduced in propitious circumstances; projects are invariably under a variety of pressures and under stress people inevitably revert to working patterns that they are familiar with. Introducing agile for the first time is no exception and we felt that utilizing DICE® would give us an indication of the areas that would need closer supervision during the process.

Our initial application of DICE® was at a general level against the two agile practices we planned to use, Extreme Programming and Scrum [8]. Table 1 shows the basic characteristics of XP, Scrum and Waterfall against the criteria laid down by the DICE® framework.

In DICE®, a project with an index of between 7 and 14 is considered a Win, 14 – 17 is a Worry and 17 – 28 is a Woe. Using the base values given for the DICE® criteria in Table 1, both the agile practices evaluated to 9 whilst a waterfall-based project is 20. This does not mean that a waterfall project will invariably fail, or that an agile based project will definitely succeed, but it does illustrate that given equal circumstances an agile based project has a better chance of succeeding than the same project run under a waterfall methodology.

The more interesting exercise was to perform a DICE® evaluation of the overall goal of the project, the introduction of XP and Scrum.

Table 1. XP and Scrum versus Waterfall

DICE® Criteria	XP	Scrum	Waterfall
Duration	Delivery in one to four weeks. Team meeting daily.	Delivery in one month. Daily review of progress.	Long duration of each phase. Milestones far apart.
D Factor	1	1	4
Integrity	Team is self-organizing, people only commit to work they have skills for.	Team is self-organizing, people only commit to work they have skills for.	A process cannot start until the previous one is completed. Team composition changes based on the current phase of the project.
I Factor	1	1	2
Management Commitment	Good. Frequent involvement of customer and product management in decision process.	Good. Product Owner decides on what is in each phase. All stakeholders review progress	Reviews of progress. 'Lines written'
C1	1	1	4
Team Commitment	Reinforced working practices. Everyone commits to his or her tasks and only to tasks they can do.	Daily commitment to team actions. Processes to supply input to team.	Mainly written documents between phases. Good between team members.
C2 (Team)	2	2	3
Effort	More effort writing tests, pair programming. Design as you go.	Design as you go. Review meetings.	Effort considered as normal.
E	2	2	1
DICE® Factor = D + 2I + 2C1 + C2 + E	9	9	20

The development team consisted of some employees who were experienced programmers and some fairly new employees who were relatively new to the company, but had good programming skills. There were also a number of consultants who were selected for their high programming skills, some had utilized eXtreme Programming on previous projects, some had not, but all expressed an interest in trying out XP. One of the consultants was employed specifically because he had strong XP coaching skills.

Taking these circumstances into account we determined the overall DICE® factors shown in Table 2.

Table 2. DICE® score of the agile project

Criteria	Factor	Comment
Duration	1	Series of 5-week iterations, with intense Sprint Planning and Sprint Review sessions at the start and finish.
Integrity	2	Most team members keen to utilize agile, some reluctance from one or two. Tendency to revert when pressures high.
Management Commitment	2	Fair. Strong initial focus and support from high management. Good long-term support from team management.
Team Commitment	1	Excellent. Team members interact well, good communications on technical matters.
Effort	2	Good effort put in at the start of the project. More perceived effort in putting XP practices in place.
DICE® Factor = D + 2I + 2C1 + C2 + E	12	That clearly puts the project in the Win zone.

4 Fine Tuning the Factors

From the conception of the project there was a strong commitment and focus, so the result of the DICE® evaluation came as no great surprise but it did give us a worse position than we originally anticipated given the original Scrum and eXtreme Programming evaluation (cf.: Table 1). Decisions were made to introduce some activities that would reduce the values for some of the factors. We considered the impact on the DICE® parameters of each change before we carried it out and only implemented changes that would have positive impact on the values.

Our iteration length was strongly time boxed by the main project schedule and could not be altered. However, it was felt that intensifying the Sprint Planning and producing higher detail story-based tasks [6] would improve the commitment to the project, both at management and team level. We also made the results of the daily automated build, unit and FIT-like [7] end-to-end testing available on the internal web. This helped to make the project progress more visible to management and had the effect of improving the integrity of the team. No one wanted to be the one with failing unit tests in the daily build.

The application of DICE® gave us a good feel for the areas that we needed to concentrate on, other projects may not have the strengths that we had in different areas. Given the weighting of the factors concentrating on Integrity and Management Commitment would give the project a more significant improvement than focusing on Duration, Team Commitment, or Effort. However, some of these are easier to work on.

4.1 Duration

We had a four-week iteration plus one week of review and planning. Halfway through the iteration there was a sanity check to review our ability to meet the iteration goal. Moving to a one week cycle with weekly planning as recommended in [2] was not recognized as an improvement if it comes to DICE®. If the time between project reviews is less than two months, the project gets the maximum Duration value of 1.

4.2 Integrity

Some ways of increasing the team's integrity would be to drive home the advantages of eXtreme Programming practices, like test-driven development [9], to increase developers' confidence and ensuring that the team gets good coaching in them. Skilled Scrum masters [10] effectively remove the impediments, motivate the developers, and make sure that code quality reaches the acceptable standards. They also ensure that the team maintains the optimum momentum.

The weight of Integrity is high in the DICE® framework and only having a capable leader, skilled and motivated team members working more than 50% of their time on the project gives a maximum value of 1 to Integrity score.

4.3 Senior Management Commitment

Making internal review processes visible and that the goals are being met helps to increase management participation in the project. We had a senior manager host the end of iteration demonstration to all the stakeholders in three countries simultaneously, more than 100 people each month saw what we had achieved in that iteration.

The weight of this factor is high in DICE® and senior management commitment shall not be underestimated. In case the agile practices are introduced by the senior management (i.e., top-down approach) this factor gets a maximum score of 1. If, however, the agile practices are driven by the development team (i.e., bottom-up approach) the initial score of 4 applies and the team leader's main goal should be to increase senior management commitment.

4.4 Team Commitment

Listening to and, responding to problems quickly, especially in the daily stand-up meetings has a positive effect on the team. At the end of iteration, everyone in the team participated in the Sprint Reflections session where problems got aired and resolved. The first level management took these reviews seriously and that helped to increase the team commitment factor.

Ensure people get variety of in what they are doing. We needed a large amount of documents to communicate our interfaces to associated projects and we made sure that several people wrote them, so no single person got locked into doing just documentation.

The Team Commitment factor is valued as 1 if the team is eager to take on the change initiative. If the team is only willing the score is 2. By responding to problems quickly and by ensuring tasks variety, the leader is able to change team's willingness into eagerness and drive up the score.

4.5 Effort

One concern early in the project was over the time spent pair programming. Programmers were loathed to do it due to the perceived increase in the time to complete tasks. We addressed this in the effort estimates by reducing the number of Ideal Engineering Hours [1] available per day. Instead of 4 hours a day we reduced the number to 2.5 and that allowed for pair programming hours in the overall project plan.

A second issue was to make sure that only what was needed at that point of time was written. There was a tendency by some of the more experienced programmers to make the initial implementation more complex than strictly necessary. We addressed this issue by introducing and coaching test-driven development [9] and encouraging the architects to use the agile modeling practices [11].

Despite the long-term benefits of pair programming that include knowledge sharing and buddy-reviews of the code, the initial effort for learning and coaching was more than 10%. Hence, the score 2 for our project. As soon as the test-driven development and agile modeling levels out the additional cost of pair programming, the DICE® score for Effort factor will reach its maximum value of 1.

5 Limitations of the DICE® Framework

A major weakness of the DICE® framework is the subjectivity of the scoring. There are no hard and fast rules for assigning of the scores, and their values depend more on the skills of the evaluators than any rigid criteria. In our case there was a large amount of experience in both Agile and Waterfall projects and whilst the figures were subjective they were backed up with long-term experience.

One method to overcome this would be to adapt one of the Agile estimating techniques, such as the Wideband Delphi [12] or the Planning Poker [13], and use that to obtain a consensus figure for each value between all the evaluators.

Another limitation of the DICE® framework is its simplicity. The method does not deal with the soft change factors, although they are important.

In order to overcome the limitations of the framework, the evaluators or the change agents should calculate the DICE® scores for the on-going project at the end of every iteration. That would give a continuous picture of the odds of the change initiative.

Finally, to provide a broad assessment of any change initiative, the change agents should use more than one evaluation technique. Hence, the use of DICE® framework can be coupled with, for example, the application of the Formula of Change [14], to find out if the change is possible on the general level. This formula provides a model to assess the relative strengths affecting the success or failure of the organizational change programs. The change is only possible if the product of three factors: dissatisfaction of how things are now, vision of what is possible, and initial, concrete steps that can be taken towards the vision, is greater than the resistance towards the change.

Another technique to be coupled with the DICE® helps determining the relative suitability of agile or plan-driven methods for a particular project. It is based on evaluation of the Five Critical Factors [15], which are the project's size, criticality, dynamism, personnel, and culture factors. This technique does not explicitly predict the outcome of change initiatives but helps finding out if going agile is a good idea, in the first place.

The last option would be to use a formal evaluation method such as the Capability Maturity Model for Software (SW-CMM) [16]. However, the authors feel that this method is too heavy-weighted for Agile projects. The application of the DICE® framework coupled with the evaluation of the Formula of Change and the Five Critical Factors should be sufficient for most of the projects.

6 Conclusion

The results of applying the DICE® framework to agile projects came as no surprise to us as we were acting as change agents and our opinions were biased. However, it was essential to evaluate the change initiative using the tools coming from the outside of the software development world in order to communicate the need of change to senior management and gain their commitment.

The weakest factor of waterfall projects is the time between project reviews or milestones, which can span from 3 months to more than a year (D=4). The management commitment is weak as waterfall projects are recognized as 'business as usual', i.e., if there was a strong need for a change, very likely some other practices were used (C_1=4). There is usually no additional effort as the working practices are pretty much the same as in previous projects (E=1). A team's commitment and its ability to accomplish the goal depend on the same factors as within the agile projects.

From the Equation 2 it is visible that the overall DICE® score for waterfall projects is north of 19 (assuming the average values of 2 for integrity and team's commitment). Hence, such projects are in the Woe zone and have low chances of success.

$$\text{Waterfall} = D + (2*I) + (2*C_1) + C_2 + E = 4 + 4 + 8 + 2 + 1 = 19 \tag{2}$$

The strongest factor of agile projects is the duration, as the time between reviews varies from one to five weeks (D=1). There is usually some additional effort due to learning curve connected to new working practices (E=2). If the team drives the change initiative, then the team commitment factor gets the maximum score (C_2=1) and the senior management commitment is recognized as neutral (C_1=3). Else, the senior management commitment factor gets the maximum score (C_1=1) and the team commitment is average (C_2=2). The integrity does not depend on the process so the average score is taken into calculation (I=2).

$$\text{Agile bottom-up} = D + (2*I) + (2*C_1) + C_2 + E = 1 + 4 + 6 + 1 + 2 = 14 \tag{3}$$

As the Equation 3 shows, the overall DICE® score for agile projects is, either south of 14 for bottom-up change initiatives (i.e., neutral senior management and top team commitment), or south of 11 (cf. Equation 4) for top-down approach (i.e., high senior management and average team commitment). Hence, the agile projects are in the Win zone and have high chances to be successful.

$$\text{Agile top-down} = D + (2*I) + (2*C_1) + C_2 + E = 1 + 4 + 2 + 2 + 2 = 11 \tag{4}$$

Based on our experience we claim that agile projects are better positioned for success than the waterfall projects according to the DICE® framework. Moreover, we hope that the readers will use the results of our study to drive the change initiatives in their organizations and will fine-tune the four factors so that their projects are successful.

References

1. Larman, C.: Agile and Iterative Development: A Manager's Guide. Addison-Wesley Professional, August 2003
2. Beck, K.: Extreme Programming Explained: Embrace Change. Addison-Wesley Professional, November 2004
3. Sirkin, H.L., Keenan, P., Jackson, A.: The Hard Side of Change Management, Harvard Business Review, October 2005, pp. 108-118
4. The Boston Consulting Group, www.bcg.com
5. Kotter, J.P.: Leading Change: Why Transformation Efforts Fail. Harvard Business Review, March 1995
6. Cockburn, A.: Writing Effective Use Cases. Addison-Wesley Professional, October 2000
7. Mugridge, R., Cunningham, W.: Fit for Developing Software. Prentice Hall, July 2005
8. Beedle, M., Schwaber, K.: Agile Software Development with Scrum. Prentice Hall, October 2001
9. Beck, K.: Test Driven Development by Example. Addison-Wesley Professional, November 2002
10. Schwaber, K.: Agile Project Management with Scrum. Microsoft Press, March 2004
11. Ambler, S.W.: Agile Modeling. John Wiley & Sons, April 2002
12. Stellman, A., Greene, J.: Applied Software Project Management. O'Reilly Media, November 2005
13. Cohn, M.: Agile Estimating and Planning. Prentice Hall PTR, November 2005
14. Beckhard, R.: Organization Development: Strategies and Models, Addison-Wesley, 1969
15. Boehm, B., Turner, R.: Balancing Agility and Discipline: A Guide for the Perplexed. Addison-Wesley, August 2005
16. Paulk, M., et al.: The Capability Maturity Model for Software V1.1. CMU/SEI-93-TR-24, DTIC Number ADA263403. Pittsburgh: Software Engineering Institute, Carnegie-Mellon University, February 1993

Agility in the Avionics Software World

Andrew Wils, Stefan Van Baelen, Tom Holvoet, and Karel De Vlaminck

K.U. Leuven DistriNet
Department of computer science
Celestijnenlaan 200 A, 3001 Leuven
{andrew.wils, stefan.vanbaelen,
tom.holvoet, karel.devlaminck}@cs.kuleuven.be

Abstract. This paper[1] takes a look at how XP and other agile practices can improve a software process for the development of avionics software. Developers of mission critical airborne software are heavily constrained by the RTCA DO-178B regulations [8]. These regulations impose strict rules regarding traceability and documentation that make it extremely hard to employ an iterative software development process. In particular, the extra validation overhead increases the time spent on small iteration cycles (for example, a bug-fix) to several weeks.

Currently, this sector is also pressed to switch to a more agile, customer driven approach. In this paper we investigate how to speed up development and cope with changing requirements using agile techniques. The research was carried out in cooperation with Barco, a major Belgian avionics equipment supplier. We explain why certain agile techniques have less effect as the project progresses. We point out the stadia in which each XP practice is beneficial and where XP practices might cause a slowdown.

1 Introduction

The upcoming popularity of agile software development is creating a pressure for application domains where less flexible software development processes are currently used. The avionics software industry is experiencing demands for a more customer oriented, agile software development approach. More specifically, this industry is confronted with late requirements changes and asked to shorten release cycles. While eXtreme Programming (XP) [1] and other agile practices seem the obvious solution to deal with these demands, at the same time people are cautioned and advised to consider a more disciplinary approach for the development of mission-critical software. For example, Boehm and Turner [3] advise a more plan-driven approach when the software could involve loss of lives. Alistair Cockburn's crystal methodology [5] states that increasing criticality level means increasing the hardness of the method, resulting in more rigor, tighter

---

[1] The described work is part of the EUREKA-ITEA AGILE project, and partly funded by the Flemish government institution IWT (Institute for the Promotion of Innovation by Science and Technology in Flanders).

P. Abrahamsson, M. Marchesi, and G. Succi (Eds.): XP 2006, LNCS 4044, pp. 123–132, 2006.

control and less tolerance. Unfortunately, due to a lack of experience with life-critical software development, the crystal level L (Life critical) is not discussed in more detail. The fact that people suggest a plan-driven approach does not necessarily indicate a lack of trust in agile methods, but more an observation that certain plan-driven methods have been proven to provide software that passes certification.

Indeed, the mission critical nature of this software has lead to stringent procedures and plans that could specifically exclude the use of agile methods. In this paper, we will show that for the avionics software world, agile improvements can be made while still respecting the RTCA DO-178B certification guidelines. To verify this, we worked together with the Belgian avionics equipment supplier Barco for a thorough analysis of a DO-178B compliant software process. The company was assessed with the following goals in mind:

- show how to optimize the software development process and still have full documentation and traceability at the end;
- enable late integration of requirements changes with minimal re-verification efforts.

While this assessment was focused on the DO-178B standard, our findings may be useful in general for mission-critical software development.

The paper itself is organized as follows. The next section takes a closer look at the DO-178B standard. This document imposes the most important software development constraints for the avionics sector. We explain in Section 3 how we came to the results of our study. We looked at team activities, team communication, the software process structure, project artifacts and project management. We found that a modified XP based process can shorten iteration cycles, provided that a number of technical obstacles can be solved. The availability of the right tools will be even more important than in traditional agile software development. The results are broken down in an analysis of the agile principles in Section 4 and a discussion of agile opportunities throughout the entire development process in Section 5.

2   Avionics Software Development

Avionics software development is heavily constrained by a simple, yet inflexible goal: *to prevent the loss of human lives*. This mantra rightfully adds suspicion to anything that may compromise the safety and security of aircraft personnel and passengers. For software, this resulted in the establishment of some strict guidelines for the development processes. Produced by Radio Technical Commission for Aeronautics, Inc. (RTCA), the DO-178B document has become the de facto standard of such guidelines. The USA's Federal Aviation Administration and many other national certification authorities regard this document as a necessary means to certify avionics software; this is specified in FAA Advisory Circular 20-115B.

The DO-178B document dates from 1992[2]. Fortunately, it does not impose a specific software development life-cycle process. The document specifies (a) objectives for software life-cycle processes, (b) descriptions of activities and design considerations for achieving those objectives and (c) descriptions of the evidence that indicates that the objectives have been satisfied. In practice, this requires the delivery of multiple documents and records to verify traceability and testing of all requirements. These documents include:

- plans for verification, quality assurance and development;
- all requirements, software and the source code tree;
- problem reports, verification cases, procedures and standards.

The objectives are grouped according to levels of potential danger if the developed software should fail: A (catastrophic), B (hazardous-severe), C (major), D (minor), or E (no-effect). The most stringent levels (A and B) demand amongst others:

- independent reviews of tests and of requirements compliance;
- traceability of system requirements to the source code.

In addition, the DO-178B standard includes strict guidelines concerning tool use and reuse of software. If software artifacts are reused between projects, the certification evidence of these artifacts should be integrated in the certification evidence of the new project. It should also be of the correct rigor required for the targeted safety level. If a tool is used that in one way or another eliminates or automates compliance to certain objectives, certification evidence for such a tool is also required. A distinction is further made between verification tools and development tools. Certification evidence for a development tool should be of the same rigor as required for the targeted safety-level as such a tool can directly introduce a bug into the airborne-system. A verification tool may be developed to a somewhat lower standard as it can only fail to detect a bug in the airborne system.

3   Industry Assessment

The avionics division of Barco develops man machine interface solutions for the avionics domain. Barco desired to improve the time-to-market and wanted to respond more quickly to customer requirements changes. However, it turned out that an agile methodology such as XP did not offer the necessary improvements, mainly because it addressed problems that were entangled with other aspects of avionics software development, and the DO-178B standard. We then performed an assessment consisting of the following activities:

- seminars and workshops about the DO-178B standard and the internal software process;

---

[2] A newer version is being prepared and will be called DO-178C.

- short interviews with all team members and longer discussions with developers, project leaders, selected team members and reviewers;
- visits to development labs and plant.

Apart from this, Barco performed an analysis of the impact of software changes and did an internal survey to find productivity impediments.

While looking for bottlenecks in software development, we found that development gets more and more dependent on hard to control external factors as the software project progresses. An example factor is hardware co-development. While software development could be made on a simulated hardware platform, testing for certification always needs to be done on the final product. For example, automated environmental tests can still take up to several days. We will see that these factors have a major impact on the overall agility of the project.

4   Agile Principles

The agile principles lie at the heart of most agile methodologies. They are defined alongside the *Agile manifesto* [2]. Before trying to bring agility into a software process, we first check whether the agile principles support avionics software development. Also, they must not contradict or interfere with the DO-178B standard. It turns out that most principles can be applied in a certification driven process without any changes. We needed to reinterpret 3 principles. However subtle these changes are, they will still have an effect on how agility can be applied to an avionics software process. These are the subtle yet important comments on the principles:

Principle: Our highest priority is to satisfy the customer through early and continuous delivery of valuable software.
This principle applies, but valuable avionics software means software suitable for flight operation and eventually certification, which needs much more work than the ordinary, "tested" software that was targeted by this principle.

Principle: The most efficient and effective method of conveying information to and within a development team is face-to-face conversation.
This principle applies, but much information that is exchanged needs to be logged and documented. Face-to-face, informal communication is hard to capture in documents, and could in fact contradict the produced documents.

Principle: Working software is the primary measure of progress.
This principle only partly applies: certification leads to additional non-software milestones in the project.

Principle: Agile processes promote sustainable development. The sponsors, developers, and users should be able to maintain a constant pace indefinitely.
The avionics sector is indeed trying move to a more constant development pace. However, the next section will show that this cannot be maintained indefinitely.

5   Agility Analysis and Opportunities

To see what bottlenecks we can alleviate with agile techniques, consider Figure 1. Since a traditional software process suffers from its complexity, the effort needed to add functionality increases as the project progresses. This defines the Boehm curve that is already 20 years old [4]. Agile processes such as XP aim for an ideal, flattened curve, allowing a constant development pace [1].

At the beginning of a project, certification driven software development follows these curves. We call this the *software phase* of the project. A first divergence can be seen in the figure when deployment tests begin: the software is prepared to get tested in the field. Here, the process slows down because of hardware dependencies and (partly automated) acceptance testing. These issues are common in embedded software development (e.g., see [7]). Hence, we call this the *embedded phase.* An even more significant slowdown is encountered when the software is ready to be certified. In this stadium, that we call *certification phase,* the software is presumed bug-free, but much documentation and manual testing is needed to provide the artifacts that are necessary for certification.

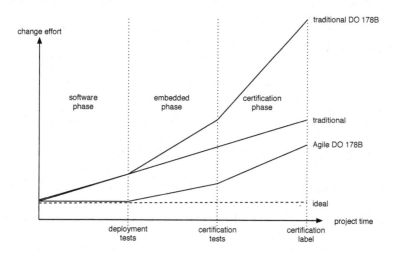

Fig. 1. Software processes compared

For simplicity, the figure does not indicate what happens after the certification itself, after which every modification needs to be recorded in a change request. Even more, the impact on all artifacts needs to be analyzed and documented.

Table 1 presents for every phase what XP practices can be applied. In addition, we discuss the most important agile opportunities for every phase. Together with the risks and weaknesses they define a new curve for an agile DO-178B driven process.

5.1 Software Phase

Software development in this phase is not yet affected by other issues or constraints - the software is developed independently. In this phase, all agile practices may be used. Requirements changes - even hardware changes - are welcomed. User and acceptance testing can be fully automated within the context of the software.

5.2 Embedded Phase

In this phase, the software must be deployed and tested on the target hardware. There are no fundamental reasons to abandon agility. However, there may be some repercussions on activities that depend on the developed software as input. Example activities include continuously installing the software on the target hardware, retesting the hardware, environmental tests and generating documentation. The opportunities in this phase mainly consist of automating these tasks. Also, feedback and communication become more important in this phase, in order to cope with the dependencies between and coordination of software and other activities. Agile practices to consider for facilitating this are daily stand-up meetings and post-iteration workshops.

5.3 Certification Phase

This phase brings with it many additional tasks that need to be executed upon each software change. Code coverage and non-functional requirements (such as maintenance) need to be analyzed. Traceability needs to be established and manual testing and reviewing is required. The evidence of all these activities needs to be collected and reported.

A logical measure here is to limit the amount of changes. First, to keep the requirements changes to a minimum, the customer can write their own acceptance tests. Regarding traceability, there is an opportunity to handle and manage documents more as source code, so that agile code-centric practices can also be applied to them. In particular, one can apply the following practices:

- auto-generate not only code, but as much documents as possible;
- include all documents in a version control system;
- manage their dependencies, so that it is immediately clear what document parts are affected by an artifact change.

This will reduce the time spent on creating, managing and reviewing documents. For documents that cannot be auto-generated, an agile document preparation practice may be useful, such as RaPiD7 [6]. In RaPiD7, documents are made in workshops where multiple stake-holders are present. Reportedly, it speeds up the document development process significantly (with speedups varying between 15 and 96%).

For independent reviewing, pair programming may offer a solution. In a way, a paired programer continuously reviews the other person's work. Frequent changes in pairs should guarantee independence, as people get to see a lot of other people's mistakes and gradually become expert reviewers. Collective code ownership also benefits this reviewing process.

The development of automatic test suites is an intensive task. Auto-generation of test code will speed-up the testing process considerably. For manual acceptance testing, there is an opportunity to automate some tests, although this may need special hardware. One would have to operate inputs (such as the control panel of a flight display) and capture the output of the system (such as the pixel values of a display).

6 Weaknesses and Risks

With the agile opportunities of the previous section, we considerably flatten the steep curve of a regular DO-178B driven process, as Figure 1 shows. However, a software process is as slow as its weakest link.

Agility relies on coping with complexity, and most agile practices focus on software complexity. For the software itself, this benefits the project up to the certification phase, because once software gets installed in production type aircraft, it does not need to be updated that often.

As a project progresses, software changes create complexity that is not handled by agile software practices. Managing traceability, even with requirements tools (such as Telelogic DOORS) may remain difficult. It may not be possible to automatically generate certain written documents. The earlier mentioned automation using agile tools is has much less value if certification regulations require the results of uncertified tools (for example, test suites) to be manually verified.

At a certain point in time, reducing complexity of the software may even cause greater complexity, because of the ramifications on traceability, documentation and testing. That is why practices such as refactoring are discouraged in the certification phase.

To summarize, although we expect significant speedups by applying the agile opportunities, a daily integrated system build process will most likely be unfeasible once these external factors come into the picture. Hence, the principle "Requirements changes are welcomed" will be hard to maintain in the certification phase, if at all.

This defines the Agile DO-178B curve in Figure 1. It is not flat, since a sustainable development pace will remain a hard to reach ideal for the avionics domain. Still, great improvements can be made compared to the traditional way of handling a DO-178B driven process.

7 Conclusions and Future Work

This analysis confirms that while a process such as XP can be applied to many domains, it is targeted at software development processes that are not hindered by or dependent on factors external to the software. While general statements cannot be made based on this single assessment, it seems that most agile principles are still valid and beneficial in the avionics world. In addition, although avionics software development is clearly dominated by the plans and documents that go with it, there is room to apply agile practices. However, because of the large certification overhead, it will not be possible to "flatten" the Boehm curve [4] as XP evangelists claim. To show this, we defined 3 development phases in which changes are increasingly hard to embrace. Thus, if agility is a must, it is best to remain in the early phases as long as possible.

This said, our most important observations for improvement are the following:

Software phase: communicate regularly and early in the development process and deliver incrementally functional prototypes. This will reduce the requirements changes later in the project, when they are more difficult to apply.

Embedded phase: add more communication, transparency and feedback to the project by applying project feedback based practices, such as daily meetings and post-iteration workshops.

Certification phase: treat documents like source code and apply continuous integration, ultimately enabling shorter iterations. For testing and reviewing, apply pair programming, collective code ownership and test-first programming.

Of course, most practices are already best applied at the start of the project. Table 1 summarizes the suitability of XP practices for every phase.

In the future, we hope to further concretize the risks and utility of the agile practices, select the best practices, and apply them in a number of projects.

Finally, we state that as the pressure for iterative and customer driven software development will further increase, the industry has no choice but to adapt their processes accordingly. Not only the customer has to accept new responsibilities for an agile approach to work. Certification authorities will need to acknowledge that agile software development can yield software that is at least as safe as before. However, providing the authorities with evidence of this remains a task for the industry. We can only guess the timeframe of these changes. As it took some time for the certification authorities in order to accept certain object-oriented development techniques for avionics software, we expect that agile practices will soon also be recognized by the certification authorities as useful practices within an avionics software development process.

Acknowledgments

We would like to thank the people from Barco for their time and feedback, especially Stijn Rammeloo for his active participation in this assessment and for his insights on the avionics software domain.

References

1. K. Beck. *Extreme Programming Explained: Embrace Change.* Addison-Wesley, 2000.
2. K. Beck and et al.   Manifesto for agile software development.   http://www.agilemanifesto.org, 2001.
3. B. Boehm and R. Turner. *Balancing Agility and Discipline: A Guide for the Perplexed.* Addison-Wesley, 2003.
4. B. W. Boehm. *Software Engineering Economics.* Prentice-Hall Advances in Computing Science & Technology Series, 1981.
5. A. Cockburn. *Agile Software Development.* Addison-Wesley Professional, 2001.
6. R. Kylmäkoski. Efficient authoring of software documentation using RaPiD7. In *ICSE '03: Proceedings of the 25th International Conference on Software Engineering*, pages 255–261, Washington, DC, USA, 2003. IEEE Computer Society.
7. P. Manhart and K. Schneider. Breaking the ice for agile development of embedded software. In *Proceedings of the 26th international conference on software engineering (ICSE)*, 2004.
8. RTCA. DO-178B: Software considerations in airborne systems and equipment certification, 1992.

A   Appendix

Table 1. XP practices (continued on next page)

Practice	Description	Software phase	Embedded phase	Certification phase	Comments and risks
Customer available	Customer is available for the team to make questions etc.	×	×	×	Commonly, avionics development starts off with a detailed requirements document from the customer. This practice could reduce the customer start-up effort and move back the start date for a project to create more room for development and certification.
Metaphor	Simple story of the purpose of the application.	-	-	-	A metaphor is not really necessary as the domain applications are very similar.
Short releases	The product is done in iterative style and new versions are "published" rapidly.	×	×	-	This is a necessary practice, but difficult to maintain towards the end of the project.

Practice	Description	Software phase	Embedded phase	Certification phase	Comments and risks
Planning game	The way for customer and the team to plan and communicate which tasks are to be implemented in each iterations.	×	×	×	As the project advances, this practice becomes essential to limit change.
Pair programming	Coding is done in pairs using one computer.	×	×	×	This practice could help comply with the DO-178B standard, because the latter mandates that all code should be proof-read by a separate person.
Collective code ownership	No one owns the code and everybody is allowed to change any parts of the code.	×	×	×	
Unit testing	Unit tests are written before the actual code.	×	×	×	
Acceptance testing	Customer writes the acceptance tests	×	×	×	These tests could seriously reduce further requirements changes. Problems arise when testing high level requirements, as the DO standard states the necessity for these to be verified by a human being.
Refactoring	Remove duplication and add simplicity.	×	×	-	This practice is not recommended late in the development process: refactoring after certification procedures would add weeks to the certification cycle.
Simple design	Tasks are solved with the simplest possible way to avoid unnecessary complexity.	×	×	×	Simple design could improve the testing cycle and reduce low level requirements.
Continuous integration	New code is integrated as soon as it is ready.	×	×	×	Recommended, as this finds bugs early.
Coding standards	Coding rules that everybody follows.	×	×	×	This is necessary for DO-178B certification.
40-hour-week	Avoiding working overtime.	×	×	×	This is mainly useful in conjunction with pair programming.

Architecture and Design in eXtreme Programming; Introducing "Developer Stories"

Rolf Njor Jensen, Thomas Møller, Peter Sönder, and Gitte Tjørnehøj

Department of Computer Science, Aalborg University
Fredrik Bajers Vej 7E, 9220 Aalborg Ø, Denmark
{rolf, molz, sunlock, gtj}@cs.aau.dk

Abstract. This article introduces a new practice to eXtreme Programming (XP): Developer stories. The goal of these stories and their creation process is to incorporate architectural planning to XP thus ensuring a viable architecture. By conducting a small development project using XP, we find that establishing a viable architecture might be problematic. Arguing that architectural quality criteria in XP are traceable to traditional criteria, and by pointing to related work regarding incremental continous design, requirements management and large-scale refactorings, we find support for this claim. We proceed by describing the new practice ensuring that it embraces the values, and supports existing practices of XP.

1 Introduction

Since the late 90's there has been a huge interest in the field of lightweighted methods. These methods are best known as agile methods, where XP has attracted the most attention. XP emphasizes on close collaboration between the developer team and the customer through face-to-face communication, frequent delivery, self-organizing teams, and rapid response to changes in requirements[1].

As a contrast to agile development, non-agile software methods produce substantial documentation during the development, and the architecture is laid out in the beginning of the process – based upon a fixed set of requirements determined as one of the first activities. XP produces no other documentation than the code itself, and due to core practices such as weekly cycles, incremental design, test-first programming, and continuous integration, XP is able to respond without significant overhead to changes in requirements focusing on what to produce, but not on how to do so.

XP is creating design and architecture by constantly redesigning through refactoring [1]. This way the architecture will keep on improving throughout the development phase, but only on demand. XP prescribes using the YAGNI principle ("You Aren't Going to Need It") as mentioned in [2], ensuring that futile development due to wrong predictions of requirements does not happen[1].

Several publications have expressed doubts regarding the quality of the architecture produced by XP compared to other methods - e.g. architecture-centric Rational Unified Process (RUP) [3].

P. Abrahamsson, M. Marchesi, and G. Succi (Eds.): XP 2006, LNCS 4044, pp. 133–142, 2006.

The approach to design in XP is radically different than in previous methods – which naturally has spurred several publications on the subject of continous, incremental design. The role of design in XP has been elaborated and compared to traditional ways of design amongst others, by Fowler [2]. Shore focuses on continuous design in [4], listing design goals and rules of thumb.

However, an experiment using XP showed us that the produced architecture in XP is not necessarily a viable architecture. Furthermore, Fowler suggests that the approach to design in XP might be too restrictive hinting that there might be room for design specific considerations [2]. By investigating similarities between criteria for architectural quality from traditional development methods versus criteria from XP we see that some properties of "good" architecture are inherent in the architecture – being the same no matter which development method is used, and that the criteria to evaluate design in XP is indeed traceable to traditional criteia.

To improve the likelihood of producing a viable architecture using XP, we seek to modify XP – and introduce a practice that systematically draws the focus of the developers onto the developed architecture. The process of the practice springs from traditional development methods, but is in every way designed to be not only non-conflicting, but also supporting the values, principles and practices of XP.

The suggested practice is a new kind of stories – developer stories. Unlike the stories described by Beck in [1] which are written by users (from now on referred to as user stories), developer stories are written by the developers. The developer stories express changes (refactoring) to the existing code, aiming to improve the existing architecture. The process of writing developer stories occurs before the meeting initiating the weekly cycle.

Does the new practice then violate the XP spirit? By evaluating the developer stories in XP, we determine that this new practice does not conflict fundamentally with XP – it even embraces all of the values, and takes its own place in the synergetic mesh of the XP practices.

2   Experiment

Initially we set out doing a small-scale software development project using XP, to discover potentially problematic processes. The project aimed to develop a search engine able to search across several SOAP sources. Performing the experiment was five developers following XP. The project scope allowed for two XP iterations.

2.1   Result of Experiment

When evaluating the experiment, there was one underlying theme in the deficiencies we experienced. After careful review of the architecture and design of the application, it was clear that the the architecture was sub-optimal. Even though there had been several occurrences of refactoring, some of the highest-level modules had high coupling, making possible future refactoring unnecessarily hard to achieve. Moreover, none of the upcoming user stories (that had not been chosen for the performed iterations) seemed to trigger refactorings of the architecture.

Reflecting on our experiment, we pose the question: *Does XP have a weak side concerning establishing a viable architecture?*

While the experiment presented a faulty architecture, and while further analysis pointed towards i.a. lacking communication regarding architectural matters as one reason, we still conduct a litterature review to assert independently from our experiment that XP does have a weak side concerning establishing a viable architecture.

Before reviewing related work we present a discussion of the term architecture, assessing that a "good" architecture indeed possess some inherent properties that are regardless of the development method.

3   Architecture and Design

What is architecture? What is design? Before we proceed investigating related work, it is necessary to understand what software architecture is. One way to describe software architecture is as a view of the software on a scale with one extreme being the concrete implementation, and the other extreme being the architecture. Moving from implementation to architecture along the scale (with design somewhere in between), the level of abstraction is heightened, hiding trivial details, and enlightening basic structures. Another view of architecture promoted by Fowler in [5] is:

> *In most successful software projects, the expert developers working on that project have a shared understanding of the system design. This shared understanding is called architecture.*

Viewing the architecture as a shared understanding causes the practices supporting inter-team communication about software design to become more important and embracing the underlying value *communication* even more so.

Beck does not rigorously differentiate between the concepts design and architecture. Where he mentions design [1], we often interpret it as architecture.

But what is a viable architecture? XP [1] uses the term *Simplicity* as the main guiding principle for design (architecture), with the following criteria *Appropriate for the intended audience, Communicative, Factored* and *Minimal* that can be used to evaluate the design.

Properties of architecture have been subject to much work. One property stems from the work of Alexander (originally on physical architecture, but since then widely adopted in software engineering) stating that a good architecture is characterized by the absence of essential weak points [6]. Other properties used in object-oriented development methods like RUP [3] originate in work from the 70's on software metrics [7]. Although not all of the criteria for a good architecture is directly evident in XP, some of them are. *Easy to understand* [3], for example, maps to *Communicative* and *Appropriate for the intended audience.* Coupling and cohesion are also among the very central principles [8] in object-oriented architecture, and can be re-found in the properties implied by *Factored* and *Minimal*. So even though XP is by no means an architecture-centric development method, the criteria given to evaluate design (or architecture) are traceable to criteria found in other non-agile methods. This seems to indicate that there are some common properties that an architecture fulfills, if it is viable. This indicates that it is no less relevant to consider architectural quality in an XP setting than in any other setting.

4   Related Work

Beck published the first descriptions of XP in the late 90's (see [9][10]). In these first descriptions of XP, the *Metaphor* was the only practice addressing architecture directly. The purpose of the Metaphor was to "*... guide all development with a simple shared story of how the whole system works...*" and "*The metaphor in XP replaces much of what other people call "architecture"...*".

Many people have, however, found the Metaphor concept hard to grasp [8], and in the latest book on XP [1], the Metaphor is no longer a practice. Lippert *et al* introduces Metaphor Design Spaces [11], giving a methodical approach to finding a good metaphor, and letting it guide the architecture. West and Solano argue that it was wrong to abandon the Metaphor as a practice [12], and advocates a more systematic discussion of how Metaphor informs development.

A common trait in the work done regarding the Metaphor suggests that albeit many developers seemingly have failed to grasp and therefore benefit from the Metaphor practice – it still addresses a need to focus on a shared understanding of important elements of the software – effectively the architecture.

The lack of explicit requirements management in XP has spurred some considerations. It has been argued that several aspects of requirements engineering are suitable for agile methods, and that where quality is a concern, agile methods may benefit from some requirements engineering practices [13][14].

Traditionally requirements are used as basis for constructing an architecture in architectural-centric methods – and we believe that concerns expressed regarding the lack of explicit requirements management in XP is partly due to an uncertainty as to whether XP produces a viable architecture.

One of the core tools of XP is refactoring, and it is a necessity to achieve continuous design. Since Fowler published "Refactoring" [15], much work has been done in the field, enhancing and describing new design patterns for different application domains. Lippert acknowledges the difficulties of performing large-scale refactorings within agile development, and presents approaches to integrate large-scale refactorings into the daily work [16].

We believe that the work done regarding the Metaphor practice, lack of explicit requirements, and troublesome large-scale refactorings point to a common problem in XP concerning the architecture of the system.

Beck has recently revised his description of XP [1], giving among other issues new attention to design, pointing to *Simplicity* as the fundamental principle. Here Beck also states that the XP design strategy is "Enough Design Up Front", and continuous incremental design. Moreover, Beck states that XP should be adapted to the environment – adding and modifying new practices which are needed to support the underlying values and principles. One of the additions to XP in the new revision, is the role of the Architect, described as such: *"Architects on an XP team look for and execute large-scale refactorings..."*. Although the role of the architect is described, the architect is not given any setting in which to communicate with the team about the possible need for large-scale refactorings.

Reviewing related work, and considering the revision of XP we believe that while Beck has acknowledged the need for a focus on architectural quality [1], there is still a need for a practice supporting the inter-team communication about architectural quality and planning of both normal and large-scale refactorings.

5   Developer Stories

We proceed by presenting a new practice to XP, which provides the development team with an opportunity to consider the architecture of the application. One of our premises is, however, to let the practice follow the general look and feel of XP – it is not an attempt to insert a "Big Design Up Front" phase into XP. We call the practice "Developer Stories", and the stories are analogous to user stories - but are written by the XP development team, and describe refactorings, large or small scale, aiming to improve the architectural quality. Given that traditional development methods have numerous approaches to working with the architecture, we lend an ear to these traditional approaches.

5.1   What Are Developer Stories?

Developer stories are, as mentioned, analoguous to user stories. The developer stories describe (changes to) units of developer-visible properties of the software. In contrast, user stories describe units of user-visible funtionality of the software. The physical representation of a developer story is an index card, which may have another color than user stories, making it easy to distinguish them from each other.

The purpose of the developer stories is two-fold. On one hand they are a tool for planning and express concrete demands for refactoring. On the other hand their creation process make the developers reflect upon the design of the system, and effectively build a shared understanding of the important elements – the architecture.

5.2   When to Write Developer Stories?

The developer stories are written before the meeting that starts the weekly cycle – fig. 1. The authors of a developer story are all the programmers in unison. The outcome of the creation process is (possibly) a number of developer stories that are prioritized. The developer stories are added to the set of available stories, and the customer is able to choose them for implementation during the upcoming iteration together with the user stories. The customer needs to be informed about the new developer stories, and the development team's view of their importance. This means that it becomes clear to the customer which refactorings are necessary, and since the whole team has written them together, they are also able to explain to the customer why these refactorings are necessary. Why does the customer get to choose? Because while the development team is able to recognize the need for architectural change, it is still the customer that is capable of determining the business value of the developer story by virtue of the fact that the customer is knowledgable of the context of the product.

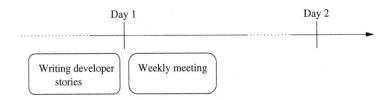

Fig. 1. Writing developer stories every week

Maybe attempting to write the stories reveals that the architecture is just fine. Either way, the development team has an opportunity to communicate about the architecture – heightening the overall level of knowledge of the architecture within the team.

5.3   How to Write?

But how are the developer stories written? Figure 2 shows the four stages of the writing process. The participants are the whole development team. Even though we describe them as stages, we envision the process as quite fluent, with rapid (and to the participants imperceptible) changes between the stages.

Discover and describe: The architect has during previous iterations acknowledged that some problems exist with the current architecture – this is the input to the process. To contribute, everyone else may express their ideas and worries about the architecture of the application.

Write developer stories: This is an iterative step. Having acknowledged and described the problems, the team now has to express the problems as requests for refactorings and new development – the developer stories. During this phase, several tools can be used – UML diagrams, CRC cards, collaboration diagrams, etc. but for the purpose of clarification and communication – not for documentation.

Estimate developer stories: After writing the developer stories, they have to be estimated. The estimation process makes the team consider how they can be implemented – either heightening the level of confidence in the stories – or spurring a rewrite of one or more stories.

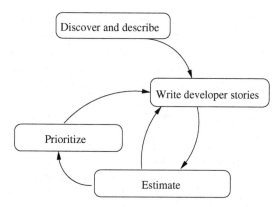

Fig. 2. The four stages of the writing process

Prioritize stories: Having completed the estimation of the developer stories, they can be prioritized, letting the team agree on which problems are in most need of being addressed. The team also needs to identify whether there are any stories that are mandatory to choose for implementation in the upcoming iteration. Maybe the prioritization reveals that the developer stories must be rewritten or specified. A heuristic that can easily be applied during the prioritization of the developer stories is the YAGNI principle. If someone can argue that some particular story quite simply describes superflous, uncalled-for architectural changes – then You Aren't Going to Need It.

Hopefully, many developer story sessions will be very short – due to a lack of problems with the architecture of the application. However, the process of discussing the architecture and letting the architect interact with the rest of the team on architectural matters may give the team courage to face problems – and give the customer an opportunity to act upon them.

6   Discussion

How does developer stories extend XP – in alignment with the XP spirit? Augmenting XP with new or altered practices is supported by Beck in [1], provided that the new or altered practices support the underlying values and principles of XP. Sharp and Robinson also conclude that the practices of XP may be altered or replaced, as long as the underlying values are supported by the new practices [17]. The values of XP are the ones that the development team have to embrace to actually do XP. However, the values are not close enough to the daily development to provide guidance in everyday problems.

6.1   Embracing the Values

In the following we will go through the values of XP, considering how developer stories fits.

Communication: The developer stories strengthen communication. It is an enabling practice because it encourages and strengthens inter-team communication between the team members regarding the design and architecture. Letting the whole team communicate about views of important elements of the system supports the pair programming practice, and enhances the collective understanding of the project. Having everyone collaborating on writing the stories supports spreading knowledge of design decisions beyond the affected programming pairs.

Simplicity: Writing the developer stories encourage simplicity. It is the governing design principle. Whenever the design of the application grows complicated, e.g. with high coupling and/or low cohesion, the developer stories provide the team with a possibility to do something about it.

Feedback: The feedback values evolves around one of the key features of XP, *Embracing changes*. Embracing change leads to the need for feedback: Was the change right? By having the development team constantly assessing that the architecture is viable and asking themselves whether it can get better, the feedback cycle gets even more intense.

Courage: It gives self-confidence and courage to do something about architectural courage. The developer stories also benefits from courage, because it takes courage to act upon problems with the architecture and give feedback to the architect. They are willing to write the developer stories, and redesign the application. Courage is the investment the team must take when writing – and an investment that is repaid when the quality of the application improves.

Respect: Equality of the team members and respect for the project is a value that lies below the surface of the previous values. If the stories are written by everybody with everybody participating, it does not violate this value – it might even support it.

6.2   Interacting with Other Practices

Like every other practice, we believe that developer stories work only poorly by themselves, but used together with the other practices of XP, the collective effect is much better. Figure 3 shows the interaction of developer stories with the practices *Incremental Design*, *Pair programming* and *User Stories*.

Incremental Design: As our experiment hinted, and as related work supported, incremental design may falter [2], in which case the developer stories support by letting the team take a collective overview of the architecture, considering possible major changes. Developer stories on the other hand get support from incremental design since the whole development team has witnessed the design grow little by little – everyone has had their influence on the design, and is therefore able to contribute in the collective writing process. Using incremental design, small refactorings become an integrated process, but it is harder to achieve large-scale refactorings. Developer stories alleviate this difficulty, providing a visualization and planning of the large-scale refactoring process.

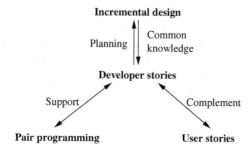

Fig. 3. Developer stories depend heavily on interaction with other practices

User stories: While user stories express units of user-visible functionality, developer stories express developer-visible properties of the software. The difference between these requirements may well be compared to the difference between functional and non-functional requirements. This way, developer and user stories complement one another.

Pair programming: Without pair programming, knowledge would not spread as thouroughly throughout the development team, and the necessary shared responsibility enabling the writing process of the developer stories would be impossible. By writing developer stories on the other hand, knowledge that might not disseminate (or only disseminate slowly) through pair programming, rapidly reaches each developer.

If a team adopting developer stories does so in the spirit of XP, we believe that it can fit into the practices of XP, making XP even better. As Beck writes in [1], different application domains present different challenges. In application domains where a viable architecture is essential for the application being developed, the developer stories might prove their usefulness.

7   Conclusion

Using XP in an experiment developing software, we found that it did not lead to a viable architecture. Inspired by the experience we searched and found support in the literature that XP does indeed have a weak point concerning establishing a viable architecture. However XP supports adding new practices and we introduce a new practice: Developer stories – aiming to strengthen the architectural focus by enabling inter-team communication. After a careful review we believe that the new practice can work in the spirit of XP, and coexist in synergy with existing practices.

7.1   Future Work

The prescribed "how" and "when" are only speculations. Therefore whether developer stories should be a core practice or a corollary practice is up to future testing. By having too much focus on the developer stories one might see that changes to the architecture will be done too often and take too much time. On the other hand, using developer stories as a corollary practice might mean that, when eventually writing them, the produced architecture will be the cause of major refactoring throughout the entire system – which might have been avoided if the developer stories where given more attention.

As always, reality beats theory, so testing developer stories in the wild is bound to be a learning experience.

References

1. Beck, K.: Extreme Programming Explained: Embrace Change. 2 edn. Addison-Wesley (2004)
2. Fowler, M.: Is design dead. (2004)`martinfowler.com/articles/designDead.html` (2004)(2004)
3. Larman, C.: Applying UML and Patterns. 3. edn. Prentice Hall (2004)
4. Shore, J.: Continuous design. Software, IEEE **21**(1) (2004) 20–22
5. Fowler, M.: Who needs an architect? IEEE Software **20**(5) (2003) 11–13
6. Alexander, C.: Notes On The Synthesis Of Form. President and Fellows of Harvard College (1994)
7. Gilb, T.: Software Metrics. Winthrop Publishers Inc. (USA edition) (1988)
8. Fowler, M.: Design: Reducing coupling. IEEE Software **18**(4) (2001) 102–104
9. Beck, K.: Embracing change with extreme programming. Computer **32**(10) (1999) 70–77
10. Beck, K.: Extreme Programming Explained: Embrace Change. Addison-Wesley (2000)
11. Lippert, M., Axel, Schmolitzky, Züllighoven, H.: Metaphor design spaces. Volume 2675 of Lecture Notes In Computer Science., Springer-Verlag (2003) 33–40
12. West, D.D., Solano, M.: Metaphors be with you! In: Agile2005. (2005)
13. Eberlein, A., do Prato Leite, J.C.S.: Agile requirements definition: A view from requirements engineering. In: TCRE'02. (2002) http://www.enel.ucalgary.ca/tcre02/.
14. Paetsch, F., Eberlein, A., Maurer, F.: Requirements engineering and agile software development. In: Twelfth International Workshop on Enabling Technologies: Infrastructure for Collaborative Enterprises. (2003) 308
15. Fowler, M.: Refactoring. Addison-Wesley (1999)
16. Lippert, M.: Towards a proper integration of large refactorings in agile software development. In: Lecture Notes in Computer Science. Volume 3092., Springer-Verlag (2004) 113 – 122
17. Robinson, H., Sharp, H.: Xp culture: Why the twelve practises both are and are not the most significant thing. Proccedings of the Agile Development Conference (2003)

Towards a Framework for Integrating Agile Development and User-Centred Design

Stephanie Chamberlain[1], Helen Sharp[2], and Neil Maiden[3]

[1] Bit10 Ltd, Sovereign Court, Sir William Lyons Road, Coventry CV4 7EZ, UK
stephanie.chamberlain@gmail.com
[2] Centre for Research in Computing The Open University, Walton Hall, Milton Keynes,
MK7 6AA, UK
h.c.sharp@open.ac.uk
[3] Centre for HCI Design City University, Northampton Square London
EC1V 0HB, UK
n.a.m.maiden@city.ac.uk

Abstract. Due to a number of similarities between user-centred design (UCD) and agile development, coupled with an appreciation that developers are rarely usability experts, it seems attractive to integrate these two approaches. However, although agile methods share some of the same aims as UCD, there are also distinct differences. These differences have made the use of these methods on development projects problematic. This paper reports a field study designed to investigate the use of agile methods alongside UCD in one particular organization. The aim of the study was to develop a framework for use by project teams wishing to integrate UCD practices with agile development. The study, its findings and five principles for integrating UCD and agile development arising from this work are discussed.

1 Introduction

The importance of knowing who the users are, understanding their priorities and goals, and actively involving them in uncovering requirements (e.g. [10]) is well understood in software engineering. However the role they should play, how they should be involved, and how much they should be involved has been a matter of dispute (e.g. [6, 9]). User involvement is also a central concern of HCI, and the importance of integrating software engineering and HCI methods has been recognised for many years (IFIP WG 2.7/13.4). The Agile Manifesto emphasises the importance of involving the customer in a development project, but this practice is proving to be problematic (e.g. [12]), and it is rare for a real end-user to take the role of customer.

"User Centred Design" (UCD) is an approach which aims to involve the users in a meaningful and appropriate way throughout a system's development (e.g. [5], [15]). Gould et al [5] first proposed three principles of UCD in the mid-1980s, and in the 20 years since then, various techniques for involving users successfully have been developed. Integrating UCD and agile development therefore has the potential to help agile developers with the difficult practice of involving customers, and the wider concern of how to integrate HCI concerns with software engineering.

P. Abrahamsson, M. Marchesi, and G. Succi (Eds.): XP 2006, LNCS 4044, pp. 143–153, 2006.

The purpose of the study described in this paper was to identify and investigate the issues faced by a project team trying to integrate UCD and agile development. The study reported was conducted within one organisation where Scrum, XP and UCD were being used. We report the study and its findings, and extract five principles which appear to be significant for successfully integrating UCD and agile methods. In the rest of this section, we explore UCD, other approaches to integrating agile methods with UCD principles, and compare UCD and agile approaches. In the next section we describe the method, and in section 3 we present our results. Section 5 presents the five principles, and the paper concludes with some practical suggestions.

1.1 User-Centred Design (UCD)

The term UCD refers to both a collection of techniques and the philosophy at the heart of these techniques. The overall philosophy of UCD is to place the user at the centre of the design process through the use of rigorous methods. For instance, the designer tries to "get to know" the users initially through techniques such as interviews, direct observation in context, forums and questionnaires, before moving on to design prototypes for the users to test within a real-life context. Often the first "prototype" is simply a paper one which the designer constructs through an analysis of the tasks that the user will perform. As development progresses and more sophisticated prototypes are developed, the user may be asked to perform tasks using the prototype with only minimum guidance from the tester. The results are then fed into an iterative process which continues until a final version of the system emerges.

1.2 Integrating UCD and Agile Development

The potential of XP to provide a bridge between software engineering and HCI is not a new idea. A discussion between Kent Beck and Alan Cooper [13] concluded that there were indeed strengths of Interaction Design and XP that could be combined. Beck and Andres [3] acknowledge this by including an interaction designer in the agile development team; personas are now commonly used in agile projects (e.g. [1]).

Several other approaches to integrating HCI and agile concerns have been suggested. For example, Kane [8] proposed how 'discount usability' [14] may be integrated with agile development. Ambler [1] suggests several models which can be used to facilitate interaction between users and developers and shows how these can be used in an agile project. Holtzblatt et al [7] have proposed a modified version of contextual design (rapid contextual design) which is appropriate for projects with a shorter timescale, including agile development [4].

1.3 Similarities and Differences Between UCD and Agile Development

A project involving both Agile Methods and UCD becomes a challenge because although there are several similarities, there are also distinct differences (e.g. [17]). The three main similarities are:

1. They rely on an iterative development process, building on empirical information from previous cycles or rounds. For instance, one of XP's values is feedback ([2:20]), and the idea of refactoring code is an embodiment of this value. In UCD one of its founding principles is iterative design.

2. Agile techniques place an emphasis on the user, encouraging participation throughout the development process. For instance, in Scrum, user evaluation of the product is encouraged on a monthly basis as users are ideally present during the sprint review ([16:54]) and the "Product Owner" is responsible for the requirements and feature prioritisation for the product. A second founding principle of UCD, is early and continual focus on users.

3. Both approaches emphasise the importance of team coherence. Beck states that one of the purposes of the planning game is to "bring the team together" ([2:85]). One of the features of the UCD approach is that the whole team should have the user in mind while developing the product.

The two main differences are:

1. UCD advocates maintain that certain design products are required to support communication with developers, while agile methods seek minimal documentation.

2. UCD encourages the team to understand their users as much as possible before the product build begins, whereas agile methods are largely against an up-front period of investigation at the expense of writing code.

2 Fieldwork

2.1 Method

Three project teams in one organisation were observed for around 2-4 hours per week on site by one individual for a period of 6 months. The organisation hosting these projects was a large media company with a tradition of employing a user-centred approach to development. The organisation had a clear distinction between 'designers', who were responsible for user-centred activities, and 'developers' who produced the code. The observer was a member of staff at the organisation, but not a member of any of the project teams that formed the basis of the study.

The study period was divided into two parts. During the first part, which lasted about a month, the researcher identified some themes which appeared to be significant to the projects being observed. These themes were then used as a framework for a more in-depth investigation which took up the remainder of the observation period.

The initial approach to observation was ethnographic in nature in that the researcher approached the activity as 'strange' and had no *a priori* hypotheses to test. The initial themes emerged over the first period of study. The observation strategy combined shadowing of individuals with site or situation observations such as meetings (14 observation sessions in all). Ten interviews were carried out in order to gain further insight into the observations and therefore not all of the team members were interviewed, although care was taken to gain as much of a cross-section as possible across all teams. Most regular meetings for all three teams were attended and some unannounced visits were made in order to gain a deeper insight into the day to day workings of the teams. At the start of each meeting or observation the method was briefly explained. The team knew they could cease the observation at any point and that the observer would leave without need of an explanation.

Contemporaneous notes, photographs and some video recordings were used to record the interviews and observations. After each session, a summary of key points was written. The environment, interactions and process were recorded by the observer.

Documents helped to provide evidence that the processes which had not been observed but were reported through interviews, e.g. maintaining a sprint backlog graph, were actually being carried out and documented.

2.2 The Project Teams

Three projects formed the main focus of the field study work. Here we refer to them as Project I, Project S and Project M. Each team contained developers (coders) and designers (those who traditionally worked on the user research and usability). Table 1 summarises the projects and their approach to integrating agile and UCD.

Table 1. A summary of the three projects observed through our study

Features	Project I	Project S	Project M
Project Application	Website to involve people in local civic life, including online community to promote and re-engage a political audience.	Interactive TV application: a two-video stream interactive quiz designed to complement a TV programme.	Web-based message board facility for the study organisation.
Methodology followed	UCD and Scrum	UCD and XP	UCD and Scrum
Main User Group	Members of the public	Members of the public	Members of the public
Other Users[1]	Content editors for the website	Administrators/ Editors	Administrators/ moderators[2] The "product owner"[3]
Distribution of the project team	All on the same floor	Spread over two floors	Seated together

All three teams had experience of using agile methods with UCD in the past, and had developed their own approaches to integration, which were observed in this study. These are described below.

The designers of Project I had reported problems on previous agile projects where they had used Scrum. They believed that these stemmed from the inclusion of the design team in the Scrum from the outset of the project. They also felt that they needed an "upfront" period of user research. On previous projects, few usability recommendations had been implemented and the team felt they had been lead by technical requirements over and above user and business requirements. Consequently, Project I decided to change their approach so that the designers did not enter the Scrum until there was clear value in doing so. The team envisaged:

---

[1] Observations showed that users within the organisation were often seen to be user representatives on all three projects.
[2] The employees within the organisation that supported the message-boards by ensuring no illegal or inflammatory content appeared.
[3] This person's job was to ensure the requirements for both the moderators and the end-users were fulfilled.

- A separate "up front" period of user requirements gathering and research which took place before development began.
- A prototyping stream where the developers and designers worked together.
- A three-man design team where one designer fed the Scrum with prototypes while the other two designers carried out user research.
- The use of iterative usability testing with constant feedback throughout the development phase.

In Project M, the designers had found attending the Scrum with developers on past projects to be unhelpful and so they ran their own UCD process in parallel to the developers' use of Scrum.

Project S were part of the Interactive Television Department where they were required to deliver within very tight timescales due to fixed transmission dates. They had found that XP worked best for them and the team were using this approach when the observations took place. During the study the team admitted that some UCD tools and methods are occasionally overlooked as a result of external time pressures.

The three projects therefore had different approaches to using UCD with an agile approach. Project I attempted to integrate UCD and Scrum, Project M used UCD and Scrum in combination and tried to align the processes, and in Project S the designers used UCD and activity progressed quite separately from XP development.

3 Results

Four themes emerged from the initial observation period: user involvement, collaboration and culture, prototyping and the project lifecycle. These appeared to be significant issues faced by the project teams in working within UCD and agile development. The meaning of these themes, and the results of further investigations focused around these themes are presented below.

3.1 User Involvement

Through our observations, user involvement was characterised as being where:

- the users were invited to give opinions or test prototypes
- the users were interviewed, observed or questioned for research purposes
- the user's interaction with the product was considered in detail

Each team used different tactics for ensuring that they had suitable user involvement. Project I developed personas based on earlier user research, and then developed a user journey, i.e. usage scenario, for each persona. They also analysed usage patterns taken from the existing version of the website. This gave them an idea as to how far the users were getting through certain processes such as setting up a campaign. Usability issues were raised in meetings by editorial staff.

In Project M we only saw one user testing the system during the observation period. As Project M involved the development of an internal system for managing web message boards, the user in this case was an editor within the organisation. Interestingly a member of the team said that the testing was being carried out "for the developer". The Editor was testing a part of the system to ensure it fulfilled her team's requirements before it was released. The Product Owner was observed attending the sprint review and following this, there was a demo of the work carried out in the sprint. This was mainly for the benefit of the Product Owner who asked questions and the developers proudly showed off the work they had done. This was done at the desk and in an informal way rather than through a formal presentation. It was one of the Product Owner's responsibilities to prioritise features within the sprint.

Fig. 1. Sprint Backlog

An example "Sprint Backlog" on a whiteboard is shown in Fig 1 from Project M.

Project S showed the least evidence of user involvement. However, the user's interaction with the product was seen to be important and the user's needs were often represented by user representatives taken from the team. For instance, the broadcast assistant was observed playing the role of the customer in order to carry out what appeared to be user acceptance testing before the product went to the dedicated QA team. The functional specification was said to be made up of a variety of "user experiences". Stories were written out on cards against the functional specification as the development producer explained what happened at each stage in user terms. The specification was written from the user's perspective.

3.2 Collaboration and Culture

Collaboration was observed with relation to:

- The collaboration between individuals within the team
- Specifically, the collaboration between designers and developers
- The culture that the chosen methodology created

Project I held cross-functional meetings which included representatives from the development, design and editorial teams. The team worked collaboratively in the meetings and requirements were captured from all team members. There had been problems with collaboration between developers and designers in the past; in this project, the Design Lead commented that "we need to get everyone involved in the user journeys as this was the problem before". There was evidence of a struggle for power between the two groups, as shown by this exchange recorded in our notes:

The Scrum Master claims that a developer has already done the back-end work. The Design Lead asks incredulously "based on what spec?" One of the developers replies that it was based on the spec provided by the technical lead. It was agreed that a general meeting was required amongst the leads of the project over this particular issue.

Each group seems to be guarding themselves against having to deal with decisions being made by one group at the expense of another. However, later this defensiveness is displayed again by the Scrum Master who objects to the Product Owner asking probing questions about estimating during a Sprint Review.

The Product Owner refers to the graph and says that the shape of the graph seems to indicate that generally there is an under-estimate of how much work there is to be done. The rather defensive retort from the Scrum Master is that the estimates are not inaccurate but that the requirements change. He adds that if there hadn't been so many small tasks to complete on top of the list of tasks for the sprint, then the team would have delivered all of the tasks by the end of the Sprint. The Product Owner states that there is always new work that crops up therefore it might make sense to say that a certain % of time is allocated for these changes. The development producer adds that there are two options: Either we need to accept that this happens and plan for it or stop it happening if it stops people working effectively. The Scrum Master again defensively says that they already are working effectively.

On Project M there were similar issues between the designers and developers. However, in this project the design team split away from Scrum altogether - this was only used by the developers. The developers sometimes pair-programmed in order to solve hard problems but this was ad hoc, not regular. Many of the problems encountered with collaboration were not to do with the use of Scrum or UCD on this project but largely due to other factors such as lack of people resources.

On Project S communication between the designer and developers was mostly informal. Meetings involving the designer and developers together were scarce. Team meetings often did not involve the designer because they were arranged at the same time as other meetings she had to go to. As a result, there was a disconnection observed between the designer and the developers.

3.3 Prototyping

Each of the projects used prototyping; Project M used an evolutionary approach, Project S used a throw-away approach, and Project I used a combination of both evolutionary and throw-away prototyping.

Project I faced timescale pressures which left little time to handle prototyping effectively. For example, the client-side developer noted that there was not much time for reviewing things as "priorities on the project have been set elsewhere". The cycle of prototyping and feedback didn't work in the way that had been envisaged.

Project M also faced time problems with prototyping, but caused by the different timescales associated with paper prototyping versus development prototyping. This meant that the designers had a shorter iteration cycle than the developers. Ultimately this may have contributed to the abandonment of Scrum by Project M designers.

The Usability Engineer observed that "design prototyping is faster than development prototyping as the <development> languages we use are too slow to prototype in. You ask for a prototype and 6 weeks later you get it." The designers worked at a different pace to the developers which made it hard to iterate around versions of software or designs.

On Project S, the broadcast assistant and a developer used a paper prototype to test that the application supported users' tasks as expected. This prototype was a series of storyboards and flows.

3.4 Project Lifecycle

The different projects exhibited different ways of combining the traditional lifecycle phases with the agile approach. For instance, Project M dedicated a whole sprint to requirements gathering at the start of the project. Some development was planned during this time but the phase was named a "business analysis phase" to indicate that the emphasis was on requirements gathering.

On Project I, the designers advocated "up-front design methods" where significant user research is carried out before any coding is done. The designer's tasks at the start of the project were to: analyse usage patterns, create user journeys (including personas), map the user's mental model and create a high level specification. Based on this information they then prioritised the task list and sent it to the rest of the team.

This activity itself wasn't observed in our study although the resulting artefacts and their use were in evidence (see Figure 2). The lead interaction designer was keen to get the whole team involved in the user journeys as not doing this had caused problems on previous projects. Each area such as technical, editorial and design had a "Discipline Lead" who looked after the interests of that particular group within the project. Requirements gathering was carried out by all of the discipline leads together.

Fig. 2. Results Board (from user research in Project I) showing user opinions

In Project S, an application functional specification was produced before the "planing game" and this provided the basis of discussion. User journeys had also been produced at this stage. Project S were unhappy making decisions on the customer's behalf.

For instance, during an observed multi-disciplinary team meeting, a developer suggests that they should plan a story around the 'red button' (which navigates to interactive TV from linear TV channels) but others are unwilling to do so until requirements had been gained from the customer.

In Project M, a whole sprint was given over to requirements gathering. Some development was planned during this time but the phase was named a "business analysis phase" to indicate that the emphasis was on requirements gathering.

4 Discussion

All projects had some degree of design before coding started but the one most loyal to XP (Project S) had the shortest design period. It also had the least user interaction. However, it must be noted that this project had a much shorter timescale than the others observed.

Project I seemed to have least problems with collaboration which may have been related to the fact that UCD and agile principles were well integrated.

Project M suffered from a detachment of the development and design methodology which as a result tended to operate separately. There was a culture of defensiveness which may have grown up out of this segregation of the two disciplines.

In reviewing the three projects it seems that a fundamental problem of communication exists between the developers and designers within each team and the subject of power within the project is a tricky one. Designers within a project defend their discipline in response to decisions made by the developers, and vice versa.

The power aspects of UCD and Agile are interesting as part of the reason these methodologies came about was because each discipline needed a defence mechanism against other disciplines such as management, or the business taking away their power. Consequently, some kind of balance needs to be put in place to ensure that this power struggle is controlled on a project.

Prototyping also appears to be problematic due to the timescales involved in developing an application in comparison to the design of a paper prototype. However, this may be ameliorated if the designers were managed differently so that other projects were interspersed for the designers and there didn't seem to be so much lag between feedback and implementation.

5 Five Principles for Integrating UCD and Agile Development

Based on our observations and the themes discovered, we have evolved a set of five principles which are significant where UCD and agile methods are to be integrated:

1. **User Involvement** – the user should be involved in the development process but also supported by a number of other roles within the team, such as having a proxy user on the team.
2. **Collaboration and Culture** – the designers and developers must be willing to communicate and work together extremely closely, on a day to day basis. Likewise the customer should also be an active member of the team not just a passive bystander.
3. **Prototyping** – the designers must be willing to "feed the developers" with prototypes and user feedback on a cycle that works for everyone involved.
4. **Project Lifecycle** – UCD practitioners must be given ample time in order to discover the basic needs of their users before any code gets released into the shared coding environment.
5. **Project Management** – Finally, the agile/UCD integration must exist within a cohesive project management framework that facilitates without being overly bureaucratic or prescriptive.

Although these principles have arisen through the observation of one particular organisation attempting to integrate agile methods with UCD, they can go some way to offer other teams a framework with which to begin. More research is required in this area through the observation of further organisations and project teams.

6 Conclusion

User-centred-design and agile methods are compatible, and they can work together but they can also provide problems if the key principles aren't addressed. For instance, the two methodologies can be at odds due to:

- Power struggles between developers and designers
- Time differences between designers' and developers' capacity to create tangible outcomes from each iteration round. Development usually takes more time
- Communication issues if members of the team don't take part in some elements/phase of the project
- A reluctance to understand the needs of each element of the project
- The extent to which the user is able/willing to contribute to the project

However, these can be overcome if:

- There is some balancing role or mechanism put in place to ensure that each discipline has equal power on the team
- Resource management and project management ensures the management of time and resources equate to utilised resources that don't become frustrated whilst waiting for results
- All members of the project team are available/involved at each key point of the project
- The user plays a part in the project so that their requirements are catered for and that the end-product works in a realistic situation

If agile methods and UCD are successfully integrated within a project team, the evidence from our observations suggest that it will be more likely to deliver benefits to the business and most importantly to the user as well.

References

1. Ambler, S. (2002) *Agile Modeling*, John Wiley and Sons
2. Beck. K. (2000) *Extreme Programming Explained_* United States and Canada, Addison Wesley.
3. Beck, K. and Andres C. (2005) *eXtreme Programming Explained: embrace change* (2nd edition), Addison-Wesley
4. Beyer, H. Holtzblatt, K. & Baker, L. (2004) An Agile Customer-Centered Method: Rapid Contextual Design, in *Proceedings of XP/AU 2004,* eds C. Zannier et al, LNCS 3134 Springer-Verlag.
5. Gould, JD and Lewis, CH (1985) Designing for Usability: key principles and what designers think, *Communications of the ACM*, 28(3), 300-311.

6. Heinbokel, T., Sonnentag, S., Frese, M., Stolte, W. & Brodbeck, F. C. (1996) Don't underestimate the problems of user centredness in software development projects - there are many!, *Behaviour & Information Technology*, 15(4), 226-236.

7. Hotlzblatt, K., Wendell, J.B. and Wood, S (2005) *Rapid Contextual Design: A How-to Guide to Key Techniques for User-Centered Design*, Morgan Kauffman.

8. Kane, D. (2003) Finding a place for discount usability engineering in agile development, *ADC 2003*, pp40-46.

9. Keil, M. & Carmel, E. (1995) Customer-Developer Links in Software Development, *Communications of the ACM*, 38, (5), 33-44.

10. Kotonya, G. & Sommerville, I. (1998) *Requirements Engineering: processes and techniques*, John Wiley & Sons.

11. Kujala, S. (2003) User involvement: a review of the benefits and challenges, *Behaviour & Information Technology*, 22(1) 1-16.

12. Martin, A., Biddle, R., and Noble, J. (2004) The XP Customer Role in Practice: Three Studies, in *Proceedings of ADC 2004*, Salt Lake City, June.

13. Nelson. E. (2002) [Internet] *Extreme Programming vs. Interaction Design* http://www.fawcette.com/interviews/becknelson_cooper/ [Accessed September 2004]

14. Nielsen, J. (1993) *Usability Engineering*, Morgan Kaufman.

15. Preece. J., H.Sharp and Y.Rogers (2002) *Interaction Design: Beyond Human Computer Interaction* New Jersey, John Wiley & Sons. Inc.

16. Schwaber. K. and M.Beedle (2002) *Agile Software development with Scrum* New Jersey, Prentice Hall.

17. Sharp, H.C., Robinson, H.M. and Segal, J.A. (2004) "eXtreme Programming and User-Centred Design: friend or foe?" in *HCI2004 Design for Life*, Vol 2.

Security Planning and Refactoring in Extreme Programming

Emine G. Aydal[1], Richard F. Paige[1], Howard Chivers[2], and Phillip J. Brooke[3]

[1] Department of Computer Science, University of York, UK
{aydal, paige}@cs.york.ac.uk
[2] Department of Information Systems, Cranfield University, UK
hrchivers@iee.org
[3] School of Computing, University of Teesside, UK
p.j.brooke@tees.ac.uk

Abstract. Security is a critical part of systems development, particularly for web-based systems. There is little known about how to effectively integrate security into incremental development processes such as Extreme Programming. This paper presents the results of a project that used Extreme Programming practices and deferred consideration of security until system functionality was complete. The findings suggest that refactorings within incremental development processes are capable of delivering high quality security solutions, and provide insights into how security requirements can be incorporated in the planning game.

1 Introduction

Security is an important part of system development. For web-based applications, such as those that use Web Services, or for distributed systems with dynamic reconfiguration capabilities, such as Grids, security requirements will be of substantial importance to customers. Established processes and practices for delivering security requirements are typically evidence-based, and demonstrate process compliance, usually by a process of inspection (e.g. the Common Criteria (CC) [11]). The tension between established security practices and the incremental and iterative delivery offered by agile processes is now well understood.

Satisfying security requirements with agile processes is challenging; Fowler suggests that security may be hard to refactor [3]. Moreover, evidence suggests that security is difficult to retrofit to a system, because of the system-wide nature of security properties [2,7,13]. Despite this, there is room for optimism, for example, the notion of 'good enough' security [5], and the idea that an incremental security architecture [2] can be used to identify the need for security refactoring.

This paper reports on a practical project, which applied Extreme Programming (XP) practices for building a web-based system. The novelty with this project was that consideration of security requirements were *deferred* until functionality was complete. That is, additional XP iterations were applied to satisfy security requirements, given a fully functional system. In these iterations, the system architecture was refactored to

P. Abrahamsson, M. Marchesi, and G. Succi (Eds.): XP 2006, LNCS 4044, pp. 154–163, 2006.

include security features, following standard XP practices used in a novel way. Though this may appear to be a contrived process, late security requirements are representative of many large projects, and agile processes are intended to be able to deal with changing requirements. Developing the system in this way explored the effectiveness of security refactoring, and provided the opportunity to consider how different types of security requirement can be incorporated in the planning game.

The finding of this project is that it is feasible to deal with security requirements during XP, by making using of refactoring. It is also possible - and effective - to incorporate security vulnerability assessments and risk analysis during the Planning Game. Moreover, refactoring is essential to security quality, particularly for simplifying the relationships between security mechanisms and the system goals they support.

We commence with a brief overview of related work, and then summarize the project, its iterations, and the refactorings. We conclude with a summary of the project and its contributions, and make several key observations pertaining to our understanding of agile security development.

2 Background and Related Work

The purpose of security is to mitigate the risk of *threats*, which result from potential *attacks* that may exploit features or vulnerabilities in a system, resulting in specific unwanted outcomes to stakeholders' assets. Security requirements can in part be determined by identifying potential attacks and attackers, as well as the threats that may arise while the system is in use. The system must also be secured from *security vulnerabilities,* i.e., "security holes that makes a system more prone to be attacked by a threat or make an attack more likely to have some success or impact" [8].

Common security requirements include:

- **Authentication:** that data actually originates from the claimed person or system.
- **Authorization:** actions, operations or data that are permitted to authenticated users.
- **Integrity:** that data are managed to ensure that only appropriate modifications are possible (e.g. prevent modification in transit, or maintain consistency with an external process).
- **Confidentiality:** that data are not shared with unauthorized entities.
- **Nonrepudiation:** that a sender/receiver is not able to later claim that they did not send or receive the message.

The international standard for security development is the Common Criteria [11], derived from the US TCSEC and the European ITSEC; it is an evaluation standard, and facilitates an inspection process. It corresponds to quality assurance practices in which documented evidence demonstrates process compliance.

The CC addresses assurance, but does not help in selecting appropriate security features. The normal way to do this is by risk analysis, which considers systematic features such as business security goals and the attack environment. Generally, two aspects of the system are considered: its design and normal use by users and organizations; and the possibility of technical defects or vulnerabilities that may facilitate unexpected paths of attack. The first requires a structural argument that security features contribute to system-level goals, whereas the second motivates security features that mitigate known defects. Both these types of requirement are a challenge to accommodate using agile processes.

2.1 Security in Agile Processes

Security, like any other system property, must be supported by the practices of the development process. In order to establish acceptable levels of security within a system, certain tasks must be accomplished during different phases of the project lifecycle and the process followed must be flexible enough to support and achieve these tasks.

The Risk Analysis and Management Methods, such as Hazard and Operability Analysis (HAZOP) [14], Failure Mode and Effect Analysis (FMEA) [9] and traditional security practices involve detailed investigation of a system's architecture. Examples of these include formal validation of design and implementation, static analysis of software, change tracking, and internal and external reviews. Beznosov and Kruchten [4] conclude that *"approximately half of the conventional assurance methods and techniques directly clash with the principles and practices of agile development"*. XP-based projects develop the simplest system in each step, without considering functions that will be needed in future iterations. This view conflicts with traditional security practice, which is essentially a top-down development, or at the very least an early definition of the security infrastructure on which a system will be based. A case study which contrasted incremental and top-down architectures [2] concluded that Agile Security can be achieved by using an Incremental Security Architecture (ISA). Moreover, [2] states that, *"instead of following traditional techniques, [an Agile process] must have its own, agile, security practices"*.

In agreement with this idea of new practices, Beznosov examines XP and introduces the concept of eXtreme Security Engineering (XSE) [5] and explains how these practices could be applied in the security domain. XSE aims to deliver 'good enough' security without defining it *a priori*. The objective of *Planning Game,* one of the XP Practices, is defined so as to plan small releases in short iterations while delivering 'good enough' security through tested functionality units. The paper also gives the extended definitions of other practices such as testing, continuous integration, simple design and refactoring which are adapted to XSE.

In summary, several researchers have considered the problem of achieving security through agile processes; however, there are few concrete case studies that either demonstrate new, agile security techniques, or explore the use of current Agile practices for introducing security mechanisms and satisfying security concerns. In this paper, we are aiming at exploring security in systems developed using agile processes, and are not intending to try to generate documentation in order to meet current certification standards.

2.2 Refactoring in Agile Processes

Refactoring is a disciplined approach for supporting change in systems [6]. Refactoring can be expensive in model-based development, where amendments in code can lead to modifications in related documents and diagrams. By contrast, refactoring is an important practice in agile processes. For example, code simplicity is achieved by different sized refactorings; refactoring may mean small design changes such as 'Pull-Up Field' or 'Extract Method' [3], but it may also mean substantial restructuring of a superclass, which may then affect subclasses with many references.

Some of the activities that can be put into practice when refactoring is required are listed below; these will be important for the discussion of security to follow.

- The communication level must be increased: When a refactoring decision is taken, all the programmers whose code may be affected from the change must be included in the refactoring process and the changes applied to the system must be made explicit to everyone in the team.
- Simplicity must be maintained: When a refactoring goes beyond small or pattern-based refactorings, the refactoring must be done in smaller steps. This will not only ease the understanding of individuals about the changes done, but also allows backtracking in case an incorrect amendment is made.

Determining a "Refactoring Route" [10] may also help manage the tasks introduced through a Refactoring pattern. The aim of this is to define a route from the current design to the desired one. It describes the refactoring steps, each of which should be achievable in one or more integration steps, and which ultimately result in the desired design. In order to adhere to agile process principles, each step must result in a working system.

The next section places these concepts in context by providing a concrete example where security requirements are introduced to the system under design in a later stage, through refactoring methods.

3 Case Study

This section gives an overview of the steps of a practical project carried out to explore the effective usage of refactoring techniques in agile processes, in particular to integrate security at a late stage in software development. The intention was to fit iterations focusing strictly on security concerns into a traditional XP development.

The project aimed to produce an online estate agency for buying and selling properties, e.g., apartments and houses. This web-based application provides a service to users where they can search through properties listed on the site, subscribe to the site and contact the estate agency that owns the site, by using a messaging service provided by the agency. The system requires users to register in order to conduct transactions beyond simple searching for properties.

There were two main deliveries. The first occurred when the application met all the service-related requirements and second delivery integrated solutions for security requirements on top of this system.

We present the case study in two sections, the first outlining how system functionality was developed (where security concerns were ignored), and the second describing how the security mechanisms were injected into the system by using refactoring patterns. The XP practices followed in the case study will also be mentioned where necessary. The reader is referred to [1] for further details.

3.1 First Delivery

The project began with the preparation of story cards as the 'Planning Game' practice suggests. The estate agency services to be delivered were written in story cards in detail and prioritized according to their importance. These story cards roughly determined the milestones of the project and the contents of each iteration. According to the story cards, 2 releases were planned for the first delivery, of which the first included 8 iterations and the second completed the remaining 3 iterations. However, more iterations than identified on the story cards were needed, in order to simplify individual iterations, establish infrastructure, and allow for refactoring. In total the first release needed 15 iterations, and the second release required 8 iterations. Table 1 gives the iteration list for the first delivery, i.e., for the first and second release. The estate agency itself is referred to as *Housing* within this table.

Each iteration consists of straightforward XP design, testing and implementation phases, ignoring all security concerns. A template was used to record a short summary of actions and alterations in each iteration; see [1] for examples.

The Stories marked with an asterisk in Table 1 are those, which weren't discussed in the Planning Game phase of the project, but became necessary along the way. For example, no database (DB) consideration was necessary until Iteration 3. Following

Table 1. Iteration List for Release 1 and Release 2

Iteration no.	Story Name	Story no.	Priority
R1-I1	Form the skeleton*		
R1-I2	Search Criteria	S2	1
R1-I3	DB Design – Property Table*		
R1-I4	Search	S1	1
R1-I5	Subscription Criteria	S3	2
R1-I6	DB Design – User Table*		
R1-I7	Subscribe	S4	2
R1-I8	Sign In Criteria*		
R1-I9	Sign In	S5	2
R1-I10	Member Page*		
R1-I11	DB Design –UserMessage Table*		
R1-I12	User Message Display	S8	3
R1-I13	Buy property	S6	2
R1-I14	Sell – Information given*		
R1-I15	Sell property	S7	2
R2-I1	Housing – Form the Skeleton*		
R2-I2	Sell (Housing) – Reply Message	S8	3
R2-I3	Sell (Housing) – Forward Message	S8	3
R2-I4	Sell (Housing) – Modify Property	S8	3
R2-I5	Sell (Housing) – Activate Property	S8	3
R2-I6	Sign Out	S9	3
R2-I7	Read Message	S10	3
R2-I8	Delete Message	S11	4

the design of the 'search' page, different DB servers were compared, an appropriate one for the system was chosen and a table to hold the property records was created.

Eight of the aforementioned iterations made use of refactoring patterns in order to introduce a new feature or to simplify the code. 'Hide Delegate' and 'Extract Method' [3] are examples of the techniques used.

After the first delivery, the system satisfied all functional requirements. The users could search the site for available properties, subscribe to email notifications of interesting available properties, send messages to the estate agency in order to buy/sell properties, and reply to messages from the agency by using the services on the site. However, security had been ignored. For example, anyone who knew a member's username could access that member's home site and display their messages. These concerns were dealt with in the second delivery.

3.2 Second Delivery

Introduction of security requirements late in a project lifecycle potentially imposes many changes to the system. To manage various types of change at the same time, we extended the Planning Game to incorporate security requirements. This section gives a summary of this approach, with its application to adding security mechanisms to the online estate agency. The reader is referred to [1] for further details.

First, the *'Define and Partition'* strategy is used in order to divide the system into smaller, but manageable pieces. This approach is similar to the one explained in [2] where partitioning is proposed in order to implement security requirements incrementally. In the estate agency, the assets, operations and technical features were taken as the entities to be defined and partitioned. *Assets* are defined as data to be protected; these are divided into two categories:

- Data that should not be accessible through any service (though it may be used by the system during service provision) and whose existence creates a threat for the system, such as passwords.
- Data that is accessible through some operations.

Partitioning helped to observe the behaviour of the system from different angles, i.e., the type of data saved within the system, the tasks carried out by the system by using the data and the relations of the system with exterior components that support the functioning of the system. *Operations* are services provided by the software and they are classified according to user access. *Technical features* are defined as the points where the system may suffer due to the development environment and/or the tools used. For the estate agency, the technical features determined were:

- Browser-related issues
- Web Server-related issues
- DB Server-related issues
- Programming Language-related issues

By defining the assets, the scope of the system was circumscribed in terms of data; this effectively determined security requirements using a conventional risk-based analysis. Defining the operations determined the scope of the system in terms of functionality; this identified an appropriate authorization, or access policy, for system users. Finally, reviewing the technical features of the system allowed security requirements to be introduced to protect, or eliminate, potential vulnerabilities.

These categorizations can be extended for different applications. The ones presented were specifically considered for the system under discussion.

Following the above process gave rise to the security requirements in Table 2.

Table 2. Security Requirements and to-do list

Purpose	Risk Type	Security Requirement
Encapsulate the data that is defined as 'should not be reachable'	Browser-side SQL-Server side	Confidentiality (asset)
Make sign-in secure (to ensure that anyone who knows the URL of the member home page can not display it)	Browser-side	Authentication (technical feature)
Avoid multiple concurrent access by one user	Browser-side SQL-Server side	Authorization (operation)
Provide required functionality to Housing	N/A	Authorization (operation)
Provide required functionality to Agents	N/A	Authorization (operation)
Avoid insertions to DB by unauthorized users through browser with a direct link to JSP page.	Browser-side	Authorization (operation) Confidentiality (technical feature)
Avoid deletions to DB by unauthorized users through browser with a direct to link to JSP page	Browser-side	Authorization (operation) Confidentiality (operation) (technical feature)
After signing out, the user shouldn't be able to turn back to his home page	Browser-side	Authentication (technical feature)
Prevent output being cached by the browser	Browser-side	Confidentiality (technical feature)
Avoid invalid users	Browser-side	Authentication
Make subscription through a secure channel	Browser-side Web Server-side	Confidentiality (technical feature)
Secure the accesses to MySQL	DB Server-side	Confidentiality (technical feature)

Due to time constraints, only the security requirements in Table 2 could be implemented; additional iterations could improve on the overall security mechanisms and coverage of requireements. Our intention was not to show how to implement each and every possible security requirement, but rather to demonstrate that the process of securing a system can be integrated with XP practices.

The strategy described above served as the Planning Game for this phase and the decisions taken at this stage were defined and prioritized according to customer needs and choices. In this way, the Planning Game was able to incorporate three critical sources of security requirements:

- a user authorization policy
- a risk-based assessment of system assets
- a review of technical vulnerabilities

Once the security requirements were known, the next step was to prioritize them and to take the required actions in order to avoid these vulnerabilities.

The following section explains how refactoring patterns were used to implement the changes to the system listed in Table 2.

3.3 Refactoring in Late Security Integration

Each *purpose* field in Table 2 was analyzed and feasible solutions were proposed. Here is a list of security mechanisms introduced and the refactoring techniques applied in order to adjust the system to these alterations smoothly:

Table 3. Security Mechanisms introduced

Security Mechanism	Refactoring Techniques Applied (taken from [3])
Encryption of Password	Replace Method with Method Object
Session ID	Replace Data Value with Object
Session Check	Extract Method
Active User	Extract Method
Provide Extra Functionality to Housing	Substitute Algorithm Extract Class / File Usage of Middle Man
Provide Extra Functionality to Agents	None
Request Owner Check	Extract Method
Provide Proper Sign-out	None
Prevent Caching	Extract Method

As shown in Table 3, modifications required to deliver the security for this project are achieved through small releases and short iterations by using relevant refactoring techniques. Each iteration introduced a new security mechanism or extended the coverage of an existing one. As XP suggests, the software was in working condition after the completion of each iteration.

4   Conclusions

We have outlined the results of a concrete study to evaluate the use of Extreme Programming practices for introducing security concerns late in development. Our experience suggests that XP practices, in particular the Planning Game and Refactoring, can be used to achieve an appropriate degree of security. In terms of achieving security requirements within XP, we make the following observations:

- Introduction of security requirements late in the project lifecycle potentially imposes many changes to the system. To manage various types of changes at the same time, an elaboration of the Planning Game was used. Conceivably, this idea could be used to achieve other system-wide requirements, e.g., dependability.

- The Planning Game can play a substantial role in establishing security requirements within Extreme Programming, via partitioning over assets, operations, and technical features of a system. This in effect provides a new, agile practice for achieving security within an iterative and incremental development, and is compatible with the ideas in [2], since the security views created in this modified Planning Game are effectively small incremental security architectures.
- Refactoring can be integrated smoothly with this lightly modified Planning Game practice, where refactorings are applied to introduce security mechanisms whose need was identified during prioritization and vulnerability assessment.

Instead of attempting to create the documentation demanded by conventional processes and assurance standards, we have focused on how agile practices can be used to build fit-for-purpose secure software that meets the most important security requirements from accepted practice – that is, our definition of "good enough" security is that security mechanisms in our system are motivated by a user's authorisation policy, risk analysis, and vulnerability assessment. The results of our work suggest:

- The need for a mechanism, namely an incremental security architecture to show how security features are structured to deliver system level security goals, and act as a trigger for refactoring.
- That it is possible to incorporate vulnerability assessment, as well as risk-analysis, in the Planning Game.
- That refactoring is central to security quality, both to implement security features, and to re-structure or partition the system to simplify the relationship between security mechanisms and the system goals they support.

We are continuing to explore the use of XP practices for achieving complex (and potentially system-wide) refactorings. We have completed preliminary experiments on refactorings to produce Web services from web applications using XP practices. In these experiments, the classes and methods used in a web application directly drive the production of methods exposed in Web services. Of course, this approach to producing Web services is incomplete as not all features of a web application are implemented as individual methods: some are emergent features that result from a collaboration among methods. Our observation so far is that the traditional XP lifecycle can be followed in producing Web services from web applications (e.g., each Web service can be described in separate story cards). We observe that if production of Web services from a web application is known to be intended at an early stage of development, then it would be a good practice to note this in the story cards for the main application. This new practice reminds developers that such annotated story cards should be encapsulated in order to generate services when the time comes.

Acknowledgement. This work was supported by EPSRC grant GR/66421/01.

References

1. Aydal, E. G., Extreme Programming and Refactoring for Building Secure Web-Based Applications and Web-Services, MSc Thesis, University of York p. 102. 2005. http://www.cs.york.ac.uk/~aydal/thesis.pdf
2. Chivers H., Paige, R.F., and Ge X., Agile Security using an Incremental Security Architecture, *Extreme Programming and Agile Processes in Software Engineering in The 6th International Conference of XP*, LNCS 3556, Springer-Verlag, 2005
3. Fowler M., *Refactoring*, Addison-Wesley, 1999.
4. Beznosov K., Kruchten P., Towards Agile Security Assurance, in *Proc. New Security Paradigms Workshop*, 2004.
5. Beznosov K., Extreme Security Engineering: On Employing XP Practices to Achieve "Good Enough Security" without defining it, *The First ACM Workshop on business Driven Security Engineering (BizSec)*, ACM Press, 2003.
6. Fowler M., Refactoring Home Page. http://www.refactoring.com/, 2005.
7. Paige, R.F., J. Cakic, X. Ge, H. Chivers, Towards Agile Re-Engineering of Dependable Grid Applications. In *Proc. Genie Logiciel & Ingenierie de Systemes et leurs Applications (ICS-SEA'04)*, CNAM, 2004
8. Introduction to Risk Analysis, http://www.security-risk-analysis.com/introduction.htm
9. Failure Mode and Affects Analysis, http://www.parnassus.org/FMEA_top.pdf
10. Lippert M., Towards a Proper Integration of Large Refactorings in Agile Software Development. University of Hamburg, 2004.
11. The Common Criteria, Common Criteria Support Environment (CCSE), August 1999. http://www.commoncriteria.org/cc/cc.html.
12. Beck, K. *Extreme Programming Explained*, Addison-Wesley, 1999.
13. Wäyrynen, J., Bodén, M., and Boström, G. Security Engineering and eXtreme Programming: An Impossible Marriage?, *Proceedings of the XP/Agile Universe 2004: 4th Conference on Extreme Programming and Agile Methods*, LNCS 3134, Springer-Verlag, 2004.
14. Kim, S., Clark, J.A., and McDermid, J.A. Rigorous Generation of Java Mutation Operations using HAZOPs, in Proc. Genie Logiciel & Ingenierie de Systemes et leurs Applications (ICS-SEA) 1999.

Divide *After* You Conquer: An Agile Software Development Practice for Large Projects

Ahmed Elshamy[1] and Amr Elssamadisy[2]

[1] ThoughtWorks Inc.
Chicago, IL 60661 USA
Aselshamy@ThoughtWorks.com
[2] Valtech Technologies
Addison, TX 75001 USA
Amr@Elssamadisy.com

Abstract. Large software development projects are not agile by nature. Large projects are not easy to implement, they are even harder to implement using agile methodologies. Based on over 6 years of experience building software systems using agile methodologies we found that we can modify agile methodologies to be successfully applied to large projects. In this paper, we will introduce a development practice, which we call *Divide After You Conquer* to reduce some of the challenges during the development of large agile projects. By solving the base problem first with a smaller development team (*Conquer phase*) before expanding the team to its full size (*Divide phase*) we can solve many of the problems that occur with larger projects using agile methodologies.

1 Introduction

Large software development projects have their own set of problems that need to be addressed [2,3,4,6,8,9]. Roughly speaking, we consider a development project *large* if the development team is anywhere between 50 and 100 people (includes developers, testers, business analysts, and managers). Many of the standard development practices in agile methodologies do not provide their expected consequences [1,2,9].

In this paper we describe a development practice that we have used on several different projects at multiple companies. This development practice, which we name 'Divide After You Conquer', solves many of the base problems first before expanding the team to its full size. This practice is related to much work that has been done before in non-agile development processes [6,7,10] – i.e. this is not a new problem. These practices and processes include prototyping, architecture-driven development, and a full upfront high level design as recommended by the Unified Process to name just a few. *Divide After You Conquer* is however different from each of these practices in that it is permanent and not throw-away like prototypes and is done in a test-driven manner as opposed to upfront design as suggested by the Unified Process [6].

2 Challenges in Applying Agile to Large Projects

One of the aspects common to many agile development methodologies is that the entire team (business analysts, developers, and testers) collaborate very heavily. With

P. Abrahamsson, M. Marchesi, and G. Succi (Eds.): XP 2006, LNCS 4044, pp. 164–168, 2006.

a large project, this type of collaboration is difficult at best. What we have found again and again that we tend to break up into subteams for better communication. The downside to subteams is the possibility that the subteams build stove-piped sub-systems if communication is insufficient among the teams. Even if the group communication is successful we can have problems of consistency and duplication that goes undiscovered. Of course, there are other practices that help alleviate these problems such as rotating team members among the subteams, having an overall design document, etc. [4,6]. We are not invalidating these techniques, but in our experience they are not sufficient to alleviate the problems typical when separate subteams build separate parts of the system. Another way to state this problem is that the different subteams may result in a non-homogeneous and inconsistent architecture.

Also, as we have indicated above, large projects using agile methodologies may not be as amenable to recognizing and responding to change. Specifically there are two different aspects, i.e. the recognition of a change and the response to that change.

2.1 Recognizing Change

The first part, of recognition of change, is greatly affected by the size of the team and the size of the artifacts (code, use cases, tests). As we have more people, whether or not we have multiple subteams, it is more difficult to determine if a change in one part of the system affects other parts of the system. The standard way that this has generally been addressed is either upfront design to make sure that everything matches and extensive documentation. With typical agile development practices upfront design is looked down upon because of the cost of design carry and the fact that requirements change. Agile development methodologies also tend to be light on documentation, and non-agile methodologies that are not documentation-light have documentation that frequently is out of synch with the project.

2.2 Responding to Change

The second part, responding to change, is usually done via refactoring. Refactoring is a good solution that relies on a large test framework as a safety net. There is nothing wrong with this, refactoring is very efficient in general. There are, however, large refactorings which are difficult and expensive to perform – so we want to minimize these refactorings. We have the non-agile solution to this problem which is design upfront, but designing upfront generally results in a design that is more complex than that needed by the exact system causing a design carry cost throughout the lifetime of the project. This particular problem, that of upfront design, has been discussed extensively in the agile development community. We need to find another way to solve our large refactoring problem other than upfront design.

3 Divide After You Conquer

Basically, instead of dividing the work first and then solving each sub-problem, the starting team is a core team (usually about 20-30% of full team) that has the most experienced developers, testers, and business analysts and it builds out the main business cases in a test-driven manner. This first phase lasts a non-trivial amount because we want to build out enough of the project that we touch all of the primary business areas (without dealing with alternative/exceptional scenarios) and build out most of the architecture. Because we have a small team, a full agile methodology works without modification. We end the first phase when we have a stable code base with a significant portion of the architecture built out and a broad swathe of business built. At this point we have *conquered* the problem and now it is time to *divide* by growing the development team and splitting up into smaller subteams to grow the project into a fully functional software system. Because the architecture has been built out in a test-driven manner we have the amount of complexity needed but no more. Teams now have a homogeneous architecture in the different subprojects. We want to stress that this is not the *only* practice needed for agile development with large projects, but it is a significant one. Unlike [2] we clearly define when we reach a stable architecture. [2] recommends just declaring the architecture is stable to give the courage for developers to work on the existing code.

3.1 The Conquer Phase

The conquer phase of the project will introduce a stable working example of the architecture and system design. This working example is built iteratively with constant refactoring and ensures that the design works for the current requirements. The system design may include layering, object models and screen layouts. All that would be a starting seeds for other subteams to follow and build upon. Creating the design through an iterative process according to the business need reduces the risk of redesigning the system when a standard upfront design approach is used.

The team will define a set of use cases that are broad enough to touch/interact with most parts of the proposed system. These use cases have to be useful to the business and simple enough to be implemented within a few months. The goal of the conquer phase is to implement these use cases in an iterative and a test-driven manner.

Testers and business analysts will come up with standards/working examples for story cards, testing criteria, testing framework that would be followed after the split. This work will act as the basis for later work by the larger team. This can be seen by many as 'reinventing the wheel' and that these standards can be set upfront. We found out that building a set of experiences for this specific project that can be reused by the larger team in the divide phase is more effective than reinventing the agile development process for each sub-project.

The initial development team (developers, testers, business analysts) that started on that early project they would have a very good over-all picture of the project. They were involved in the implementation of the simple business cases that touch most if not all business areas. They also understand the overall flow of the application. This knowledge will enable a better split into teams when we reach the divide phase. This group will also work as mentors for the remaining team in the next phase.

Finally, the starting project is not a prototype. It is a set of production quality stories, code and tests that will be used as the basis for building out the entire system. In this case the conquer phase has the same goals as the elaboration phase in a development process like the Unified Process [10] – namely to flush out the architecture and address any high-risk areas. Some problems may not appear unless we try to implement a real life situation with a complicated enough business use case.

3.2 The Divide Phase

Divide Subteams by Business Areas: The divide phase starts when the project is divided into sub-teams, which is a common practice for large projects. Sub-teams are more manageable and they can adapt to change more easily. A common practice also is to split based on business areas. Dividing into business areas helps understanding the business within a business area – understanding the business is of prime importance to a successful project. The business functionality will also drive the code, which is a major benefit of applying agile methodologies. Jutta Eckstein [2] shows similar practice. Eckstein recommends starting small and growing slowly. It did not emphasize on when to start dividing into subteams or when to start to grow the team. We clearly recommend splitting the teams after completion of the broad business case and the team will only grow after the division into subteams.

Staff gradually: Staffing the sub-teams would be by assigning members of the existing team (the team on the conquer phase) to sub-teams. New team members will also be assigned to sub-teams. No specific requirement on the newly joined members, except being open for using agile methodologies. The staffing may occur as initial staffing to start the sub-teams and gradually add new team members to sub-teams as needed. Staffing gradually would help the knowledge transfer to be done smoothly, releasing the load on the conquer team to do knowledge transfer properly to new team members. The initial staffing should allow for pairing between members of the conquer phase and newly joined members. Pairing may include developers, BA and QA team members as well.

Transfer Knowledge: In the beginning of the *Divide Phase* knowledge needs to be transferred from the core team members to the additional team members. There are several ways that we have seen this done: code reviews, pair programming, and mentoring are three of the most common techniques. Code reviews are not necessarily one-shot deals but can be done repeatedly until the expanded team becomes cohesive. Pair programming is not always the easiest practice to implement depending on the environment of the company, but when allowed has been one of the most successful techniques we have seen. Finally, mentoring lies somewhere between the two extremes where the core team members take on the role of mentors to the new members to transfer business, testing, and design knowledge.

Rotate team members from the newly staffed members: During the course of project rotation of team members between sub team will be helpful to transfer knowledge between sub-teams. Members rotated to new teams may work on interfaces between the two sub-teams, the one they were originally on and the newly joined. This also helps maintain the consistent and homogenous architecture that we built in the *Conquer* phase. By rotating the team members they are exposed to the entire system which allows for a large project version of the eXtreme Programming practice of *Collective Ownership*.

4 Challenges in Applying This Practice

The practice mandates having a highly skilled set of developers at the beginning of the project (the conquer phase). The high skilled developers should be available for the rest of the project. In the beginning of the divide phase staffing with other developers, business analysts and testers should start. In some situation this staffing pattern may not be applicable, due to some organizational structure of the company. Still in some other companies as it's the natural way to staff a large project. Companies will give much attention to large projects and they would staff them with their best team members in the beginning. As the team grows they may staff the project from new hires, consulting companies or developers that are freed from other projects. This common scenario may match the staffing time line proposed.

Defining the use cases or the core part of the system is the main challenge when applying this practice. Some systems may have convoluted set of functionality with high interaction. Finding a simple business case that satisfies the core system is hard is such systems.

Knowledge transfer between subteams is still a challenge. Members' rotation is still not enough to ensure successful communication between subteams. Other practices must be involved to enhance the communication between subteams and ensure proper interfaces between teams. These practices like [8] are out of scope of this paper.

References

1. Cockburn, A. Agile Software Development, Pearson Education, Indianapolis, IN. (2002).
2. Eckstein, J. Agile Software Development in the Large: Diving into the Deep, Dorset House Publishing, New York, NY. (2004).
3. Elssamadisy, A. XP on a Large Project- A Developer's View, in Extreme Programming Perspectives, eds. Marchesi et al., Pearson Education, Indianapolis, IN. (2003).
4. Elssamadisy, A. and Schalliol, G., Recognizing and Responding to "Bad Smells" in Extreme Programming, presented in International Conference on Software Engineering 2002.
5. Evans, E. Domain-Driven Design: Tackling Complexity in the Heart of Software, Pearson Education, Indianapolis, IN. (2004).
6. Jacobi C. and Rumpe, B., Hierarchical XP: Improving XP for Large-Scale Reorganization Processes, in Extreme Programming Examined, eds. Succi et al., Pearson Education, Indianapolis, IN. (2001).
7. Larman, C. Applying UML And Patterns, Prentice Hall, Upper Saddle River, NJ. (2001).
8. Rogers, O., Scaling Continuous Integration, presented in XP 2004, (2004).
9. Schalliol, G, Challenges for Analysts on a Large XP Project, in Extreme Programming Perspectives, eds. Marchesi et al., Pearson Education, Indianapolis, IN. (2003).
10. Scott, K. The Unified Process Explained, Pearson Education, Indianapolis, IN. (2001).

Augmenting the Agile Planning Toolbox

J.B. Rainsberger

Independent Consultant
me@jbrains.info

Abstract. Agile approaches including XP and Scrum grew out of one particular team's practice, so its advice contains hidden assumptions we need to identify. If we do not, we risk seeing these techniques fail a team, or a team fail with these techniques. This report describes one team's experience learning adaptive planning, and the steps it took to augment the out-of-the-box process that the agile literature suggests. It shows how the team's environment has motivated these changes while allowing the team to continue to engage in an evidence-based continuous improvement program.

1 Project Background

I joined this project approximately three months after it began. Although the team had completed some good work, they were unable to run their product from end to end when I asked them to. They had built their product in layers, rather than shipping small, working stories. They had a product backlog and sprint backlogs, but with items estimated anywhere from a few hours to thousands of hours. Since the team was not delivering working product increments as Scrum suggests[5] and some increments were estimated with such high risk of error, it was not clear when the team completed any individual backlog item. This made it difficult to know when they had completed enough features for a suitable public release. I felt that measuring velocity for this team was meaningless, given the way they were writing and implementing stories, so I recommended they start again. We did that, starting with one, simple story running from end to end.

2 Planning Techniques

After completing the first few stories, we started with a simple set of agile planning techniques slanted towards Scrum, the agile flavor the company was adopting. My goal was to guide the team to deliver on a predictable schedule to help management plan releases with confidence. We started with these techniques:

1. Writing stories
2. Estimating in points
3. Product backlog

P. Abrahamsson, M. Marchesi, and G. Succi (Eds.): XP 2006, LNCS 4044, pp. 169–174, 2006.

4. Measuring velocity per calendar-month sprint
5. Sprint backlog
6. Projecting velocity using Yesterday's Weather[2]

In keeping with the spirit of the *YAGNI* principle[3], we began planning and tracking the project with this minimal toolbox. Within the first few days, it became clear that these techniques would not suffice on their own. One of the central assumptions of agile planning is that over time, teams are allowed to converge to a consistent pace otherwise it is difficult to project accurately the contents of a release. Well-known agile planning practices rely on statistical effects such as the central-limit theorem to simplify the planning process[1]. They recommend delivering small stories, estimated on a small scale of 1–3 points and assuming that the team's throughput in the next sprint will be the same as its throughput in the last sprint. They assume that the average cost of a story point converges quickly, but the kinds of instability this team experiences increases the variance of the cost of each story point completed. Two instabilities stand out in their effect on this team: availability of people and understanding of stories.

3   Team Continuity

This team endures unusually high **personnel instability**, having a higher member turnover rate than I have ever seen. Support works commonly pulls team members away from their primary project for days, even weeks at a time, with at most a few days' notice. The irony, of course, is that this causes even more support work on future releases. While losing people for extended periods is jarring enough, we cannot even rely on the availability of those "core members" of the team from day to day. Ongoing team members are commonly **distracted** with duties that fall outside the team's mandate, and to a degree I have never seen before. Early on, when I arrived to coach on a given day, it was common for at least one person not to be there who had been there the day before. I began to track on a whiteboard when each team member would be out of the room that day, and there would be 3–6 entries each day, making a team of 6–8 programmers act more like a highly unstable team of 3 or 4. A story might go through three different owners on its way to completion, allowing details to fall easily through the cracks.

These instabilities have caused precisely the problems one would expect. **Multitasking** at the individual level is known to lower productivity[4]. This team's imposed multitasking has had predictable results: their velocity remained entirely unpredictable. Even as we looked at how to solve this problem, we found another, more basic issue that made velocity a meaningless measure for this team.

4   Difficulty with Stories

When it first began working with stories, I counseled the team to keep stories small enough for a pair to complete in 3 days. Since they were learning test-driven development, this meant stories were at times impossibly small–much smaller than the size needed to represent tangible progress to the end user. This gave the team's analysts fits as they learned how to be good XP customers. We have combined story-writing workshops with sheer determination on their part to learn to deliver software with stories, including how to split larger ones into small, "vertical" slices, rather than into technical layers. Unfortunately, agreeing on how to write a story is only half the problem.

While struggling with what stories meant, the team has also struggled with the meaning of **done**. Recalling my first day on the job, I had asked the team's then-Scrum Master what one problem he would most like me to try to fix. He asked me to teach the team what it meant to be done a piece of work, including code, tests, customer acceptance and deployment. The team continues to struggle with this, most recently encountering problems trying to deploy their work. They had lost focus on the importance of deployment and fooled themselves into believing they had completed stories that did not work during sprint review demonstrations. This imprecise working definition of "done" contributes to the variance in velocity as the team effectively borrows time from future sprints to "clean up" the work from the previous sprint.

5   Fixing the Cost of a Story Point

In order to make some sense of how quickly the team is going, I knew we had to normalize the team's velocity somehow, taking into account its personnel instability and continuing distraction. I began simply, by counting the amount of time each person spent in the room each day, then keeping a running total along with the total of story points delivered. This resulted in data such as "25.5 people have delivered 8 points," meaning that the team delivered 8 points' worth of stories while expending the equivalent of 25.5 person-days' worth of effort. This allowed us to compute the team's velocity in terms of the number of actual people available, rather than assuming the size and availability of the team is stable. We found that indeed the number of available people-days varied so much from week to week that projections several sprints into the future could not be believed. We have brought this up repeatedly to management, but they have not yet made it a top priority to stabilize the team. Even after accounting for this difference, velocity per available person-day was still not converging, so the current Scrum Master began to look for a way to make sense of how the team was progressing.

In response to these problems, the current Scrum Master has developed a planning template that provides much-needed additional information with a low cost of operation. The team now counts both the number of story points completed and individual, daily team member availability, which the team calls "actuals." Each day at the daily scrum, the Scrum Master asks each team member how much time they spent working on the current project, rather than outside the project. Each person reports their time spent in $\frac{1}{2}$-day increments, from 0 to 2, in case someone works overtime. With this information, the Scrum Master is able to compute the cost of each story point in person-days, which he calls the team's **load factor.** He also notices trends in the availability of each person and uses this information in sprint pre-planning to present concerns to management about their degree of distraction in the previous sprint. During this meeting he gathers information from the managers of each team member about how available they can be expected to be in the coming sprint. With this information he *subjectively* adjusts the team's availability so he can project the team's velocity in the coming sprint. His calculations run as follows:

1. **maximum capacity** is working days × number of people.
2. **planned capacity** is maximum capacity − planned absences.
3. **actual capacity** is the sum of team actuals.
4. **availability factor** is actual capacity ÷ planned capacity.
5. **load factor** is points completed ÷ actual capacity.
6. **projected availability factor** is estimated by adjusting the previous availability factor in light of management's best guess about each person's availability for the coming sprint.
7. **projected load factor** is previous load factor × projected availability factor ÷ previous availability factor.
8. **sprint budget** (in points) is planned capacity ÷ projected load factor.

He generates along with the usual Story Burnup chart a *Resource Burnup*, which compares actual personnel availability not only to the maximum possible, but to what everyone had expected during sprint pre-planning. This feedback shows management with hard data one of the driving forces keeping the team's velocity down. As the Scrum Master told me, he wanted to turn a *gut-feel* discussion into a *fact-based* discussion, a sentiment clearly aligned with the tenets of adaptive planning. Much like the shape of a Story Burnup highlights certain problems with a team's performance, the shape of the Resource Burnup alongside the Story Burnup clarifies for all involved the effects of management's decisions to deploy people inside and outside the team. All this work clarifies the average cost of a story point, reducing the team's tendency to overcommit, one of the Scrum Master's key goals.

6   Fixing the Value of a Story Point

Aside from the usual periods of chaos associated with acquiring any new skill [6], the team has faced a serious challenge in using stories to help them deliver features: what it means to complete a story. In response to the growing number of submitted stories that were not accepted, or that failed after deployment, the team has tightened its acceptance criteria. It has encouraged the analysts to apply stricter standards when deciding whether to accept stories, which include "planned functionality must show demonstrable progress", "deployed functionality must pass all programmer and acceptance tests" and "shipped functionality must be validated by the customer or a proxy." While none of the items on their checklist are startling to the experienced agile practitioner, they represent a considerable step forward towards standardizing the value of a point. Holding each story to these standards will help stabilize the point as a currency of delivered feature so that calculating the cost of a story point, as we described in the previous section, has merit and is meaningful.

7   Conclusions and Future Work

The XP and Scrum literature strongly suggests simple planning tools, limited mainly to backlogs, story cards, points (or ideal hours) and Yesterday's Weather. It warns against teams complicating their planning process prematurely. While this team's planning process is certainly more involved than I am accustomed to seeing on agile teams, this complexity has certainly shown to be needed in light of an unusually volatile environment. The team has benefited from an increase in confidence in the plan from sprint to sprint and stakeholders now have clearer answers to the question, "Why are you not going faster?" The team is able to quantify the effects of their people deployment decisions on this project, which allows everyone involved to make the appropriate trade-offs more effectively. It will take some time for these improvements to manifest themselves in a more predictable velocity from sprint to sprint, but the team has taken a strong step in that direction by augmenting the agile planning toolbox **based on evidence that such changes were needed**.

8   Epilogue

At press time, not much has changed in the way that management assigns people to projects. The larger organization continues to struggle with individuals as bottlenecks, making it difficult to allow them to concentrate on new product development. These people continue to be the only ones who can handle certain support issues. As the organization adopts practices like automated acceptance testing and test-driven development more widely, it is hoped that the number of urgent support issues will decrease, allowing high-demand individuals to be distracted less and concentrate more on contributing to new development. While they are making small improvements in this direction, the organization remains a long way–years, perhaps–from being able to use velocity, points and Yesterday's Weather as the XP literature intends them to be used.

Acknowledgements

The author would like to thank Object Mentor, Inc. for setting up the opportunity to work with this particular team. At press time, our client had not yet approved the use of their name in this report; but in spite of this, I would like to thank the unnamed Scrum Master of this team for spending time with me to explain how he arrived at his current planning process. I would finally like to thank the members of the team for their hard work, their healthy skepticism and their receptiveness to strange ideas.

References

1. Mike Cohn, "Agile Estimating and Planning". Presented to SD West Expo 2004. http://www.mountaingoatsoftware.com/pres/sdwest040317_aep.pdf
2. http://c2.com/cgi/wiki?YesterdaysWeather
3. http://c2.com/cgi/wiki?YouArentGonnaNeedIt
4. "Executive Control of Cognitive Processes in Task Switching," Joshua S. Rubinstein, U.S. Federal Aviation Administration, Atlantic City, N.J.; David E. Meyer and Jeffrey E. Evans, University of Michigan, Ann Arbor, Mich., Journal of Experimental Psychology - Human Perception and Performance, Vol 27. No.4
5. Ken Schwaber, Mike Beedle. *Agile Management with Scrum*. Prentice Hall, 2001.
6. Gerald M. Weinberg, *Becoming a Technical Leader*. Dorset House, 1986.

Incorporating Learning and Expected Cost of Change in Prioritizing Features on Agile Projects

R. Scott Harris[1] and Mike Cohn[2]

[1] Montana State University–Billings
sharris@msubillings.edu
[2] Mountain Goat Software, LLC
mike@mountaingoatsoftware.com

Abstract. Very little has been written to date on how to prioritize and sequence the development of new features and capabilities on an agile software development project. Agile product managers have been advised to prioritize based on "business value." While this seems an appropriate goal, it is vague and provides little specific guidance. Our approach to optimizing "business value" uses tactics to minimize costs and maximize benefits through strategic learning. In order to provide specific and actionable advice to agile product managers, we present two guidelines. These guidelines are meant to provide a set of considerations and a process by which an agile product manager can achieve the goal of optimizing "business value" while recognizing that different product managers will vary in their notions of what "business value" is.

1 Introduction

Over the past seven years, agile software development processes such as Scrum [1], Extreme Programming [2], Feature-Driven Development [3], and DSDM [4] have emerged and their use has become much more prevalent. Central to these processes is a reliance upon emergent requirements and architecture. On an agile project, there is no upfront requirements engineering effort. Instead, the project begins with very high level requirements, often in the form of "user stories" [5]. The project team builds the software through a series of iterations and a detailed understanding of the requirements is sought only during the iteration in which software supporting those requirements is written.

A key tenet of agile processes is that these requirements are prioritized by a customer [2], customer team [6], or "product owner" [1] acting as a proxy for the end users of the intended system. Throughout this paper we will use the term product manager to represent this role independent of the specific agile process employed.

Product managers are given the relatively vague advice to prioritize based on "business value" [7][8]. Unfortunately, "business value" is both vague and broad whereas prioritization decision must be specific. Elsewhere, we have argued that product managers need to consider specific additional guidelines for prioritizing requirements on agile projects that lead to the fulfillment of maximizing "business value" [9]. This paper outlines those guidelines and discusses their implications for agile software development projects.

P. Abrahamsson, M. Marchesi, and G. Succi (Eds.): XP 2006, LNCS 4044, pp. 175 – 180, 2006.

2 The "Knowledge Problem" Facing Product Managers

Applying the work of Hayek [10], and Jensen and Meckling [11][12] to agile processes, we distinguish between "scientific knowledge" and "specific knowledge." The former is knowledge that is universal and can, for example, be taught in schools. In software development, knowledge of various programming languages and specific algorithms is "scientific knowledge." A challenge on any software development project is obtaining the "specific knowledge" regarding what the customer and users want. This is confounded by the fact that often users do not know precisely what they want and means not only that the customer and users must learn what they want, but that the product manager must also learn what they want.

Learning is the acquisition of knowledge. "Scientific knowledge" is learned outside of the immediate project while the bulk of "specific knowledge" must be learned during the development process and can be roughly divided into two categories: (a) learning what it is that users need and (b) learning the best way to develop software to meet those needs. Participatory design [13], essential use cases [14], and user stories [5] are techniques that have been developed to address the former; educated guessing and experimentation can be efficient ways to generate the latter. Because projects always will have emergent requirements that cannot be defined upfront, experimentation may be the cheapest way to learn what will work to satisfy a user's desires.

Others have studied the issue of prioritizing requirements and have concluded that Saaty's analytic hierarchy process (AHP) is "the most promising approach." [15][16][17]. Their focus is on upfront prioritization that implicitly assumes that ALL knowledge necessary to complete the project is given to the product manager at the beginning. Further, the focus has been on mechanics of the prioritization process and not on discussing the standards used that determine the priority order. Certainly for an agile project this is an overly simplistic view. Through its use of end-of-iteration reviews an agile team will learn more about the relative desirability of each feature and may even alter the criteria by which desirability is judged. This will (or should) alter any previous prioritization, thereby necessitating a new prioritization exercise. If it is anticipated that a significant amount of learning will take place as the project unfolds, expected repetitions of AHP or similar prioritization will be cost-prohibitive.

Our focus has been on how learning if project specific knowledge can affect product management. Any one-time upfront non-iterative approach to doing this ignores the crucial issue of learning. Therefore, we rejected the possibility of discovering or refining a static model to rank features in favor of suggesting guidelines for a dynamic process.

3 Guidelines for Prioritization

We define two issues of concern: "learning" and "the cost of change." We assert that early and low-cost acquisition of project specific knowledge and decreasing the cost of change positively impacts "business value." Though these two concepts are generally interdependent (i.e., the more one learns, the lower will be the cost of change), and related in a manner that depends on specific and particular features, we separate the issues to emphasize how to address each.

3.1 Guideline 1: Defer Features with High Expected Costs of Change

There are two aspects to what we call the expected cost of change for a feature. The first is the risk that a change will be needed; the second is the cost of making the change. The Expected Cost of Change (ECC) for a feature is the arithmetic product of the probability that change will be needed and the cost of making the change.

At any time on a project, every feature to be developed has an associated ECC. Each feature can be ordered from low to high. Those features that are both highly certain to remain unchanged throughout the project and that have a low cost of change will be the ones with the lowest ECC; those features that are very likely to change and that will impose a high cost to change will be the ones with the highest ECC. All others will fall in between.

When considering only ECC, we have demonstrated that total development cost can be minimized by developing features in order from lowest ECC first to highest ECC last [9]. This leads to our first guideline for prioritizing features.

It makes intuitive sense that if a product manager has a choice between developing features that are more likely to be changed and those that are less, it will lower overall expected costs if those that are more likely to be changed are deferred until more and better knowledge about how (or even whether) to develop them is gained. Additionally, one must consider the cost of change and defer developing those features that will be most costly to change. As the project progresses, project-specific learning will increase the probabilities that high cost-of-change features will be done correctly the first time thereby lowering the expectation of ever bearing that cost.

To implement this guideline, if one wants to plan to minimize the total expected cost of change over the scope of the project when learning takes place, sequential decisions will have to be based on (1) prioritizing activities that will have the greatest impact to lower the ECC of the deferred features and (2) deciding which remaining individual feature has the lowest ECC. In doing so, we should note that it is possible that these two criteria may not yield the same immediate priority activity. This possibility is discussed below.

Lowering the ECC of deferred features depends on the amount of specific knowledge that is generated during the immediate activity. Addressing that issue leads to our second guideline.

3.2 Guideline 2: Bring Forward Features That Generate Useful Knowledge

Just as different features will have different ECCs, each feature may have a different impact on learning. For example, developing one feature may greatly inform the product manager about the desirability of a feature set or the usability of the main user interface workflows. Developing different features will impart different amounts of knowledge to the developers creating the product. While the knowledge expected to be generated in any immediate activity will not affect the ECCs used in the prioritization calculations that decided features to develop in that immediate activity, it will affect the ECCs of delayed features. This means (a) the value of acquisition of knowledge can be viewed separately from the issue of ranking ECCs *given current levels of knowledge* and (b) "useful knowledge" may be prioritize by how it is expected to lower the ECC of the deferred features.

Prioritization based on these two guidelines may or may not agree regarding what the immediate next activity should be—in which case the product manager or agile team will have to employ additional criteria to sort out what should be done. However, the more important outcome is that prioritization using these guidelines will indicate a lot of features that should NOT be done immediately. Because the specification (and even the need for) the deferred features will be more nebulous than those to be developed immediately, learning that occurs in the immediate activity could—indeed, should—alter future prioritizations. Therefore, prioritization of features is only useful in deciding what should be done in the immediate next activity and what should be delayed. This leads to our third guideline.

3.3 Guideline 3: Incorporate New Learning Often, but Only to Decide What to Do Next

We cannot emphasize enough that learning is both important and a continuous and cumulative process that will change the priority of what is best to do next. This implies that a product manager and agile team must be nimble and constantly prepared to alter plans based on newly-acquired knowledge. Indeed, it should be clear that becoming wedded to a plan that is any longer than the next activity is both costly to formulate (if any time is spent on it) and could lead one in the wrong direction.

Because learning is a continuous process, decisions are both simplified and bounded. The sequence of decision-making only requires that one decide on the immediate project, user story, or feature to develop next and not concern oneself with the order of deferred activities. Sort the features into just two categories: what to do "now" versus "not now." Those features that are not done "now" will then be reevaluated for the next iteration when there is more knowledge upon which to base the evaluation. This is sequential planning where the "plan" is in the process and not the result. Without it, there is no agility in agile processes.

It should be noted that this guideline is consistent with and supports the agile preference for short iterations. While it is often useful to have a loosely-defined release plan covering the likely set of features to be delivered over the course of a small number of months, the detailed work of prioritizing and sequencing features should only be done an iteration at a time.

4 Implications

In this final section we consider an example of how these guidelines can be applied to the practical decisions of a project. These guidelines are presented to clients in both training classes and in consulting discussions. We have found it best to tell clients to perform a rough, initial prioritization of the desired features based on the nebulous "business value" provided by each. We stress that it is not necessary to prioritize all remaining features and normally guide product managers to plan two or three times as much as they expect the team to be able to complete in a single iteration. For these items product managers are given the guidance to think of expected cost of change and knowledge generated as "sliders" that can move a feature ahead or backward within the prioritization. Product managers then review the selected features sliding them forward and back based on considerations of expected cost of change and expected knowledge generated.

Following this process, we find that features with architectural implications that will not have exceptionally high expected costs of change but that will increase knowledge dramatically can justifiably be developed in an earlier iteration than would be justified by prioritization solely on business value. We have applied the guidelines in this way to support the early selection of a particular application server. We have also used this on projects to justify the higher prioritization of features that influenced design approaches for a security framework as well as internationalization and localization. Similarly, when applied in this way, the guidelines can support the earlier development of features that generate significant learning about the main metaphors of the user experience being designed.

On the other hand, features with a high expected cost of change that will provide little new knowledge, should be deferred. By deferring such features we put their design off to the point where our knowledge about the product and system has increased and to where we can presumably make better decisions about those features with an initially high expected cost of change. Further, since developing these features would not provide significant new knowledge to the product manager or team, we are able to defer these features while foregoing no opportunities to learn. We have applied the guidelines in this way to a project struggling to choose between three competing client technologies. This decision was deferred while maximizing the team's learning through the development of other features.

Through the application of these guidelines on commercial projects we are able to provide more guidance to agile product managers than the conventional "prioritize based on business value." We have found that instructing them to consider relative changes in the cost of change and, more importantly, the amount of knowledge generated by the development of a feature leads to better decisions. Most importantly, the guideline-based approach described here requires very little effort and allows the product manager to make easier decisions such as "what one thing should be done next" rather than the harder "what is the full set of priorities." This more iterative approach to prioritization acknowledges that learning occurs throughout a development project and is more consistent with the agile management of software development projects.

References

1. Schwaber, K., Beedle, M.: Agile Software Development with Scrum. Prentice-Hall, Upper Saddle River, NJ (2001).
2. Beck, K.: Extreme Programming Explained: Embrace change. Addison-Wesley, Upper Saddle River, NJ (1999).
3. Palmer, S.R., Felsing, J.M.: A Practical Guide to Feature-Driven Development. Addison-Wesley, Upper Saddle River, NJ (2002).
4. Stapleton, J.: DSDM: Business-Focused Development, 2nd edn. Pearson Education, Upper Saddle River, NJ (2003).
5. Cohn, M.: User Stories Applied for Agile Software Development. Addison-Wesley, Upper Saddle River, NJ (2004).
6. Poppendieck, T.: The Agile Customer's Toolkit at www.poppendieck.com.

7. Andrea, J.: An Agile Request For Proposal (RFP) Process. Proceedings of the Agile Development Conference, Salt Lake City, UT (2003) 152–161.
8. Augustine, S.: Great COTS! Implementing Packaged Software With Agility. Presentation at Agile Development Conference, Sydney, Australia (2004).
9. Harris, R.S., Cohn, M.: The Role of Learning and Expected Cost of Change in Prioritizing Features on Agile Projects, Ms (2006). Available at www.moutaingoatsoftware.com.
10. Hayak, F.A.: The Use of Knowledge in Society. American Economic Review, Vol. XXXV, No. 4 (Sept. 1945) 519–530.
11. Jensen, M.C., Meckling, W.H., Baker, G.P., Wruck, K.H.: Coordination, Control, and the Management of Organizations: Course Notes. Harvard Business School Working Paper #98-098 (October 17, 1999).
12. Jensen, M.C., Meckling, W.H.: Specific and General Knowledge, and Organizational Structure. In Werin, L., Wijkander, H. (eds.): Contract Economics. Blackwell, Oxford (1992). Also published in Journal of Applied Corporate Finance (Fall 1995) and Jensen, M.C.: Foundations of Organizational Strategy. Harvard University Press, Boston (1998).
13. Schuler, D., Namioka, A. (eds.): Participatory Design: Principles and practice. Erlbaum, Hillsdale, NJ (1993).
14. Constantine, L.L., Lockwood, L.A.D.: Software for Use. Addison-Wesley, Reading, MA (1999).
15. Karlsson, J., Ryan, K.: A Cost-Value Approach for Prioritizing Requirements. IEEE Software, Vol. 14, no. 5 (1997) 67–74.
16. Saaty, T.L.: The Analytic Hierarchy Process. McGraw-Hill, New York (1980).
17. Karlsson, J., Wohlin, C., Regnell, B.: An Evaluation of Methods for Prioritizing Software Requirements. Journal of Information and Software Technology, Vol. 39, No. 14–15 (1998) 939-947.

Automatic Changes Propagation

Maciej Dorsz

Projekty Bankowe Polsoft Sp. z o.o,
60-965 Poznań, Poland
maciej.dorsz@pbpolsoft.com.pl

Abstract. This article presents the Automatic Changes Propagation tool, which is used in one of Polish software companies. This system tries to solve the problem of introducing changes in deployed system versions when an error in the head version is found. The tool was created to speed the process of changes propagation for the application used in more than 12 Polish financial institutions. Unfortunately, the customers have different system versions and therefore it is not enough to correct only the newest one. Because the manual changes are time-consuming, monotonous and error-prone the automatic way is very desired. Moreover, the Automatic Changes Propagation tool prepares the application patches which are ready for deployment.

1 Introduction

About two years ago one of the Polish software company applications was deployed in more than 12 financial institutions. In this article it will be named: AMLPortal (Anti Money Laundering Portal). Unfortunately, almost all of the customers have got different versions of the application. Moreover, some of them have *live* and *test* environments. Therefore, the team developing this product had to organize CVS naming conventions to be able to manage each client's version [1]. Then Ant script was added to generate a ready to deploy application [2]. The product is written in Java, therefore Ant script simply generates .war file. With time, the problem of introducing changes in previous, but still used versions, appeared.

The problem of introducing changes will be shown on the example. Considering the case that one of the clients has 100 version, the second one 110 version and the third one 120 version of AMLPortal. Then, the testers find the error in the *head version* [2]. The product manager asks the programmers to correct the error. But, it means making the changes in the *head version*, and creating patches for: 100, 110 and 120 versions. In this example, the programmers have to implement the change in four system versions. But, as it was mentioned before, the system was sold to more than 12 clients...

Usually, the correction in all system versions is identical. Therefore, the programmers have to implement it in one of the versions and subsequently copy it to the others, and next, generate improved versions/patches. Such a task is quite monotonous, unnecessarily time-consuming and error-prone. After preparing the correction in one system version, the programmers have to retrieve the next one, find changed files,

P. Abrahamsson, M. Marchesi, and G. Succi (Eds.): XP 2006, LNCS 4044, pp. 181–185, 2006.

copy changes, build version, commit modifications, tag the versions and use Ant to create the patch. All the time, there is a risk that a programmer will postpone introducing the changes in system versions, and in fact he/she will forget about it. Therefore, a simple application for automatic changes propagation was proposed.

2   Automatic Changes Propagation

The Automatic Changes Propagation tool (ACP tool) makes a list of differences between two tags from CVS repository. Then ACP tool copies the changes, compiles versions, commits the changes and generates patches. In Fig. 1 the diagram outlining the process of automatic changes propagation is presented.

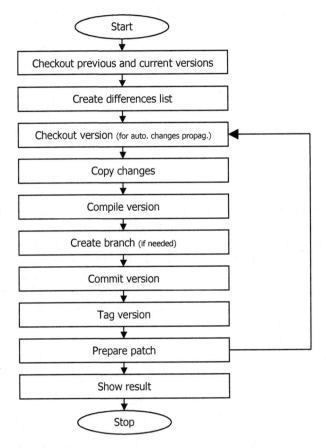

Fig. 1. The diagram outlining the process of automatic changes propagation

2.1   Marking the Current State

The computer scientist willing to introduce the change in order to correct the founded error has to tag the current system version.

2.2 Introducing the Correction

Next step, a computer scientist is obliged to comment the changed lines of code by his identifier and date or to mark the blocks of code with *start* and *end* pseudo tags. The last stage is to compile and test the code. If necessary changes to jUnit [3] tests should be added. Then the *commit* is done.

Unfortunately, to use 1.0 ACP tool version the programmer has to mark changed lines of code, Currently ASP tool is undergoing improvements in order to be able to recognize changes introduced by the programmer between system versions. It should be based on data stored in CVS repository without the necessity of commenting lines or blocks.

2.3 Using Automatic Changes Propagation Tool

The last, but not least stage, is to use ACP tool. The programmer sets system properties shown in Table 1.

Table 1. Some of the ACP properties

Property name	Value	Comment
previous_tag	125	#designates the system version with an error
current_tag	126	#designates the corrected version
patches_tags	100,110,120	#versions, to which the correction should be propagated and patches created
change_key	MD_010106	#change identification key
commit_comment	validation	#commit comment for ACP automatic commits
(...)		

Then the programmer runs ACP. ACP uses the CVS *checkout* command to obtain the versions marked with *previous_tag* and *current_tag*. Next, ACP supported by *cvs diff* creates the list of differences between those two versions. Finally, the programmer differences are filtered with *change_key* parameter. The differences are also stored in temp file named: differences_file.txt.

The next stage concerns retrieving subsequent system versions, as given in *patches_tags* parameter. For each version CVS command *checkout* is used. Next, ACP tool propagates changes by placing them according to differences list. In the end, ACP uses Ant script to compile created version. If the build result is 'success' the branch for the version is created and the changed files are *commited* to that branch. Then, the Ant script is used to generate .war file and patch is ready for deployment. If the build result is 'failed' the changes are not *commited* and the programmer must introduce changes manually. It may happen if the versions are too much different. Fig. 2 shows the example of the possible positive propagation results.

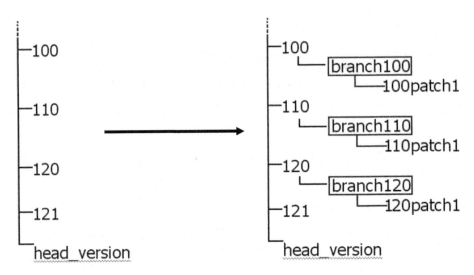

Fig. 2. The CVS result of the usage of Automatic Changes Propagation tool

It should be stated that for AMLPortal patch means the whole system version, but the patch is created in order to correct errors. Therefore, changes in patches are usually small, though patches are whole .war files.

3   ASP in Practice

The Automatic Changes Propagation tool can be used for the propagation of changes in one line of code, or the changes of one line into a block or a block into one line. Moreover, a number of changes may be introduced in one file. However, ASP can propagate the change only when it is unambiguous. It means that if there are two lines in one file which are equal, and one of the was modified by the programmer, the change won't be introduced automatically.

ASP tool is used only in one of Polish companies, whether it will be an Open Source application has not been decided yet. It would be not difficult to adapt ASP to another environments. To use it one needs CVS repository, clearly defined subsequent version tag conventions and Ant script to compile and generate versions.

The ASP tool can be used to propagate changes: the changes connected with errors, but also ones related to new functionality or source file documentation. In AMLPortal there is one *head version*, and new functionality is added only to it. However, in systems developed in many branches ASP tool could help to propagate new functionality changes automatically.

4   Summary

This article presents ACP tool, which allows one to automatically propagate changes. The changes are created on the basis of two different versions. Next, after checking that the compilation process goes smoothly, branches and patches are created.

The next development phase for ACP tool means the development of GUI side as well as improving the algorithm for propagating changes. Moreover, ASP should be able to create differences list on the data stored in CVS and to free the computer scientists from adding comments to all changed lines or blocks of code. Moreover, the better mechanism for coping changes is being considered.

Acknowledgment

The work has been supported by the Rector of Poznan University of Technology as a research grant BW/91-429.

References

1. http://www.nongnu.org/cvs/
2. http://ant.apache.org/
3. http://junit.sourceforge.net/

Making Fit / FitNesse Appropriate for Biomedical Engineering Research

Jingwen Chen[1], Michael Smith[1], Adam Geras[1,2], and James Miller[3]

[1] Electrical and Computer Engineering, University of Calgary,
Calgary, Alberta, Canada T2N 1N4
{JinChen, SmithMR}@ucalgary.ca
[2] Ideca, Calgary, Alberta, Canada
AGeras@ucalgary.ca
[3] Electrical and Computer Engineering, University of Alberta,
Edmonton, Alberta, Canada T6G 2V4
JM@ece.ualberta.ca

Abstract. A prototype test driven development tool for embedded systems has been developed with hardware-oriented extensions to *CPPUnitLite*. However *xUnit* tests are written in the language of the solution; problematic in the development of biomedical instruments as the customer, the "doctor", does not have "extensive knowledge of the domain". The biomedical application is often prototyped within *MATLAB* before movement down to the "plumbing level" on a high-speed, highly parallel, processor to meet the requirement for real-time application in a safe and secure manner "in the surgical theatre" or "on the ward". A long term research goal is an investigation of how to gain, as with standard business desktop system, the full advantage of using *Fit* and *FitNesse* as communication tools under these circumstances. We demonstrate the practical application of using indirection to permit a single set of *Fit* tests for both *MATLAB* and embedded system verification for a biomedical instrument.

1 Introduction

Imagine you are developing in a biomedical engineering environment where a reliable, high performance, medical instrument must be produced "for the surgical theatre" or "on the ward"! Signal processing algorithms will be needed to monitor, analyze and report on patient life signs. You know that some of the required algorithms have already been developed in a research laboratory (using *MATLAB*). These algorithms need to be migrated to, and then validated on, an embedded platform using a combination of *C++* and assembly code in order to meet strict time constraints.

Even in such an environment, you will still want to undertake unit testing, but now the "testing requirements" differ significantly from the standard "desktop" business problem. There have been a number of notable efforts in migrating *Agile* ideas into the embedded environment [*e.g.* 1]. However using *xUnit* embedded tools, such as *E-TDDunit* [2], to support *Agile* development is problematic in a biomedical engineering environment. The *xUnit* concept, by design, requires tests written in the language of the solution. But now this language involves *MATLAB, C++* and assembly

P. Abrahamsson, M. Marchesi, and G. Succi (Eds.): XP 2006, LNCS 4044, pp. 186–190, 2006.
© Springer-Verlag Berlin Heidelberg 2006

code. However the exploration of medical instrument development is more than just a question of unit tests since, as with the standard business customer, the bio-medical engineering customer (the "doctor") just does not have that sort of experience level in assist in product development at such a level.

Our long term research direction is to explore how to take full advantage of the *Agile Fit* [3] and *FitNesse* [4] concepts in a biomedical engineering research environment where the tables may include combinations of image comparisons, timing diagrams, image processing algorithm and data mining results together with textual information from physicians and other medical experts. However, a key short term goal is to demonstrate a practical approach to allow a single suite of such *Fit* tests to be used by "doctor" customer validation of work of the original MATLAB development code and the commercialization of such code on the medical instrument (embedded system). This paper details our experiences with taking the theoretical concept of using *Fit* simultaneously in two different development environments and demonstrates the practicality and limitations of such an approach.

2 *Fit* and *FitNesse* in a Biomedical Engineering Environment

Our long term goal is to analyze (in real-time) a series of images coming from a magnetic resonance imaging scanner used to determine cerebral perfusion parameters (blood flow) for patients suffering from stroke. Stroke is a major disabler and killer across the world; and its financial impact is staggering. Algorithms from such a study involve deconvolution, signal aliasing problems and modeling techniques, with everything running at full speed on highly parallel processors; involving issues beyond the scope of a five page report. We will therefore, for illustrative purposes, choose a greatly simplified device to illustrate some of the issues that must be overcome of communicating using *Fit* when product development occurring in *MATLAB,* C++ and assembly code.

Assume that the biomedical application requires the determination of the temperature of a doctor's stethoscope. Cold stethoscopes are a common complaint received from patients! The basic hardware involves using a *TMP03* thermal sensor [5] which produces a voltage pulse (*voltWidth*) whose width is proportional to temperature. Conversion from pulse width to actual temperature is to be performed using a function (*CalculateTemperature( )*) running on an embedded system powered by a Black-Fin (ADSP-BF533) processor using the VDK real-time operating system [5].

Fig.1 provides an overview of the biomedical *Fit / FitNesse* test and development system. The customer tests are described through tables stored on a Wiki-page. The *Runner* takes the test data and fixture name, and passes these to the *FitServer* for execution. Customized fixtures are available to use the *MATLAB* API to start and run the *MATLAB* engine to validate the *MATLAB* code associated with the code (*ConvertTemperature.m*). Additional customized fixtures are available for running the code on the embedded platform from the host computer. For this example, this required the development of fixtures to use the Visual DSP development environment (VDSP IDDE) [6] to compile code, download and run that code (*ConvertTemperature.dxe*) on the embedded platform over a communication link.

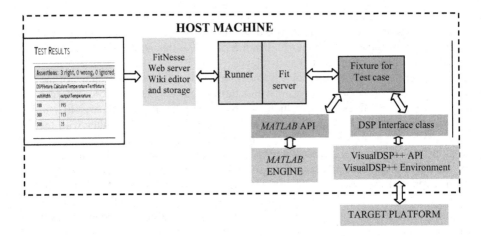

Fig. 1. Block diagram of a test environment demonstrating how *Fit* fixtures can be used to run customer tests in both the *MATLAB* environment and on an external embedded target platform

3   Using *Fit* Within a Biomedical Research Development Environment

There are a number of stages the developer must work through to use the proposed *Fit* approach to designing, developing and testing a biomedical engineering product.

1. Consulting with the customer to produce *Fit* test tables as part of development specification.
2. Developing standard fixtures to use the test data from the test tables.
3. Validating the linkage between the code under test and *Fit* through a method stub running in the same environment as *Fit / Fitnesse*.
4. Extending the method stub to use the *MATLAB* API to pass the test table data to the *MATLAB* development environment.
5. In *MATLAB*, developing the code to meet the tests.
6. Extending the method stub to use the embedded development environment's API to pass the test table data (over a communications link) to the external device.
7. This is combined with using the *MATLAB* code as a template to develop the necessary C++ and assembly code to pass the known functional tests, and any additional non-functional tests. Key test validation issue – *double precision floats MATLAB* variables become *fixed length integer* for speed on the embedded system.

Stage 1: Assume that the developer and customer have worked together to provide a two column test table (**DSPFixture.CalculateTemperatureTestFixture**) that will be used to validate the function *ConvertTemperature( )*. The columns are *voltWidth*, detailing input values from the temperature device, and *Temperature,* the expected results.

Stage 2: Standard fixture components can be used for all three platforms

```
#include "necessary_Fit_includes.h"
class CalculateTemperatureTestFixture: public ColumnFixture {
// Make voltWidth variable and outputTemperature( ) function known to Fitserver
    public: explicit CalculateTemperatureTestFixture (void){
        PUBLISH(CalculateTemperatureTestFixture, unsigned, voltWidth);
        PUBLISH(CalculateTemperatureTestFixture, float, outputTemperature);
    }
    private: unsigned voltWidth;
    float outputTemperature (void){ // Call the function to calculate temperature
        return(CalculateTemperature (voltWidth));
    }
};
```

Stage 3: Validation of the fixture code through a method stub

```
float CalculateTemperature (unsigned voltWidth){
    // Necessary code to simulate calculation of temperature using voltWidth
    return dummy_temperature;
}
```

Stage 4: Extending the method stub to activate the *MATLAB* Engine requires a series of calls through the *MATLAB* API to first activate, then to transfer data to global data within the *MATLAB* environment, run the code and finally retrieve the result.

```
#include "API_interface.h"        // API Environment
float CalculateTemperature (unsigned voltWidth) {
// Create an API application project, then build the code.
    API_Interface  API
    API.CreateADSPApplicationProject ( );
    API.BuildAndLoadProgram ( );
// Transfer voltWidth value. Use a communication link on embedded system
    API.PUBLISH (voltWidth,"API_voltWidth");
    API.RunProgram ( );        // Run the code
// Read (transfer) the test result (From embedded platform back over the COM link)
    float outputTemperature = API.PUBLISH ("API_Temperature");
    return outputTemperature;
}
```

Stage 5: The reader is referred to [6] for a comprehensive example of developing *MATLAB* algorithms for an assisted hearing device using *Fit*.

Stages 6 and 7: Extending the method stub to activate the embedded platform is equivalent to **Stage 4** except this stage uses the VDSP embedded API rather than the *MATLAB* API. The communication between the fixture (on the host machine) and the external embedded platform (Blackfin ADSP-BF533) is through global variables.

```
.byte4 _Embed_voltWidth, _Embed_Temperature; // global variables changed by Fit
_main:                                        // PUBLISHed over COM link
```

```
// Pass global variable as a parameter to CalculateTemperature( )
P0.L =  lo(_Embed_voltWidth);     P0.H =  hi(_Embed_voltWidth);
R0 = [P0];
CALL _CalculateTemperature;   // Perform required function
// Prepare result from Calculate Temperature( ) for Fit access over COM link
P0.L =  lo(_Embed_Temperature); P0.H =  hi(_Embed_Temperature);
[P0] = R0;
RTS;
```

4 Discussion and Conclusion

We have demonstrated a working *Agile* tool with *Fit* fixtures modifications that permit one set of *Fit* tables, constructed by the biomedical customer and technical developer, to be used to test both *MATLAB* developed code and commercialized embedded code. However based on this initial experience, many driver extensions are needed to make the approach practical. The development of customized column fixtures is one possible solution. An alternative is to take a different approach where, instead of direct interfacing of *Fit* and *FitNesse* into these environments, fixtures are developed to allow use of the *xUnit* tools *MATLABUnit* [*e.g.* 7] and *E-TDDUnit* [2]. Financial support was provided by University of Calgary, Analog Devices and the Natural Sciences and Engineering Council of Canada through a Collaborative Research and Development grant. MRS is Analog Devices University Ambassador.

References

1. Van Schooenderwoert, N., Morsicato, R.: Taming the Embedded Tiger – Agile Test Techniques for Embedded Software, Agile Development Conference (2004) 120 – 126.
2. Smith, M, Kwan, A., Martin, A., Miller, J.: E-TDD – Embedded Test Driven Development: A Tool for Hardware-Software Co-design, 6th International Conference, XP 2005, Sheffield, UK (2005) 145 – 153.
3. Ward Cunningham:Fit: Framework for Integrated Test (2002): fit.c2.com/wiki.cgi?FrameworkHistory (Accessed, January, 2006).
4. FitNesse: http://fitnesse.org/FitNesse.UserGuide (Accessed, January, 2006).
5. Analog Devices: www.analog.com/processors (Accessed January 2006).
6. Geras, A.: Fit and MatLab   http://www.ucalgary.ca/~ageras/testml/ (Accessed, January 2006)
7. Dohmke, T. *mlUnit*, thomas.dohmke.de/en/projects/mlunit (Accessed November, 2005)

Sprint Driven Development: Agile Methodologies in a Distributed Open Source Project (PyPy)

Beatrice Düring

Change Maker, Järntorget 3, 413 04, Gothenburg, Sweden
bea@changemaker.nu

Abstract. This paper describes the practices created, adopted and evolved in a Distributed Open Source Project (PyPy) project. PyPy is a hybrid project, combining the different aspects of Agile and Distributed Development within the context of an Open Source community. The project is partially funded by the European Commission through the 6th Framework Program. Influences and adoptions of techniques such as "sprinting" has been a core balancing act for the project since its inception. "Sprints" in the Python community differs from the Scrum version of sprints and in this paper we will present how this evolved agile method acts as a primary method of quality assuring the aspects of distributed and dispersed work style of the PyPy project and insures an ongoing interaction with the Open Source aspects of the project.

1 Introduction

There are different methodologies and practices in use in PyPy – such as Agile and Distributed development, F/OSS culture and the management practices in use in EU-projects in the 6th Framework Program. It should be noted that most of the techniques in use in the PyPy project evolved into practice inspired by success stories from other projects in the F/OSS community and "word-by-mouth". It has rarely been the case that methodologies have been researched and applied through formalized decision procedures in the PyPy project. Rather the approach has been that of trial and error and customizing certain practices to fit the needs of the project when actual need arose.

PyPy has the goal of implementing a highly flexible and fast Python implementation written in Python. The project received EU-funding 1 December 2004 and will continue for two years. The partial funded part of the project concists of 14 work packages and 58 deliverables. A consortium of 8 partners was constructed to fullfil the contract (for more information about the project, see http://codespeak. net/pypy, www.pypy.org).

2 Agile Influences

Within the Agile development portfolio there are a multitude of techniques, tracing it´s roots to the software experiences of the 70´s and 80´s. During the late 90´s the first agile development methodologies were published such as eXtreme Programming,

P. Abrahamsson, M. Marchesi, and G. Succi (Eds.): XP 2006, LNCS 4044, pp. 191 – 195, 2006.

Crystal and others and the collaboration between the instigators and authors resulted in the Agile Manifesto, published 2001.

The values stated in the Agile Manifesto (2001), stating the following central traits for Agile Development:

* Individuals and interactions over processes and tools
* Working software over comprehensive documentation
* Customer collaboration over contract negotiation
* Responding to change over following a plan

Research on two established Agile Development Methodologies, eXtreme Programming and Scrum shows large similarities between practices used in PyPy and practices advocated in these methodologies, although there are also crucial differences based on the unique environment of the PyPy project.

In Scrum the following similarities can be found with the PyPy project regarding practices and processes - the key one being "sprints" [1]. Although none of the roles in Scrum or documentation such as Product Backlog and Sprint Backlog are implemented in PyPy sprints. (see more on this in Section 3. Sprint Driven Development).

In eXtreme programming the following practices can be found which are also employed in the PyPy project:

* simple design
* testing
* refactoring
* pair programming
* collective ownership
* continuous integration
* coding standard
* just rules

The PyPy project has been "test-driven" from the very start and it has employed automated test suites for language compliance tests (Python) and unit tests. This test framework together with an extensive "coding style" guide (covering style of code, style of tests, naming conventions etc) and version control support (Subversion) created the platform that allows for continuous integration into the code base. During sprints "pair programming" is used systematically - not only between core developers sharing an interest in a specific task but also for mentoring newcomers by pairing them with core developers.

The aspects of "simple design" can be found within the Python community (Zen of Python) as well as being supported by the iterative approach being used within PyPy (iterations from the end of one sprint until the end of the next sprint - ca 6 weeks). Some PyPy-specific rules regarding design and testing such as focusing on rapidly achieving functioning semantics and concepts and then, during refactoring focus more on optimization of the working code.

As for the aspects of "collective ownership" and "just rules", the PyPy development process is open for anyone who is interested in participating:

• The sprints are open for any developers interested in PyPy and Python (although experience as well as costs could be limiting factors).

- The automated framework for testing and version controls allows for a more relaxed approach regarding distributing commit rights to newcomers.
- The open and transparent communication in the development process (on line via mailing lists and IRC as well as during sprints)
- The accessability of the core developers for answering questions and mentoring (on line via mailing lists and IRC as well as during sprints)
- The weekly synchronization meetings via IRC, open for all interested developers to participate
- The documentation and tutorials available on line

These are all key factors, creating and maintaining an atmosphere of "collective ownership". This has also been crucial for evolving the community of PyPy from a few core developers to almost 350 subscribers to the development list as well as increasing the amount of developers with commit rights to access and make changes to the code base from a few core developers to almost 50 people (during the period of 2003 to 2006).

Some of the practices in eXtreme programming have created challenges in the PyPy development environment:

* small/short releases
* 40 hour week
* on site customer
* open workspace
* pair programming

The shared denominator regarding these challenges is that they in most cases are tied to the fact that PyPy is working distributed/dispersed as well as agile. During sprints the work style is both developer-driven, self organized as well as collaborative (pair programming and open workplace). Between sprints this process remains developer driven and self organized but the open workspace shifts into virtual workspaces.

If the community can be viewed as the actual customers (developers interested in a flexible and fast Python implementation, written in Python) then there is constant communication regarding prioritized functionality in current iterations and upcoming ones (both during sprints and in between sprints – on line). Due to both the community interaction as well as the continuous integration of code (as it is being written) there have only been 3 major releases in the PyPy project during the period February 2003 and October 2005.

The reason for having larger releases and so few during this period was that PyPy is a language implementation project (not application level) and this created the need to reach a "stable" platform (release 0.6, May 2005). After this was achieved two more releases followed quickly (release 0.7 August 2005.

Aspects such as process terminology found in eXtreme Programming are not used in the PyPy project (planning game and metaphors) as well as the phases and roles specific to XP.

A open question regarding the comparison of practices in eXtreme Programming and those employed in the PyPy project is the reference to Kent Beck´s focus on teams being situated physically close in order to facilitate understanding and communication. This is an non-negotiable core aspect of XP, although Beck himself states that you might still be working geographically distributed and XP-style if it concerns "two teams working on related project with limited interaction" [2].

In the case of PyPy this is made more complicated because not only are the core developers working distributed, sometimes in pairs of two at the same location - they are also working dispersed - as is the rest of the PyPy community. The main strategy in PyPy to handle this challenge and risk to the development process is to sprint systematically, using sprints not only for iteration purposes but also to provide an accelerated and collaborative physical practice.

The question, whether this sprint driven approach in a distributed F/OSS team still would be considered as being within the scope of eXtreme Programming, is an open one and should be studied together with other aspects of hybrid practices evolving around Agile, Distributed and F/OSS teams.

3 Sprint Driven Development

PyPy first started during a one-week meeting, a *"sprint"*, held at Trillke-Gut in Hildesheim February 2003. The sprint was inspired by practices used by other Python projects such as Zope3. Originally the sprint methodology used in the Python community grew from practices applied by the Zope Corporation. Their definition of a sprint was: *"two-day or three-day focused development session, in which developers pair off together in a room and focus on building a particular subsystem"* [3]. Inspired by practices such as pair programming in eXtreme Programming sprints were first used within the commercial work and later tried and used within the Open Source context around Zope development. There seems to be no specific sources relating the Zope/Python version of sprinting to the terminology used in Scrum, signifying an iteration around a specific increment – lasting up to a month [4].

The Zope sprint approach focuses indeed on just writing code and has one "formal" role tied to it – the role of the "coach". The coach prepares the content of the sprint and manages and tracks the work during the sprint. Tutorials are done during the first day and the suggested limit of people is to be no more than 10 people participating during a sprint.

The method evolved rapidly and sprints done in connection to conferences were more "open" and tutorial oriented, as opposed to sprints were only experienced developers in the Zope domain participated. Sprinting spread through the Python community and today almost all Python projects in the Python Open Source community sprint at least once every year.

Sprinting up to a week became the initial driving factor in developing the code base and the community/people around PyPy.   Sprints gave the opportunity to both help, participate and influence the ideas within PyPy. PyPy sprints was then as now a developer driven effort and the role of coaches are not in use in PyPy. Sprint preparation and planning as well as the actual organizing rotated between the developers, using their contacts and networks to identify locations and facilities to sprint in to as low costs as possible for both travels and accommodation for the sprint attendants. Already from the start the strategy to travel and sprint, visiting different local communities and "recruiting" contribution was a conscious one – also for the reason of "justly" distribute the load of travel costs in the developer community.

Why did PyPy choose sprinting as a key technique in the beginning of the project? It is a method that fits distributed teams well because it gets the team focused around visible challenging goals while working collaboratively (pair-programming, status meetings, discussions etc) as well as accelerated (short increments and tasks, "doing" and testing instead of long startups of planning and requirement gathering).   This means that most of the time a sprint is a great way of getting results and getting new people acquainted - a good method for dissemination of knowledge and learning within the team.

References

[1] "Agile project management with Scrum", Ken Schwaber, Microsoft Professional 2004
[2] "eXtreme programming explained", Kent Beck, Cynthia Andres, 1999
[3] http://www.zopemag.com/Guides/miniGuide_ZopeSprinting.html
[4] "Agile project management with Scrum", Ken Schwaber, Microsoft Professional 2004

Storytelling in Interaction: Agility in Practice

Johanna Hunt, Pablo Romero, and Judith Good

University of Sussex, UK

1 Author Summary

Johanna Hunt is a first year DPhil researcher and Associate Tutor at the University of Sussex, and a Research Assistant in Algorithms at the University of Hertfordshire.

Her research is concerned with investigating the community of Agile Systems practitioners. She is particularly looking at notions of identity, boundary, communication and space as demonstrable in conversational storytelling and personal narratives from this practitioner-group.

2 Extended Abstract

One of the stated beliefs common to practitioners of all the agile methodologies is that "the most efficient and effective method of conveying information to and within a development team is face-to-face conversation."[1] This view is pervasive throughout Agile Systems techniques and approaches.

There is starting to be some interest and in-depth investigation into the nature of programmer interaction and dialogue within the case of pair-programming [2] as well as larger scale ethnographic studies of XP practice [10]. Although interesting metaphoric features have already been found in the language of expert software developers [12][8][7], more detailed qualitative analysis can also be made into the nature of such communication.

Narrative analysis [9] is an in-depth qualitative analysis methodology, and focuses on the ways in which people make and use stories to interpret the world. Storytelling and its role for communicating social tacit knowledge and historical and organisational identity is well recognised [4]. So far there are fairly few cases where narrative analysis has been applied to Information Systems (an analysis of these are given in Wagner [11]), but it is beginning to find popularity within the information systems community as it has proved particularly useful when considering tacit knowledge transfer and related communication issues, especially during periods of organisational change [1][5].

Narratives are considered to be social products within specific contexts, and an interpretive device through which people communicate knowledge and define their own identity. It is arguable that the most basic and prevalent form of narrative arises as the product of ordinary conversation [6]. As Gregori-Signes [3] points out "We tell stories to each other as a means of packaging experience in cognitively and effectively coherent ways, or [...] as a way to test the

---

[1] http://agilemanifesto.org/principles.html

P. Abrahamsson, M. Marchesi, and G. Succi (Eds.): XP 2006, LNCS 4044, pp. 196–197, 2006.

borderlines between the exceptional and the ordinary." Conversational stories are "negotiable and collaboratively developed between more than one speaker – although one speaker usually has a predominant role."

A pilot study, incorporating narrative interviews supported by observational data, of a small software development company in the South of England has recently been conducted. Preliminary analysis supports the view that this qualitative technique, when further applied to the community of Agile Systems developers, will provide potentially interesting results.

Acknowledgements

This work is being conducted in the Informatics Department at the University of Sussex under the supervision of Pablo Romero and Judith Good.

References

1. Rosio Alvarez and Jacqueline Urla. Tell me a good story: Using narrative analysis to examine information requirements interviews during an erp implementation. *The Data Base for Advances in Information Systems*, 33(1):38–52, 2002.
2. S. Bryant. Double trouble: Mixing qualitative and quantitative methods in the study of extreme programmers. In *VL/HCC*, pages 55–61, 2004.
3. Carmen Gregori-Signes. Conversational storytelling (website lecture notes 2004), 2005. Retrieved 10/11/2005, 2005, from the World Wide Web: http://www.uv.es/g̃regoric/Clases/CA_2004/4b_storyCA_04.doc.
4. Helena Karasti, Karen S. Baker, and Geoffrey C. Bowker. Ecological storytelling and collaborative scientific activities. *ACM SIGGROUP Bulletin*, 23(2):29–30, 2002.
5. Charlotte Linde. Narrative and social tacit knowledge. *Journal of Knowledge Management*, 5(2):160–170, 2001.
6. Elinor Ochs. Narrative. In Teun van Dijk, editor, *Discourse as Structure and Process*, pages 185–207. Sage, London, 1997.
7. M. Petre. Team coordination through externalised mental imagery. *International Journal of Human-Computer Studies*, 61(2):205–218, 2004.
8. Marian Petre and Alan F. Blackwell. Mental imagery in program design and visual programming. *International Journal of Human-Computer Studies*, 51(1):7–30, 1999.
9. C. Reissman. *Narrative Analysis*, volume 30 of *Qualitative Research Methods*. Sage, London, 1993.
10. Helen Sharp and Hugh Robinson. An ethnographic study of xp practice. *Empirical Software Engineering*, 9(4):353–375, 2004.
11. Erica L. Wagner. Interconnecting information systems narrative research: An end-to-end approach for process-oriented field studies. *Global and Organizational Discourse about Information Technology*, pages 419–435, 2002.
12. Julian Weitzenfeld, Tom Reidl, Charles Chubb, and Jared Freeman. The use of cross-domain language by expert software developers. *Journal of Metaphor and Symbolic Activity*, 7(3-4):185–195, 1992.

Towards an Agile Process for Building Software Product Lines

Richard F. Paige, Xiaochen Wang, Zoë R. Stephenson, and Phillip J. Brooke

Department of Computer Science, University of York, UK
xcwang1981@yahoo.co.uk, {paige, zoe}@cs.york.ac.uk
School of Computing, University of Teesside, UK
p.j.brooke@tees.ac.uk

Abstract. Software product lines are sets of software systems that share common features. Product lines are built as if they were a family of products, identifying those features that change and those that can be reused. There is an evident incompatibility between the requirements of software product lines and agile practices. We report on experiments that used Feature-Driven Development to build software product lines, and describe the minor extensions that were useful for developing software product lines.

Software product lines (SPL) [4] are collections of software systems that share a common set of *features*. SPLs are an emerging software paradigm allowing for large-scale reuse for companies, since software is built as if it were a *family* of products rather than an individual product. A family is a set of products that have common aspects and predicted variability [4]. Once an SPL has been developed, the process of *software development* is one of tailoring and configuring a product line, rather than building a product wholesale. Examples of products that have been considered as SPLs include engine controllers, type managers, and anti-lock braking systems. Noteworthy amongst many of these systems is their embedded nature.

SPL development is usually a time-consuming and extremely expensive process. Key challenges include identifying features and variation points, capturing the product line architecture, and managing the configuration process. Approaches used for developing SPLs are typically architecture-based, particularly those for safety critical systems such as aero-engine controllers [5]. Models are considered helpful to assist in the feature identification process and in highlighting configurations.

Agile development methods, such as Feature-Driven Development (FDD) [3], have evolved to meet a need for increased productivity, while dealing with challenges such as changing requirements. SPL methods have evolved to increase productivity, ideally via increased reuse. However, there is an apparent incompatibility between agile practices, and what is needed to develop SPLs. In particular,

- The agile principle of emphasising simplicity, and implementing functionality that satisfies the current instead of future requirements, goes against the requirement to support different variation points and configurations in SPLs.
- The agile principle of delivering working software frequently contrasts with the substantial up-front development time for an SPL in order to provide infrastructure, which can thereafter be configured and deployed.

P. Abrahamsson, M. Marchesi, and G. Succi (Eds.): XP 2006, LNCS 4044, pp. 198–199, 2006.

Despite these apparent incompatibilities, we believe that the SPL development process can benefit from agile development techniques. To evaluate this, we have carried out several experiments in using an agile process to build a SPL [1]. Our approach was to first assess existing agile processes to determine which might provide suitable practices for identifying SPL features, configurations, and variation points. We selected FDD because of its lightweight modelling capabilities, and because it provided substantial guidance on identifying system features, something that must also be done in SPL development. We then applied FDD directly to building a microwave oven software product line. Variants of a microwave considered included one with only a simple cooking facility, one with a weight sensor to gauge temperature and cooking time, and one with built-in recipes.

We encountered two difficulties in applying FDD to building SPLs: integrating SPL architecture design into FDD; and incorporating component development in FDD. An architectural description is important for SPL development since it is a part of the SPL core assets and is reused by product development. Architecture and component development were integrated into FDD with minor extensions to the overall process; architecture is considered incrementally, following [6], and SPL variations are generated as a result of the agile refactoring practice.

As a result of this case study, we constructed an extension to FDD. Two new phases were added: one for consideration of architecture (based on the Architectural Tradeoff Method [2]) and one for SPL component design. An argument as to why this remains an agile process is laid out in detail in [1], but a key point of note is that the architectural and component models that are produced are the simplest and smallest that help in identifying variation points in SPL development.

We then applied the revised process to a further case study - an e-commerce system - in order to validate and further explore the approach. Our observations are that an agile process like FDD, which explicitly considers features as first-class artifacts in system development, is well-suited to SPL development, as long as additional consideration of SPL architecture and SPL component design is added to the approach. Full details of the case studies can be found in [1].

References

1. X. Wang. Towards an Agile Method for Building Software Product Lines, MSc Thesis, University of York, UK, September 2005.
2. L. Bass et al. *Software Architecture in Practice* (2nd edition), AWL, 2003.
3. S. Palmer and J. Felsing. *A Practical Guide to Feature-Driven Development*, Prentice-Hall, 2002.
4. D. Weiss. *Software Product Line Engineering*, AWL, 1999.
5. Z.R. Stephenson. *Change Management in Families of Safety Critical Systems*, PhD Thesis, University of York, UK, 2003.
6. H. Chivers, R.F. Paige, and X. Ge. Agile Security via an Incremental Security Architecture. *Proc. XP 2005*, LNCS 3556, Springer-Verlag, June 2005.

Extending the Embedded System
E-TDDunit Test Driven Development Tool
for Development of a
Real Time Video Security System Prototype

Steven Daeninck[1], Michael Smith[2], James Miller[3], and Linda Ko[2]

[1] NovAtel Inc., Calgary, Alberta, Canada T2E 8S5
SRDaeninck@shaw.ca
[2] Electrical and Computer Engineering, University of Calgary,
Calgary, Alberta, Canada T2N 1N4
SmithMR@ucalgary.ca
[3] Electrical and Computer Engineering, University of Alberta,
Edmonton, Alberta, Canada T6G 2V4
JM@ece.ualberta.ca

Despite the existence of 75 "different" *xUNIT* frameworks, their domain of application differs only in the programming language, compiler or operating system supported. If one is working in the embedded world, unit testing is still needed, but now our "testing requirements" differ significantly from the testing framework needed for the desktop world. Embedded systems often have significant non-functional requirements, which demand validation at the unit level. In addition, they interact intimately with hardware resources and often have only very limited input/output capabilities – imagine a *xUNIT* framework where printing to the screen is a technical challenge!

There have been a number of notable efforts in migrating Agile ideas into the embedded environment but only one or two intrepid practitioners have braved this new domain deep down towards and into the "plumbing" layer of small embedded systems. The purpose of this abstract is to demonstrate extensions of an embedded system test driven development tool (*E-TDDUnit* [1]) to permit the development of a real-time security system prototype (Fig. 1) around an Analog Devices ADSP-BF533 Blackfin Processor EZ-Kit Lite evaluation board. This initial solution and tests were successfully ported to a newly available BF537 system (with both video and Internet connection); demonstrating the practicality of the approach. *E-TDDUnit* is a customized *CPPUnitLite* version [2] adopted and modified so that the tests could run on the **real embedded system** where the timing relationships were not just seen through a simulated environment.

The code development for this project can be recognized as having two distinct stages, commonly found in embedded applications involving video and telecommunications. An attempt to run the same set of *E-TDDUnit* tests for (1) the double precision floating-point MATLAB prototyping phase (develop and test signal processing algorithms) and (2) a code migration phase, where the algorithm implementation must meet the time and precision requirements of running on a fixed point processor, was abandoned because of the impractical C++ / MATLAB interface.

P. Abrahamsson, M. Marchesi, and G. Succi (Eds.): XP 2006, LNCS 4044, pp. 200–201, 2006.

One of the reasons for choosing a *xUnit* style of testing tool is that the tests and code are written in the same language. This means that both tests and code can be run on the target machine without the overhead of communications between the host and target machines affecting the real-time performance of the target. However, this advantage has an associated disadvantage in that the tested code must fit into the embedded system memory but still function at full speed along side the test code itself. This means that a key element that distinguishes embedded system development from desk top application development is memory – size, type and location: Level one (L1) memory, connected directly to the processor core for extremely high speed; Level two more bountiful than L1 memory but slower; and Level three off-chip memory which is by comparison extremely slow. We will demonstrate in the poster how many of the memory problems associated with gaining the advantages of using Agile methodologies with embedded systems can be overcome by such techniques as customizing the macros for the standard *CPPUnitLite* test syntax for the embedded memory environment together with creative methods such as handling multiple heaps.

A key issue to handle were the testing of the many threads running on the system, essentially one thread for each of the boxes shown in the schematic (Fig. 1). All these threads, and the tests themselves, competed for the limited internal processor and external hardware resources. In conclusion, it was found that automated testing is possible for some of the real-time threads associated with the communications protocol used on the video-surveillance prototype. However, further extensions are needed before *E-TDDUnit* can test the most generally described real-time thread operation automatically.

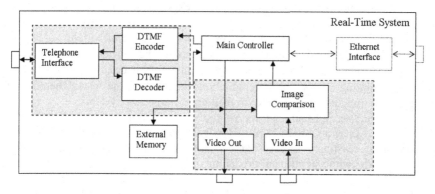

Fig. 1. Real-time security system providing video surveillance and entry detection. Each block essentially becomes a thread competing for internal and external resources.

References

[1] Smith, M, Kwan, A., Martin, A., Miller, J.: E-TDD – Embedded Test Driven Development: A Tool for Hardware-Software Co-design, 6th International Conference, XP 2005, Sheffield, UK (2005) 145 – 153.
[2] M. Feathers, "CppUnitLite Source code", c2.com/cgi/wiki?CppUnitLite (Accessed January, 2006).

Evaluation of Test Code Quality
with Aspect-Oriented Mutations

Bartosz Bogacki and Bartosz Walter

Institute of Computing Science, Poznań University of Technology, Poland
{Bartosz Bogacki, Bartosz.Walter}@cs.put.poznan.pl

1 Introduction

Along with growing popularity of agile methodologies and open source movement, unit testing has become one of the core practices in modern software engineering. It is particularly important in eXtreme Programming [1], which explicitly diminish the importance of other artifacts than source code and tests cases. In XP unit test cases not only verify if software meets functional requirements, but also enable refactoring, alleviate comprehension and provide guidance on how the production code should be used. Therefore, they contribute to many other important practices of XP, which explicitly or implicitly rely on their ability to effectively discover bugs.

Mutation testing [2] is a technique used for verifying the quality of tests. It figures out how the test cases actually react to faulty response received from deliberately altered production code. High quality tests are expected to uncover any mutation of the source code which makes it to behave even slightly differently. Such modified code (called *mutant*) is killed when it causes at least one test case to fail.

Despite of its advantages, mutation testing has not been widely adopted by software industry. The main drawback its high complexity: it usually includes multiple phases of mutating source code, compilation and running the tests. Therefore, the technique is in practice inapplicable for medium or large size systems.

In the paper we present a prototype tool for mutation testing, which employs aspect-oriented programming (AOP) [3] to generate and execute mutants. It follows the control of existing test cases and examines how they deal with the altered production code, while significantly reducing time required to create and run mutants.

2 Architecture of Aspect-Oriented Mutants Generator

In traditional model of mutation testing, mutants are generated by arbitrary or directed production code modifications, e.g. operator replacement, redefinition of a method etc. The mutations are performed in separation in order to avoid possible cross-cutting side effects. Depending on the scope of changes, they are or not externally visible to test cases through altered results of method execution. To depict the above, let us consider an exemplary source code presented at Fig. 1 and its test case at Fig. 2. Te test will fail (kill mutant) if one of three conditions is met: (1) the return value of the method Foo.bar() called with parameter 3 is different than 3000, or (2) an

P. Abrahamsson, M. Marchesi, and G. Succi (Eds.): XP 2006, LNCS 4044, pp. 202–204, 2006.

unexpected exception occurs, or (3) the parameter values 0 or 6 do not make the method to throw an expected exception. However, the mutant cannot be discovered if it does not affect the method outcome.

```java
public class Foo {
    public int bar(int a)
        throws IllegalArgumentException {
        if ((a > 5) || (a < 1)) {
            throw new IllegalArgumentException();
        }
        int c = a;
        for (int i = 0; i < a; i++) {
            c *= 10;
        }
        return c;
    }
}
```

Fig. 1. Exemplary source code under test

```java
public void testBar () {
    assertEquals (3000, new Foo().bar(3));
    try {
        new Foo().bar(6);
        fail ("Expected exception for value: 6");
    } catch (IllegalArgumentException e) {}
    try {
        new Foo ().bar(0);
        fail ("Expected exception for value: 0");
    } catch (IllegalArgumentException e) {}
}
```

Fig. 2. Exemplary JUnit test method for method *bar()* in class *Foo*

Hence, it seems sufficient to observe the reaction of test cases to such properties, without tracking individual changes in the production code and expecting the change to reveal with tests cases failures. In order to dynamically and non-invasively access the method results, we employed the capabilities of Aspect-Oriented Programming. In the example (see Fig. 2) all calls to Foo.bar() could be captured on the fly by an aspect and their actual results (return value and/or exceptions) would be replaced with mutants, just as if the mutation had been introduced directly into the source code.

The proposed prototypic tool, which exploits this observation, is actually composed of two collaborating aspects: *MutantGenerator* and *MutantExecutor*. The first one follows the original flow of a test case and captures control at every method call. In order to better mimic the normal program behavior, the aspect executes each test case twice. First, it runs the original method and stores its results and context. Secondly, it generates mutants of the results, applying typical testing rules, e.g. an integer yields following mutants: *0, –value, value ± n, Integer.MIN_VALUE* and *Integer.MAX_VALUE.*

Subsequently, the other aspect, *MutantExecutor*, wraps test code execution and runs each of the generated mutants. Its responsibility is to capture each call to the tested method in a test case and replace it with subsequent executions of the mutants generated by *MutantGenerator*. It also intercepts any exceptions that may be thrown, preventing them from being propagated to the TestRunner, which could falsely classify them as assertion failures.

It is important to notice that both aspects are core parts of the tool and do not need to be created or compiled specifically for the production code to be mutated.

4   Conclusions

To evaluate this approach, we have built a prototype based on AspectJ [4] compiler to build code and tests and with JUnit [5] as the testing library. Early experiments show that it appears to generate and run the mutants a few orders of magnitude faster that the popular Jester [6]. The savings result mainly from the fact that the tool does not require multiple mutant compilations, reduces the number of equivalent and transparent mutants, and preserves the syntactic correctness of the mutated code. However, it differs from Jester in that it learns the code usage from existing test cases, and then mutates the code. Jester, on the other hand, mutates the code insight into test cases, which allows for assessing the code coverage, but also leads to redundant or transparent mutants.

Currently the prototype deals only with primitive Java types and `null` values for objects. In future, we plan to employ an on-fly object creation with dynamic proxies and implement other mutation operators as well as perform a larger scale evaluation.

Acknowledgements

The work has been supported by the Rector of Poznań University of Technology as a research grant BW/91-429.

References

1. Beck K.: Extreme Programming Explained. Embrace change. Addison-Wesley, 2000.
2. Hamlet R.G.: Testing programs with the aid of compiler. IEEE Transactions on Software Engineering, Vol. 3(4), July 1978, pp.279-290.
3. Kiczales G., Lamping J. et al.: Aspect Oriented Programming. In: Proceedings of ECOOP 1997, Lecture Notes in Computer Science 1241, Springer Verlag, pp. 220-242.
4. AspectJ Project HomePage, http://www.eclipse.org/aspectj/ (visited in January 2006).
5. JUnit homepage, http://www.junit.org (visited in January 2006).
6. Moore I.: Jester. A Junit test tester. In: Proceedings of the 2nd International Conference on Extreme Programming and Flexible Processes in Software Engineering, XP2001.

Experimenting with Agile Practices – First Things First

Fergal Downey, Gerry Coleman, and Fergal McCaffery

Dundalk Institute of Technology, Department of Computing and Maths,
Dublin Road, Dundalk, Co. Louth, Ireland
fdown05@studentmail.dkit.ie, gerry.coleman@dkit.ie,
fergal.mccaffery@dkit.ie

Abstract. Faced with challenges in relation to interpretation of requirements, issues with build and deployment and excessive integration defects, this paper examines how a software team propose using a novel combination of Covey's 'First Things First' principle and Cockburn's Methodology Shaping, as a potential solution to examine their current process and define a new set of working conventions which will address these issues.

Keywords: Methodology, software, agile, time-management.

1 Introduction

The software team involved in this research is part of a major UK bank and is responsible for the development of eCommerce applications supporting mainly customer servicing requirements identified by each of the bank's business divisions. The team was established in 2001 but has now grown to more than sixty people which include one of the authors. The team has a strong focus on project delivery but no-one is assigned responsibility for process or methodology.

The company provides a set of Project Management Minimum Standards (PMMS) which are used for project control and these standards are based on a traditional waterfall approach to software development. The standards are generic so that they can be used independently of technology or domain, but as a result are not specific enough to be of real value.

A number of key issues are encountered to varying degrees on each of the projects undertaken by the team as follows:

1.1 Requirements Not Fully Understood

The PMMS mandates the delivery of a Business Requirements Definition (BRD). This must be signed off by the business expert and the project sponsor and as such must be at a low level of precision, sufficient to define the proposed business value and the application domain. A high precision Detailed BRD (DBRD) is subsequently produced to enable technical specifications and designs to be delivered. This is written as a set of detailed textual Use Cases and is accompanied by a "happy-path" prototype, but the sheer volume of information (the most recent project had a DBRD of almost 400 pages) and the Unified Modeling Language (UML) [1] format leads to the business expert signing off a specification that they do not fully understand in order to progress the project to the PMMS Delivery stage.

P. Abrahamsson, M. Marchesi, and G. Succi (Eds.): XP 2006, LNCS 4044, pp. 205–208, 2006.

1.2 No Integration Until After Build Completion

In order to break up the project into manageable chunks for which developers can take ownership, the project team is divided into User Interface (UI), Mid-Tier and Database sub teams. Each use case is then assigned to someone from each sub team who are then responsible for delivery of the end-to-end use case. This works to an extent, but issues are encountered when there are multiple dependencies between use cases and when these are being developed by different members of the sub teams. This leads to excessive integration defects being encountered when all use cases are delivered as an entire application at the end of the Build phase.

1.3 Build and Deployment Issues

Build and deployment of the applications developed by the software team is complex in nature due to the distributed high resilience eCommerce architecture along with the requirement to integrate with secure authentication services and legacy systems. All deployments must be automated with minimal manual intervention to ensure repeatability through each of the numerous test environments as well as preventing unnecessary access to production servers in the interest of data privacy and security. Scripting and configuration issues subsequently cause delays to the start of the formal testing phase as a result of not attempting deployment of the application until after the build has completed.

2 Methodology Shaping

The team has successfully delivered a number of large projects since its inception and as such believes that they must be doing some things well and should continue with or enhance these practices. The team also believes that some of the current practices are not adding value and these should be discontinued. The latter however must be reviewed in the context of the entire development lifecycle to ensure that discontinuing a design or build practice deemed not valuable does not have a detrimental impact on testing, implementation of maintenance.

Having some experience of Post Implementation Reviews (PIR) which are mandated under PMMS, the team agreed that input from and discussion with all members of the team was essential as well as consensus in relation to what are the most important things to address. This is consistent with the Crystal Clear technique of Methodology Shaping as described by Cockburn [2].

Using the Methodology Shaping technique, the team proposes to gather information about prior experiences of individuals and project teams. It will not be possible to get the entire team in a single workshop, nor would this be the most effective approach, so it is proposed to use a combination of interviews and workshops with the end result being two lists:

1) Disliked/Avoid – Practices that have been personally experienced by members of the team on previous projects that they would not like to repeat on the current or next project.

2) Liked/Keep - Practices that have been personally experienced by members of the team on previous projects that they would like to see repeated (and possibly enhanced).

The items on both lists will then be weighed by all individuals within the team to indicate the significance of each and the higher weighed items will be the areas to focus on initially.

Compiling both lists will ensure that consideration is given to eliminating existing practices which are not adding value instead of just enhancing existing or adding new practices.

3 First Things First

The team looked at the output from previous PIRs and these all reported that the project teams believed they could have done things better if only they had more time and resources. Two possible solutions may be considered for this complaint. Firstly, make allowances on the next project for more time and/or additional resources. Unfortunately however, these commodities are in short supply due to increasing demand from the bank's business divisions and already challenging timelines for delivery of new products or services to the bank's customers. The second solution calls for an effective time management framework in order to make better use of the time that is available by ensuring that all activities and practices are adding value and are mutually beneficial to all members of the project team.

Stephen Covey's fourth generation time management discipline which he calls First Things First (FTF) [3, 4] provides a matrix against which all activities and practices can be reviewed. Covey says that FTF focuses on preserving and enhancing relationships and on accomplishing results. This emphasis on people and evident results is consistent with the key values outlined in the Agile Alliance Manifesto [5] and is therefore an ideal philosophy to use alongside the practical approach of Methodology Shaping.

	URGENT	NOT URGENT
IMPORTANT	QUADRANT 1	QUADRANT 2
NOT IMPORTANT	QUADRANT 3	QUADRANT 4

Fig. 1. Time Management Matrix

FTF separates activities that are performed into four quadrants as shown below in Figure 1. Two factors define an activity. *Urgent* means it requires immediate attention, whereas *Importance* relates to results.

Quadrant one is the fire-fighting quadrant where things are urgent and important. In the software development lifecycle, critical defects or issues with test environments would fall into this quadrant.

Quadrant two contains activities which are important but not yet urgent. These would include code reviews or end to end integration. There are no immediate consequences of not performing these activities. However if not performed they will result in the creation of urgent and important issues as outlined above.

Quadrant three activities are urgent, but not important. These activities are usually part of someone else's agenda and not aligned with the objectives of the current project. An example may be unnecessary or irrelevant progress reporting.

Quadrant four activities are neither urgent nor important, such as spam emails or meetings with no agenda or objectives, but nevertheless result in interruptions to the important activities.

The key to effectively managing available time according to Covey, either on an individual or team basis is to spend as much time as possible on Quadrant two activities. It is essential to firstly identify and eliminate the activities which are not important (Quadrants 3 and 4), freeing up time for the important tasks (Quadrants 1 and 2). Secondly important activities should be performed before they become urgent. There will always be genuine crises and emergencies, but the emphasis is on being proactive around the opportunities presented in Quadrant 2, thus reducing the time required in Quadrant 1. For example, time spent on code reviews is likely to result in fewer defects encountered during testing.

4   Current Status and Future Work

This is part of ongoing research looking at improving the software process used by the team through experimenting with agile practices. The literature review is continuing and the Methodology Shaping workshops have been scheduled to take place during the next month. The output from the workshops will be presented in a future paper and will also provide the starting point for refining the existing set of working conventions.

References

1. Fowler, Martin, Scott Kendall: UML Distilled. Addison-Wesley (1997)
2. Cockburn, Alistair: Crystal Clear: A Human Methodology for Small Teams. Addison Wesley, (1999)
3. Covey, Stephen: Seven Habits of Highly Effective People. Simon & Schuster, (1989)
4. Covey, Stephen: First Things First. Simon & Schuster, (1994)
5. http://www.agilealliance.org

Test-Driven Development: Can It Work for Spreadsheet Engineering?

Alan Rust, Brian Bishop, and Kevin McDaid

Department of Computing and Mathematics, Dundalk Institute of Technology,
Dundalk, Co. Louth, Ireland
alan.rust@dkit.ie, brian.bishop@dkit.ie, kevin.mcdaid@dkit.ie

Abstract. It is widely accepted that the absence of a structured approach to spreadsheet engineering is a key factor in the high level of spreadsheet errors. In this paper we propose and investigate the application of Test-Driven Development to the creation of spreadsheets. Through a pair of case studies we demonstrate that Test-Driven Development can be applied to the development of spreadsheets. A supporting tool under development by the authors is also documented along with proposed research to determine the effectiveness of the methodology and the associated tool.

1 Introduction

End-user programming is the most common form of programming today [2] with spreadsheets created using Commercial off-the-shelf packages the popular example. The ubiquity of spreadsheet programs within all levels of management in the business world means that important decisions are made based on the results of these, mainly end-user developed, programs. Unfortunately, there is extensive empirical and anecdotal evidence that shows that the quality and reliability of spreadsheets is poor [4].

It is widely accepted that the absence of a structured approach to spreadsheet engineering is a key factor in the high level of spreadsheet errors. Spreadsheets have been referred to as the original agile development environment, and it has been argued that agile methodologies may be better suited to end-user development than more traditional methodologies. We therefore propose the application of the software development methodology, Test-Driven Development (TDD) [1], to spreadsheet engineering.

2 TDD and Spreadsheets

TDD is a coding technique that insists that the software developer writes the tests before they write the code. TDD, supported by a dedicated tool, has been shown in software engineering to improve the quality of code and to support the testing and maintenance of software.

The importance of tool support for TDD cannot be overstated, as manually running tests would increase project time substantially. In order to apply TDD to spreadsheet engineering we have created a tool that mimics the functionality of established TDD tools such as JUnit or VBUnit. Our tool differs from JUnit or VBUnit in that the

P. Abrahamsson, M. Marchesi, and G. Succi (Eds.): XP 2006, LNCS 4044, pp. 209–210, 2006.

developer is not required to write code when creating tests. Instead an interface allows entry of input and output values that specify a test.

Before structured experiments designed to answer the key research question "Does TDD reduce the level of spreadsheet errors?" can take place it is important to establish that TDD can be applied in the spreadsheet domain and to identify the associated issues. An initial investigation comprising two case studies by two of the authors was conducted to identify these issues.

Upon completion of the case studies, both authors felt that the methodology and tool worked well and that there was an increased confidence in the reliability of the spreadsheet following the adoption of the approach. In fact one of the authors felt that were he to start again he would write an even higher number of tests for the spreadsheet and that he would refactor a number of the formulas. The case studies also revealed a number of key issues relating to the future improvement of the TDD tool.

3   Conclusions

This paper explores the potential of Test-Driven Development (TDD), a best-practice in Extreme Programming, to improve the engineering of spreadsheets. Through two case studies the authors have increased their understanding of TDD and how it can be applied in the spreadsheet domain. Importantly, the authors have concluded that the methodology has the potential to improve the development of spreadsheets. However, the studies have revealed a number of issues with the tool and the methodology. These issues are currently being addressed before trials involving real users can be conducted to prove the effectiveness and efficiency of the innovative method.

Acknowledgments

The authors acknowledge the support of the Irish Research Council for Science, Engineering and Technology funded by the National Development Plan and the support of Co-operation Ireland and the Peace 2 programme.

References

1. Beck, K.: Test Driven Development: By Example. Addison-Wesley (2003)
2. Burnett, M., Cook, C., Rothermel, G.: End User Software Engineering. Communications of the ACM, September, Vol.47, No. 9 (2004)
3. Panko, R.: What We Know About Spreadsheet Errors. Journal of End User Computing 10, 2 (Spring), p15–21 (1998)

Comparison Between Test Driven Development and Waterfall Development in a Small-Scale Project

Lei Zhang[1], Shunsuke Akifuji[1], Katsumi Kawai[2], and Tsuyoshi Morioka[2]

[1] Hitachi (China) Research & Development Corporation, Beijing Fortune Bldg. 1701,
5 Dong San Huan Bei-Lu, Chao Yang District, Beijing 100004, China
{leizhang, sakifuji}@hitachi.cn

[2] Hitachi, Ltd., Systems Development Laboratory, 292, Yoshida-cho, Totsuka-ku,
Yokohama-shi, Kanagawa-ken, 244-0817 Japan
{katsumi, morioka}@sdl.hitachi.co.jp

In order to popularize the Test Driven Development (TDD) practice in Chinese offshore companies, an experimental research was firstly conducted to compare TDD with the traditional waterfall development in a small-scale project. Although the project scale was small and all the subjects were students, this experiment was designed very strictly to guarantee the reliable evaluation of the efficacy of TDD. Furthermore, it is also the first time to evaluate the maintainability and the flexibility of TDD by experiment.

This experiment was carefully designed to guarantee that except the development flow, other factors had minimum effects on the experimental results.

(1) *Subject*: Eight students from five universities were divided into 'T' group and 'C' group. Each group had four members with similar programming and TDD experiences.
(2) *Task*: Two groups were asked to develop the same project of 'Working Attendance Management System' at the same time. The detailed Requirement Specification and the GUI designed by the plotting tool were provided to ensure the workload of two groups as similar as possible.
(3) *Development Environment and Tools*: The development environment Eclipse and the test tool JUnit were specified. In addition, the structure was designed to be Client/Sever and the database was required to use MySQL.
(4) *Working Space*: Two groups worked in two different rooms in order to avoid the communication between them.
(5) *Development Flow*: 'T' group and 'C' group were required to develop the same project by TDD and the waterfall development, respectively. The development flow of 'T' group was 'simple design – test – code – refactor' and that of 'C' group was 'simple design – detailed design – code – test'.

In order to comprehensively evaluate the efficacy of TDD, six parameters were estimated by this experiment. The evaluation methods and the data collection processes of these six parameters were stated as follows:

(1) *Productivity*: The productivity of each group was evaluated by the total developing time, which was recorded manually by each group every day.

P. Abrahamsson, M. Marchesi, and G. Succi (Eds.): XP 2006, LNCS 4044, pp. 211–212, 2006.
© Springer-Verlag Berlin Heidelberg 2006

(2) *Reliability*: The code reliability of each group was estimated by the total bug number during the developing process, which included the bugs found by other teammates and by the daily build at 19:00 every evening.

(3) *Maintainability*: The maintainability of each group was evaluated by the time used to remove one bug. The shorter the time is, the better the maintainability is. Some Java scripts were written based on an open source tool of Bugzilla to calculate the time used to remove one bug.

(4) *Flexibility*: Several new functions were added during the developing process and the flexibility of each group was estimated by the time used to adapt to these requirement variations. The shorter time means the better flexibility.

(5) *Efficiency*: The efficiency of each group was evaluated by the code size written to implement the same functions. The smaller code size represents the higher efficiency. The code size of each group was recorded by a code-counting tool every day.

(6) *Tester quality*: The tester quality of each group was estimated by the results of the code coverage. An open source tool EMMA was used to calculate the code coverage during the developing process.

This experiment was conducted from June to August in 2005. Based on the experimental results, several conclusions were drawn as follows:

(1) The TDD developers took less time (10%) than the traditional developers. This stated that the TDD approach had higher productivity.

(2) The TDD approach appeared to yield code with the superior reliability, maintainability, flexibility and efficiency. The bugs found during the developing process were 28% less than those of the traditional group. The average time used to remove one bug in the TDD group was 8% shorter than that of the traditional group. The time used for the requirement variation of TDD was 30% shorter, and the code size was 33% smaller than those of the traditional group, respectively.

(3) The test code coverage of the TDD approach was about 10% higher than that of the traditional group.

All the above experimental results were summarized in the following table. It can be seen that the TDD group performed better on all the evaluated aspects in this experiment.

Table 1. Summary of the experimental results

No.	Evaluated Parameters	Superiority of TDD to Waterfall (Shown by Percentage)
1	Productivity	10%
2	Reliability	28%
3	Maintainability	8%
4	Flexibility	30%
5	Efficiency	33%
6	Tester Quality	10%

In the near future, we will further study the efficacy of TDD in larger scale projects and the effect of the programming experience of the subjects on the experimental results.

A Practical Approach for Deploying Agile Methods

Minna Pikkarainen and Outi Salo

VTT Technical Research Centre of Finland, P.O. Box 1100, FIN-90571 Oulu, Finland
Minna.Pikkarainen@vtt.fi, Outi.Salo@vtt.fi

1 Introduction

Over the past years, a great number of organizations have started utilizing agile prin-ciples and practices in their software development [1, 2]. Despite of the promising experience reports, the deployment of agile practices is a challenging task which re-quires adjustment and dedication from all the stakeholders involved in the develop-ment process [3, 4]. In order to fit the agile practices into organization's software development context, agile specific guidelines and methods to support their selection, deployment and tailoring are needed [5]. However, the existing software process improvement (SPI) approaches have originally been targeted for the context of the traditional software development thus lacking some central aspects such as iterative process adaptation [5] and procedures for suitable organizational learning [6]. Agile Assessment and Post-Iteration Workshops (PIWs) are technologies that can be used in the deployment of agile software development methods.

2 Agile Deployment Process and Technologies

The agile deployment process proposed here combines Agile Assessment procedures and iterative execution of process adaptation and deployment with PIWs. This pro-vides an opportunity for rapid feedback loop from the project teams to organization. At the moment, one method for assessing agile software development is an Agile Assessment [7, 8]. The approach of Boehm and Turner [9] also provides a way for assessing the agile home ground of a software development project. However, this model maintains a strict focus on assessing the agile and plan-driven risks rather than finding the weaknesses and strengths of the used practices. The new idea in the Agile Assessment approach is to make the agile principles and practices a part of the as-sessment process and to use the generated information for improving the software development processes, utilizing agility-based solution alternatives.

The iterative process adaptation within agile project teams provides project teams with a means of iterative tailoring the deployed practices during the ongoing project. The PIW method (e.g., [10]) proposes a way to conduct this activity in a rapid yet validated and systematic manner. Furthermore, the PIW method provides mechanisms for organizations to harvest and utilize SPI feedback from process deployment in projects to organizational learning [5, 6], e.g., in Agile Assessments.

Both Agile Assessments and PIWs have been successfully performed for several projects in many organizations (e.g. Agile Assessment in 8 projects in Hantro, Nokia and F-Secure and PIWs in 8 Mobile-D™ case projects). Based on the results, the

P. Abrahamsson, M. Marchesi, and G. Succi (Eds.): XP 2006, LNCS 4044, pp. 213–214, 2006.
© Springer-Verlag Berlin Heidelberg 2006

Agile Assessment has found to be an objective, lightweight approach which provides evidences of the agile technologies performance, know-how about available and suitable agile practices as well as practical, agile improvement ideas. PIWs have offered to the project teams with systematic mechanisms of effective process adaptation and organizations with an opportunity to effectively learn from the project teams conducting agile deployment.

3 Conclusions

Currently, the agile software development methods provide an attractive alternative to the traditional plan-driven software development approaches. Specific procedures are, however, needed to support a systematic selection and deployment of new agile practices as well as for tailoring them to suit individual projects. The presented agile deployment approach integrates the specific Agile Assessment and Post-Iteration Workshop technologies offering practical solutions to answer these needs.

References

[1] B. Greene, "Agile Methods Applied to Embedded Firmware Development," Agile Development Conference, Salt-Lake city, 2004.

[2] J. Highsmith, Agile Project Management, Creating innovative products: Addison-Wesley, 2004.

[3] M. Cohn and D. Ford, "Introducing an Agile Process to an Organization," *IEEE Software*, vol. 36, pp. 74-78, 2003.

[4] H. Svensson and M. Höst, "Introducing an Agile Process in a Software Maintenance and Evolution Organization," 9th European Conference on Software Maintenance and Reengineering, 2005.

[5] M. Pikkarainen, O. Salo, and J. Still, "Deploying Agile Practices in Organizations: A Case Study," EuroSPI 2005, Budapest, Hungary, 2005.

[6] O. Salo and P. Abrahamsson, "Integrating Agile Software Development and Software Process Improvement: a Longitdinal Case Study," ISESE 2005, Autralia, Noosa Heads, 2005.

[7] M. Pikkarainen and U. Passoja, "An Approach for Assessing Suitability of Agile Solutions:A Case Study," XP 2005, Sheffield University, UK, 2005.

[8] M. Pikkarainen and A. Mäntyniemi, "An Approach for Using CMMI in Agile Software Development Assessments: Experiences from Three Case Studies," SPICE 2006, 2005.

[9] B. Boehm and R. Turner, "Balancing Agility and Discipline," in *Balancing Agility and Discipline -A Guide for the Perplexed*: Addison Wesley, 2003.

[10] O. Salo, "Improving Software Process in Agile Software Development Projects: Results from Two XP Case Studies," EUROMICRO 2004, Rennes, France, 2004.

Streamlining the Agile Documentation Process Test-Case Driven Documentation Demonstration for the XP2006 Conference

Daniel Brolund and Joakim Ohlrogge

Agical AB, Sweden
daniel.brolund@agical.com
joakim.ohlrogge@agical.com
http://www.agical.com

Abstract. In far too many software projects the value of the documentation delivered is not high enough to motivate the effort spent to write it. An outdated document can be as misleading as a good, up to date one can be helpful. This demonstration will show how unit tests complemented with descriptive comments can be used to generate documentation that is constantly up to date. It is demonstrated by example how both the static and dynamic features of a software system can be salvaged with very little effort to be presented to a bigger audience as relevant, readable documentation.

1 The Demonstration

We will, by test-driving a small application, demonstrate how to use the TDDoc add-on to the RMock dynamic mock framework [1] in Java(TM) to create generated documentation (GD). The GD will be geared towards a technical audience, such as users of a framework or developers of an application. It will contain technical/API text-and-snippet documentation to illustrate the principles. We will also demonstrate how this approach is resilient to many refactorings.

2 The Rationale

The rationale of this approach is that when test-driving an application, the test cases contain a lot of information about the system, but the information is hard to come by or overview. By adding some extra information in a (sub-)suite of test cases and use them to generate the documentation, this information can be structured more human-friendly and complement API documentation such as Java-doc with a more usage/function-oriented view of the system. Since the GD originates in running code, it will also be more robust than static documents, and it will, without manual re-work, survive many kinds of refactorings and changes that would break the static document. Just as test cases are an executable specification of the implementation, they can at the same time be the executable

P. Abrahamsson, M. Marchesi, and G. Succi (Eds.): XP 2006, LNCS 4044, pp. 215–216, 2006.

specification of the documentation, hence concentrating the usage information in one place to avoid duplication.

Different projects have different requirements and motives for documentation. The net value of documentation is the gross value of the documentation minus the cost of creating and maintaining the documentation. To increase the net value of documentation one can increase the gross value or decrease the cost. By using the demonstrated approach, the GD is always up-to-date, hence increasing the gross value and the net value with it. Meanwhile, the cost of creating and especially maintaining the documents through changes and refactorings should be lower, also adding to the net value. This increase in documentation productivity could be used to document better to the same cost or to keep status quo on documentation to a lower cost.

3   Risks

One risk is that it will be cheap to create piles of unuseful, skeleton documentation. Another risk is that the comments and testcases are not maintained, or that the comments will clutter the testcases.

4   Open Discussion

Discussion about the current state of the approach:

- **What is the value of this approach in the agile context?** Is it value or waste? Who will benefit the most and the least?
- **What are the limitations and risks?** How can one assure that the comments are updated? Will the testcases be cluttered?
- **Could this approach be an XP-enabler?** Are customers more likely to use XP if they are provided with more extensive documentation? Can it be used to generate pre-sale documentation?
- **What is the relation to other frameworks, such as FIT [2]?** What benefits could be made? Are there integration issues or possible overlaps?

Discussion about future enhancements:

- **Test-driven build and deployment documentation.** Could the concept of test-driving be expanded one step further?
- **What more information can be extracted from a running system that is useful for documentation?** GUI snapshots, memory information, thread information, stacktraces. Are they relevant?

References

1. http://rmock.sourceforge.net
2. http://fitnesse.org

Open Source Software in an Agile World

Steven Fraser[1], Pär J. Ågerfalk[2], Jutta Eckstein[3],
Tim Korson[4], and J.B. Rainsberger[5]

[1] Senior Staff, QUALCOMM, San Diego, USA
`sdfraser@acm.org`
[2] Research Fellow, University of Limerick, Ireland
`par.agerfalk@ul.ie`
[3] Consultant, Objects in Action, Braunschweig, Germany
`jutta@jeckstein.com`
[4] Consultant, Korson Consulting, TN, USA
`tim@korson-consulting.com`
[5] Founder, Diaspar Software Services, Toronto, Canada
`me@jbrains.info`

Abstract. Open Source Software (contrasted with proprietary or "closed" software) has become a more widely accepted enterprise solution not withstanding some issues related to intellectual property rights and issues of liability and indemnification. Open Source Software (OSS) takes collaborative software development to a global extreme – OSS also provides a mechanism for decreasing time-to-market, improved quality, and reduced development costs. This panel will serve as a catalyst to discuss strategies, tools, and communities focused on the development and application of open source software.

1 Steven Fraser (Panel Moderator)

Steven Fraser recently (January 2005) joined QUALCOMM's Learning Centre as a member of senior staff in San Diego, California – with responsibilities for tech transfer and technical learning. From 2002 to 2004 Steven was an independent software consultant on tech transfer and disruptive technologies. Previous to 2002 Steven held a variety of software technology program management roles at Nortel and BNR (Bell-Northern Research) - including: Process Architect, Senior Manager (Disruptive Technology and Global External Research), Advisor (Design Process Engineering), General Chair (Nortel Design Forum), and Software Reuse Program Prime. In 1994 he spent a year as a Visiting Scientist at the Software Engineering Institute (SEI) collaborating with the "Application of Software Models Project" on the development of team-based domain analysis techniques. Since 1994, Steven has regularly moderated panels at ACM's OOPSLA and other software conferences – serving as OOPSLA panels chair in 2003 and as XP2006's General Chair. Steven holds a Doctorate in Electrical Engineering (software graphics standards validation) from McGill University in Montreal, Canada, an MS in Physics (Queen's University at Kingston), and a BS in Physics and Computer Science (McGill University). Steven is a member of the ACM and IEEE.

P. Abrahamsson, M. Marchesi, and G. Succi (Eds.): XP 2006, LNCS 4044, pp. 217–220, 2006.
© Springer-Verlag Berlin Heidelberg 2006

2 Pär J Ågerfalk

The open source software (OSS) is a global phenomenon with developers spread across the world. At the same time, the OSS model is an agile approach that manages to adapt fluently to changing situations and which is known for producing high-quality code with swift handling of the few bugs that remain in released software. In the proprietary world, the understanding of agile approaches in global software development is still quite limited. Hence, understanding better the interplay between agile methods, OSS and global software development is an important topic that should benefit all three 'communities' (OSS, agile and commercial/proprietary). In this panel I will draw on recent research in this area and present a number of challenges that should be part of a research agenda for the intersection of OSS and agile methods.

Pär J Ågerfalk is a research fellow at the University of Limerick and an assistant professor (universitetslektor) in informatics at Örebro University, where he heads the Methodology Exploration Lab. He received his PhD in information systems development from Linköping University in 2003. His research on systems development method flexibility, language/action based information systems theory and open source software development has resulted in more than 50 publications in a variety of journals, books, and international conferences and workshops. He has served on the committees of numerous conferences and is an associate editor of European Journal of Information systems as well as of the electronic journal Systems, Signs and Actions (www.sysiac.org). Ågerfalk is scientific manager and deputy coordinator of the EU FP6 Co-ordination Action project CALIBRE (www.calibre.ie), co-leading the distributed development work package and coordinating the scientific side of the CALIBRATION open source industry research forum. He was the lead author of the paper 'Assessing the Role of Open Source Software in the European Secondary Software Sector: A Voice from Industry', which won a best paper award at the 1st International Conference on Open Source Systems in Genoa 2005.

3 Jutta Eckstein

Open Source provides a great leverage for implementing the fist value: Individuals and interactions over processes and 'tools'. I regard this as the major reason why I have never seen an agile project without using any kind of Open Source software. Using the official purchasing department in order to acquire a new tool takes typically too long to provide the necessary quick feedback an agile team needs. On the other hand Open Source software development, although being distributed, implements a lot of agile techniques, sometimes even the agile value system. This provides for commercial agile teams great learning opportunities. Thus agile software development and Open Source form a give-and-take relationship.

Jutta Eckstein is an independent consultant and trainer for over ten years. She has a unique experience in applying agile processes within medium-sized to large mission-critical projects. This is also the topic of her book Agile Software Development in the Large. Besides engineering software she has been designing and teaching OT courses in industry. Having completed a course of teacher training and led many 'train the trainer' programs in industry, she focuses also on techniques which help teach OT and is a main lead in the pedagogical patterns project. Jutta has presented work in her main areas at ACCU (UK), OOPSLA (USA), OT (UK), XP (Italy and Germany) and Agile (USA). Jutta is a member of the board of the Agile Alliance and a member of the program committee of many different European and American conferences in the area of agile development, object-orientation and patterns.

4   Timothy Korson

I am not an open source zealot, not am I a strong proponent of any particular commercial software environment, but I do care passionately about the process of building software better, faster, and cheaper. From this perspective I believe that both the Agile community and the Open Source community have given us valuable insights about how to develop software. And these are not just theoretical insights. Both communities have demonstrated to us practical techniques that work. For example the XP concepts of pair programming and shared ownership are really taken to the extreme in the open source community. These and many other lessons are there for all of us to learn and apply in our own companies if we but have the courage to try.

Timothy Korson has had over two decades of substantial experience working on a large variety of systems developed using modern software engineering techniques. This experience includes distributed, real time, embedded systems as well as business information systems in an n-tier, client-server environment. Korson's typical involvement on a project is as a senior management consultant with additional technical responsibilities to ensure high quality, robust test and quality assurance processes and practices. Korson has authored numerous articles, and co-authored a book on Object Technology Centers. He has given frequent invited lectures at major international conferences and has contributed to the discipline through original research. The lectures and training classes he presents are highly rated by the attendees.

5   J.B. Rainsberger

I have primarily been a consumer, rather than a producer, of Open Source tools, libraries and software. As a general computer user, I rely on Open Source tools for most of my basic computing needs: e-mail, browsing, personal organization, word processing, spreadsheets. The abundance of free general-purpose tools makes it easy for me to pay for more specialized software, so I can support fellow software professionals better. In my role as a software developer, I rely on Open Source tools for my development platforms. Having used many expensive development environments, it is obvious to me that the Open Source community produces superior work overall, since in many cases, I find high defect rates much more costly than smaller feature sets, and commercial environments tend to deliver more defects in hopes of delivering more features than Open Source projects. Also, while companies believe themselves to be under continuous time pressure to deliver, the best Open Source projects tend to release more frequently, with rich feature sets and low defect rates.

I suppose it's true what "Peopleware" by DeMarco and Lister says: "teams allowed to set their own deadlines often finish sooner".

In my work as a consultant and programmer, I emphasize reusing existing libraries as a way to counter the Not invented here attitude that afflicts many software teams. I have already seen considerable improvement, as teams that build on existing work tend to learn more about what's possible for their project than those who build more for themselves. Programmers spend very little time reading code, so reusing Open Source libraries gives them an excellent opportunity to do just that. In so doing, they learn much more about their platform, about what makes good and bad design, and about what features are possible. It is a simple way to expand the team in some sense to include considerable outside expertise. While occasionally we run into libraries we wish we'd never found, I never consider that time wasted, as it sharpens each person's understanding of what makes a good or bad product. The Open Source community provides an invaluable service to those who deliver software for a living, and even to those who simply use computers on a regular basis. We owe them much for their efforts.

J. B. Rainsberger is the Founder of Diaspar Software Services, where he coaches both individual programmers and entire teams in value-driven software development practices. His book, JUnit Recipes is the top-selling book for Java programmers about JUnit, testing and test-driven development. Joe has been an XP practitioner, researcher, presenter, and author since 2000 – and in 2005 received one of the first Gordon Pask awards for contribution to Agile practice.

Politics and Religion in Agile Development

Angela Martin, Rachel Davies, Jutta Eckstein,
David Hussman, and Mary Poppendieck

Abstract. Politics and Religion are traditionally taboo topics in polite after-dinner conversation. In this panel, we are going to discuss taboo topics in agile software development. Technical teams ought to choose technology based on the immediate needs of the current project and organization. But we all know that technology and methodology choices are often driven by people enhancing their resume - this conflict can start religious wars! On agile projects, we ask our customers to prioritize stories purely by business value, as if this is a straightforward thing to do and company politics are irrelevant. We need to recognize that projects that only deliver working software can still be classed as failures from an organizational perspective. If we pretend that the political dimension does not exist on agile projects then we cannot develop and share practices that help us handle these situations. This panel brings industry professionals to share their perspectives and experiences, the audience should come prepared to both ask and answer questions.

Angela Martin (amartin@thoughtworks.com) – Panel Moderator

Being agile does not insolate us from failure, some agile projects succeed and some agile projects fail. Newsflash: the key difference between the projects that have failed and succeeded is not whether they did all of the agile practices – for example, pair programming has had little bearing on whether the project failed neither has delivering working software that delivers business value been enough – the key difference has been the presence of a political player either directly on or supporting the team. The political player keeps up with organization's politics and power structure, identifying the organisational players and the rules: Who needs to say "yes!", Who needs to stop saying "no!", Which rules to follow and finally Which rules to break. To ensure project success we need to not only get our internal practices (e.g. pair programming etc) right but also our external facing practices right, we need to recognize the importance of politics in software development.

Angela Martin, ThoughtWorks Limited: Angela Martin is a consultant with eleven years of professional software development experience; she works directly with programmers and customers on agile projects to deliver software that works. She is also completing her PhD research at Victoria University of Wellington, New Zealand, supervised by James Noble and Robert Biddle. Her research utilises in-depth case studies of the XP Customer Role, on a wide range of projects world-wide. Angela is also an Agile Alliance Board Member.

Rachel Davies (rachel@agilexp.com)

Whatever your role, you need to balance your long-term career development against short-term project constraints. When these needs are in conflict, we look for creative

P. Abrahamsson, M. Marchesi, and G. Succi (Eds.): XP 2006, LNCS 4044, pp. 221–224, 2006.
© Springer-Verlag Berlin Heidelberg 2006

ways to align them. Life is a political act. We all create and leverage alliances as part of our daily work life. I would like to be able to discuss openly issues and trade-offs that shape our technology and methodology choices on software development projects rather than leave them shrouded by rhetoric to conceal underlying motivations. I believe the agile community needs tools that help teams explore such issues in a non-confrontational way rather than denying their existence.

Rachel Davies, Agile Experience Ltd - www.agilexp.com. Rachel is an XP practitioner and makes her living training and coaching agile teams in industry. She is also a director of the Agile Alliance.

Jutta Eckstein (www.jeckstein.com, info@jeckstein.com)

I experience religion often more on "our" side: Every so often I see coaches focusing and insisting on specific practices and ignoring the fact that those (agile) practices are not appropriate for the specific team in its environment. And even worse by insisting on the use of those practices - the agile value system is completely ignored. So the focus on the practices can even undermine the value system.

I see the challenges of politics more often created by the organisation surrounding the team. For example, I saw the project management acknowledging the message of the team and the team's past achievements, but the good(?) connections way up the hierarchy ignored the team's message and promised the customer everything - this is unavoidably leading to disappointment on all sides if not to a disaster of the whole project. Agility provides the key advantage of being an early trouble detector which helps also to surface religious and politic issues early on. However, the difficulty is to address them appropriately.

Jutta Eckstein is an independent consultant and trainer for over ten years. She has a unique experience in applying agile processes within medium-sized to large mission-critical projects. This is also the topic of her book Agile Software Development in the Large. She is a member of the board of the AgileAlliance and a member of the program committee of many different European and American conferences in the area of agile development, object-orientation and patterns.

David Hussman (david.hussman@sgfco.com)

Helping companies transition to sustainable agile development means looking beyond a first project or an individual who is passionate about agile change. There is no shortage of writings which stress the importance of values and principles, yet their writings also challenge agilists to step up and address concepts difficult in our daily lives outside of the creation of software products.

Tools available to aid the agile community with this challenge – and common to many agile styles – include the many forums which allow for people to take small ventures into politically or religiously charged territory, and the role of someone who is in the community to create a space where it is safe to investigate options or alternative views (XP Coach – SCRUM Master). Similar to anyone who takes a savant leadership role, these roles do not magically remove the issues, but they go along way toward building a community that can adapt as needed to survive and succeed in the face of human challenges created, be these political or dogmatic.

David Hussman has designed and created software for more than 13 years in a variety of domains: digital audio, digital biometrics, medical, retail, banking, mortgage, and education to name a few. For the past 6 years, David has mentored and coached agile teams in the U.S., Canada, Russia, and Ukraine. Along with leading workshops and presenting at conferences in North America and Europe, David has contributed to numerous publications and several books (including "Managing Agile Projects" and "Agile in the Large"). David co-owns the Minneapolis based SGF Software, is a senior consultant with The Cutter Consortium, and has contributed to the agile curriculum for Capella University and the University of Minnesota.

Mary Poppendieck (mary@poppendieck.com)

When I heard there was going to be a panel on taboo topics, I didn't know if I had the courage to write about my most closely held taboo topic: *Some are more equal than others.* But I decided to take a deep breath and jump in. I hope the water isn't too cold.

Women: The first presentation I heard about XP discussed how pair programming was implemented at an early adopting company. Everyone was required to work fixed hours in order to be available to 'pair.' Years before, as a young mother, I had lobbied long and hard for flexible hours so I could be home with my kids in the late afternoons. Was this thing called pair programming going to take away all of the flexible working hours I had fought so hard to obtain? While I'm on the subject, when I was a young programmer, a good third of programmers were female. What's happened to all of the women anyway?

Sides: What is this nonsense called a "Bill of Rights"? Customer SIDE and Team 'SIDE'? As if the people who really understand the problem to be solved are the visitors. Oh, yes, the 'customer' may be a customer 'team', but that's a different team than the 'real' team. I don't get why there would be more than one team, more than one side. I don't get how developers think they can be successful if customers don't do their job well. I don't believe in "technical success." I can't understand why we aren't all in this together.

Managers: Why do people equate bad management with management? Why does something as important as leadership make us nervous? How do we think that changes are going to be made if we speak ill of those we need to champion the changes? How are we ever going to grow leaders if we give the impression that leadership is a bad thing?

Barnyard Language: What's wrong with the courtesy and respect shown by using politically correct language? Which indirectly brings me full circle to the first taboo....

Mary Poppendieck has been in the Information Technology industry for thirty years. She has managed solutions for companies in several disciplines, including supply chain management, manufacturing systems, and digital media. As a seasoned leader in both operations and new product development, she provides a business perspective to software development problems. A popular writer and speaker, Mary's classes on managing software development have been popular with both large and small companies. She is co-author of the book Lean Software Development: An Agile Toolkit, published by Addison Wesley in May, 2003 and winner of the Software Development Productivity Award in 2004.

How Do Agile/XP Development Methods Affect Companies?

Steven Fraser[1], Barry Boehm[2], Jack Järkvik[3], Erik Lundh[4], and Kati Vilkki[5]

[1] Senior Staff, QUALCOMM, San Diego, USA
sdfraser@acm.org
[2] Director, Center for Software Engineering, USC, LA, USA
boehm@sunset.usc.edu
[3] VP R&D Operations of Excellence, Ericsson AB
jack.jarkvik@ericsson.com
[4] Principal, Compelcon AB, Helsingborg, Sweden
erik.lundh@compelcon.se
[5] Development Manager, Nokia Networks, Finland
kati.vilkki@nokia.com

Abstract. Does the discipline inherent in Agile/XP methods change the way a company does business in contrast to the influences of "traditional" plan-driven or ad-hoc software development practices? Are there differences in strategies for customer engagement, staff resourcing, and program management? Companies live or die depending on the accuracy of scheduling/budgeting projections and the ability to do more with less. Lean development, SCRUM, XP, and other agile methods may stress companies in hitherto unanticipated ways leading to both evolutionary and revolutionary organizational change. This panel will discuss the differences and similarities between XP/Agile and more traditional software development practices with regard to their impact on companies.

1 Steven Fraser (Panel Moderator)

This panel was developed in partnership with Erik Lundh to offer a forum to discuss the impact of Agile/XP developments on organizations.

Steven Fraser recently (January 2005) joined QUALCOMM's Learning Centre as a member of senior staff in San Diego, California – with responsibilities for tech transfer and technical learning. From 2002 to 2004 Steven was an independent software consultant on tech transfer and disruptive technologies. Previous to 2002 Steven held a variety of software technology program management roles at Nortel and BNR (Bell-Northern Research) - including: Process Architect, Senior Manager (Disruptive Technology and Global External Research), Advisor (Design Process Engineering), General Chair (Nortel Design Forum), and Software Reuse Program Prime. In 1994 he spent a year as a Visiting Scientist at the Software Engineering Institute (SEI) collaborating with the "Application of Software Models Project" on the development of team-based domain analysis techniques. Since 1994, Steven has regularly moderated panels at ACM's OOPSLA and other software conferences – serving as OOPSLA panels chair in 2003 and as XP2006's General Chair. Steven

P. Abrahamsson, M. Marchesi, and G. Succi (Eds.): XP 2006, LNCS 4044, pp. 225–228, 2006.
© Springer-Verlag Berlin Heidelberg 2006

holds a Doctorate in Electrical Engineering (software graphics standards validation) from McGill University in Montreal, Canada, an MS in Physics (Queen's University at Kingston), and a BS in Physics and Computer Science (McGill University). Steven is a member of the ACM and IEEE.

2 Barry Boehm

In recent agile methods workshops with our large-company industry affiliates, the participants have unanimously agreed that agile methods have helped them become more flexible and adaptive to change. But they have also agreed that scalability and legacy practices have limited their range of adoption of agile methods. Scalability issues have included team-of-teams coordination and change management, independent–team product interoperability, multi-customer change coordination, and unscalable COTS or architectural suboptimization on early increments.   Legacy practice issues have included distributed development practices, outsourcing and contractual issues, quality factor requirements, legacy system evolution and integration, maturity model criteria, and legacy waterfall regulations, specifications, and standards. Most are exploring product and process architectures for hybrid agile/plan-driven development.

Barry Boehm is the TRW Professor of Software Engineering and the Director of the Center for Software Engineering in the USC Computer Science Department. Dr. Barry Boehm served within the U.S. Department of Defense (DoD) from 1989 to 1992 as director of the DARPA Information Science and Technology Office and as director of the DDR&E Software and Computer Technology Office. He worked at TRW from 1973 to 1989, culminating as chief scientist of the Defense Systems Group, and at the Rand Corporation from 1959 to 1973, culminating as head of the Information Sciences Department. He entered the software field at General Dynamics in 1955. His current research interests involve recasting software engineering into a value-based framework, including processes, methods, and tools for value-based software definition, architecting, development, and validation. His contributions to the field include the Constructive Cost Model (COCOMO), the Spiral Model of the software process, and the Theory W (win-win) approach to software management and requirements determination. He is a Fellow of the ACM, AIAA, IEEE, and INCOSE, and a member of the National Academy of Engineering.

3 Jack Järkvik

Applying agile techniques inspires people and organizations to speed the learning process. A focus on results emerges so staff will develop strong likes or dislikes. Agile techniques highlights that people are more important than process and puts special pressure on both artisans and managers. There is a risk – maybe all agile does is allow real performers to shine and it tends to more clearly single out the real performers from the mediocre ones? One big challenge is to avoid basing all progress on a few stars. The important task is to use "agility" to introduce new potential performers into the teams. There is always a need to grow new performers. This is true for both artisans and managers. The reason people tend to learn so quickly applying agile techniques is that feed-back is immediate. You do not learn just from project-to-project, but also from day-to-day or week-to-week. On the whole, traditional processes separate training from development, while agile does not. It is vital to create a working environment where new learning is made a part of regular working. There is room for more than one approach in a large company, especially during a crisis. Being successful at launching products excuses deviations from central directives. Homegrown agile methods can be very successful in saving failing projects. The challenge is to get people and projects to use these methods before they run into trouble. A challenge much like the XP coach attempting to introduce pair programming to the very people that always gather around one computer as soon as they get into trouble.

Jack Järkvik began his career in 1975 at LM Ericsson where he currently has executive responsibility for R&D Operational Excellence. He has a Masters in Electronics, an MBA (both from Gothenburg University) and a Masters in the Management of Technology from MIT. For ten years he ran his own consulting firm. His development experience started with programming in PLEX, Ericsson's unique telecom switch language. Since 1990 Jack has applied agile techniques within Ericsson's telecom domain on "large" multi-site software/hardware co-projects.

4 Erik Lundh

XP and the agile approaches in general have been most useful, in my work, to inspire dramatic improvements quickly. I typically spend days not months at a company. When an organization runs a successful pilot project with a highly disciplined agile method such as XP – the successful team acts as a Toyota pull system. The iterations provide "Takt" in the Toyota sense to the rest of the company. The rest of the company gets clear motivation to adapt their processes to support the successful "development engine" (the XP team). I know of no better way than XP to get management involved. Toyotas "genchi gembutsu" – gets your hands "dirty" with the decisions you make.

Erik has developed software for more than 25 years with experience that includes programming, design, architecture, sales, and R&D management. He has also served on the board of several companies. Initially, while working with cross-industrial R&D centers on software products, colleagues at Lund University brought XP to Erik's attention. Erik uses XP as a catalyst to improve the maturity of software companies. Erik, a certified SCRUM Master, combines his experience as project "supertechie" with years spent advocating classic software process improvement (SPI) within the context of CMMI process improvement. Erik has experience introducing XP in organizations that range in size from small startups to large organizations. Erik evangelizes XP and Agile development throughout Sweden – hosting industry experts such as Ward Cunningham, Mary/Tom Poppendieck and Charlie Poole. Erik is a board member of SPIN-Sweden, and an involved sponsor of most Swedish SPIN-chapters. His local chapter SPIN-SYD is the largest in Sweden, with over 40 companies including Ericsson and ABB.

5 Kati Vilkki

Agile methods put the focus back where it belongs: to people, technical excellence and co-operation. Working in self-directing teams promotes empowerment and thus increases creativity. Being successful in large-scale product development requires finding ways to enable self-directing teams to work towards a common goal without compromising empowerment and feeling of ownership in the teams - a task easier said than done. Finding the balance between agility and commonality is a dynamic process. My current interest is how to introduce agile and iterative development methods into a large organization. In my experience the way of introducing these methods should reflect the methods and the end result we want to reach, so the deployment should also be agile and iterative and strive to find the best possible balance. A big challenge is also the transformation process from more "traditional" product development towards agile and iterative development. The transformation needs to happen gradually especially when working with complex products with a lot of legacy code and it is interesting to find out the different paths to make this change. This is a huge learning process for the whole organization!

Kati Vilkki has worked for Nokia Networks since 1994 first as software and system designer, and more recently in different R&D management and development capacities. She has also a strong back-ground in change management and organizational development. She has a Masters degree in Computer Science from Helsinki University. Currently she heads the NET Product Creation Renewal Program and team, which fosters the adoption of agile and iterative development methods in large-scale programs.

Author Index

Vol. 4044: P. Abrahamsson, M. Marchesi, G. Succi (Eds.), Extreme Programming and Agile Processes in Software Engineering. XII, 230 pages. 2006.

Vol. 4039: M. Morisio (Ed.), Reuse of Off-the-Shelf Components. XIII, 444 pages. 2006.

Vol. 4038: P. Ciancarini, H. Wiklicky (Eds.), Coordination Models and Languages. VIII, 299 pages. 2006.

Vol. 4037: R. Gorrieri, H. Wehrheim (Eds.), Formal Methods for Open Object-Based Distributed Systems. XVII, 474 pages. 2006.

Vol. 4034: J. Münch, M. Vierimaa (Eds.), Product-Focused Software Process Improvement. XVII, 474 pages. 2006.

Vol. 4027: H.L. Larsen, G. Pasi, D. Ortiz-Arroyo, T. Andreasen, H. Christiansen (Eds.), Flexible Query Answering Systems. XVIII, 714 pages. 2006. (Sublibrary LNAI).

Vol. 4024: S. Donatelli, P. S. Thiagarajan (Eds.), Petri Nets and Other Models of Concurrency - ICATPN 2006. XI, 441 pages. 2006.

Vol. 4021: E. André, L. Dybkjær, W. Minker, H. Neumann, M. Weber (Eds.), Perception and Interactive Technologies. XI, 217 pages. 2006. (Sublibrary LNAI).

Vol. 4011: Y. Sure, J. Domingue (Eds.), The Semantic Web: Research and Applications. XIX, 726 pages. 2006.

Vol. 4010: S. Dunne, B. Stoddart (Eds.), Unifying Theories of Programming. VIII, 257 pages. 2006.

Vol. 4007: C. Àlvarez, M. Serna (Eds.), Experimental Algorithms. XI, 329 pages. 2006.

Vol. 4006: L.M. Pinho, M. González Harbour (Eds.), Reliable Software Technologies – Ada-Europe 2006. XII, 241 pages. 2006.

Vol. 4004: S. Vaudenay (Ed.), Advances in Cryptology - EUROCRYPT 2006. XIV, 613 pages. 2006.

Vol. 4003: Y. Koucheryavy, J. Harju, V.B. Iversen (Eds.), Next Generation Teletraffic and Wired/Wireless Advanced Networking. XVI, 582 pages. 2006.

Vol. 4001: E. Dubois, K. Pohl (Eds.), Advanced Information Systems Engineering. XVI, 560 pages. 2006.

Vol. 3999: C. Kop, G. Fliedl, H.C. Mayr, E. Métais (Eds.), Natural Language Processing and Information Systems. XIII, 227 pages. 2006.

Vol. 3998: T. Calamoneri, I. Finocchi, G.F. Italiano (Eds.), Algorithms and Complexity. XII, 394 pages. 2006.

Vol. 3997: W. Grieskamp, C. Weise (Eds.), Formal Approaches to Software Testing. XII, 219 pages. 2006.

Vol. 3996: A. Keller, J.-P. Martin-Flatin (Eds.), Self-Managed Networks, Systems, and Services. X, 185 pages. 2006.

Vol. 3995: G. Müller (Ed.), Emerging Trends in Information and Communication Security. XX, 524 pages. 2006.

Vol. 3994: V.N. Alexandrov, G.D. van Albada, P.M.A. Sloot, J. Dongarra (Eds.), Computational Science – ICCS 2006, Part IV. XXXV, 1096 pages. 2006.

Vol. 3993: V.N. Alexandrov, G.D. van Albada, P.M.A. Sloot, J. Dongarra (Eds.), Computational Science – ICCS 2006, Part III. XXXVI, 1136 pages. 2006.

Vol. 3992: V.N. Alexandrov, G.D. van Albada, P.M.A. Sloot, J. Dongarra (Eds.), Computational Science – ICCS 2006, Part II. XXXV, 1122 pages. 2006.

Vol. 3991: V.N. Alexandrov, G.D. van Albada, P.M.A. Sloot, J. Dongarra (Eds.), Computational Science – ICCS 2006, Part I. LXXXI, 1096 pages. 2006.

Vol. 3990: J. C. Beck, B.M. Smith (Eds.), Integration of AI and OR Techniques in Constraint Programming for Combinatorial Optimization Problems. X, 301 pages. 2006.

Vol. 3989: J. Zhou, M. Yung, F. Bao, Applied Cryptography and Network Security. XIV, 488 pages. 2006.

Vol. 3987: M. Hazas, J. Krumm, T. Strang (Eds.), Location- and Context-Awareness. X, 289 pages. 2006.

Vol. 3986: K. Stølen, W.H. Winsborough, F. Martinelli, F. Massacci (Eds.), Trust Management. XIV, 474 pages. 2006.

Vol. 3984: M. Gavrilova, O. Gervasi, V. Kumar, C.J. K. Tan, D. Taniar, A. Laganà, Y. Mun, H. Choo (Eds.), Computational Science and Its Applications - ICCSA 2006, Part V. XXV, 1045 pages. 2006.

Vol. 3983: M. Gavrilova, O. Gervasi, V. Kumar, C.J. K. Tan, D. Taniar, A. Laganà, Y. Mun, H. Choo (Eds.), Computational Science and Its Applications - ICCSA 2006, Part IV. XXVI, 1191 pages. 2006.

Vol. 3982: M. Gavrilova, O. Gervasi, V. Kumar, C.J. K. Tan, D. Taniar, A. Laganà, Y. Mun, H. Choo (Eds.), Computational Science and Its Applications - ICCSA 2006, Part III. XXV, 1243 pages. 2006.

Vol. 3981: M. Gavrilova, O. Gervasi, V. Kumar, C.J. K. Tan, D. Taniar, A. Laganà, Y. Mun, H. Choo (Eds.), Computational Science and Its Applications - ICCSA 2006, Part II. XXVI, 1255 pages. 2006.

Vol. 3980: M. Gavrilova, O. Gervasi, V. Kumar, C.J. K. Tan, D. Taniar, A. Laganà, Y. Mun, H. Choo (Eds.), Computational Science and Its Applications - ICCSA 2006, Part I. LXXV, 1199 pages. 2006.

Vol. 3979: T.S. Huang, N. Sebe, M.S. Lew, V. Pavlović, M. Kölsch, A. Galata, B. Kisačanin (Eds.), Computer Vision in Human-Computer Interaction. XII, 121 pages. 2006.

Vol. 3978: B. Hnich, M. Carlsson, F. Fages, F. Rossi (Eds.), Recent Advances in Constraints. VIII, 179 pages. 2006. (Sublibrary LNAI).